# Software Process Modeling

# INTERNATIONAL SERIES IN SOFTWARE ENGINEERING

Series Editor:
**Victor R. Basili**
*University of Maryland*
*College Park, MD 20742*
basili@cs.umd.edu

*Also in the Series:*
PROCESS IMPROVEMENT IN PRACTICE: A Handbook for IT Companies by Tore
Dybå, Torgeir Dingsøyr and Nils Brede Moe ISBN: 1-4020-7869-2
IDENTIFYING RELEVANT INFORMATION FOR TESTING TECHNIQUE
SELECTION by Sira Vegas, Sira Vegas, Victor Basili; ISBN: 1-4020-7435-2
MULTIMEDIA SOFTWARE ENGINEERING by Shi-Kuo Chang; ISBN 0-7923-7736-2
EXPERIMENTATION IN SOFTWARE ENGINEERING: AN INTRODUCTION by Claes
Wohlin, Per Runeson, Martin Höst, Magnus C. Ohlsson, Björn Regnell, Anders
Wesslén; ISBN: 0-7923-8682-5
NON-FUNCTIONAL REQUIREMENTS IN SOFTWARE ENGINEERING by Lawrence
Chung, Brian A. Nixon, Eric Yu and John Mylopoulos; ISBN: 0-7923-8666-3
SOFTWARE DEFECT MODELING by Kai-Yuan Cai; ISBN: 0-7923-8259-5
CONSTRAINT-BASED DESIGN RECOVERY FOR SOFTWARE REENGINEERING:
Theory and Experiments by Steven G. Woods, Alexander E. Quilici and Qiang Yang;
ISBN: 0-7923-8067-3
TOOLS AND ENVIRONMENTS FOR PARALLEL AND DISTRIBUTED SYSTEMS by
Amr Zaky and Ted Lewis; ISBN: 0-7923-9675-8
FORMAL SPECIFICATION TECHNIQUES FOR ENGINEERING MODULAR C
PROGRAMS by TAN Yang Meng; ISBN: 0-7923-9653-7

**International Series in Software Engineering** addresses the following goals:
- ■ To coherently and consistently present important research topics and their application(s).
- ■ To present evolved concepts in one place as a coherent whole, updating early versions of the ideas and notations.
- ■ To provide publications which will be used as the ultimate reference on the topic by experts in the area.

With the dynamic growth evident in this field and the need to communicate findings, this series provides a forum for information targeted toward Software Engineers.

# Software Process Modeling

edited by

**Silvia T. Acuña**
*Universidad Autónoma de Madrid*
*Spain*

and

**Natalia Juristo**
*Universidad Politécnica de Madrid*
*Spain*

 Springer

Dr. Silvia T. Acuna
Universidad Autónoma de Madrid
Escuela Politécnica Superior
Ingeniería Informática
28049 MADRID
SPAIN

Dr. Natalia Juristo
Facultad de Informatica
Universidad Politecnica de Madrid
Fac. Informatica Campus de Montegancedo
Boadilla del Monte,28660
28660 MADRID
SPAIN

Library of Congress Cataloging-in-Publication Data

A C.I.P. Catalogue record for this book is available
from the Library of Congress.

**Software Process Modeling**
edited by
Silvia T. Acuña, *Universidad Autónoma de Madrid, Spain*
*and*
Natalia Juristo, *Universidad Politécnica de Madrid, Spain*

International Series in Software Engineering        Volume  10

ISBN 978-1-4419-3710-0        e-ISBN 978-0-387-24262-0

Printed on acid-free paper.

Printed in the United States of America.

9 8 7 6 5 4 3 2 1

springeronline.com

# Contents

# 3

## Software Dependability Applications in Process Modeling          **65**

*Ray Madachy and Barry Boehm*

# 4

## Simulation Process Modelling for Managing Software Evolution          **87**

*Meir M. Lehman, Goel Kahen and Juan F. Ramil*

# 5

# Software Process Modelling: Socio-Technical Perspectives 111

*Patrick Waterson, Stephan Weibelzahl and Dietmar Pfahl*

# 6

# Motivation and Process Improvement 141

*Watts S. Humphrey and Michael D. Konrad*

# 7

## Managing Organizational Change for Software Process Improvement                                              **163**
*Deependra Moitra*

# 8

## A Workshop-Oriented Approach for Defining Electronic Process Guides. A Case Study                        **187**
*Torgeir Dingsøyr, Nils Brede Moe, Tore Dybå and Reidar Conradi*

# Contributors

## *Barry Boehm*

USC Center for Software Engineering, Department of Computer Science,
University of Southern California, Los Angeles, CA 90098-0781, U.S.A.
E-mail: boehm@sunset.usc.edu


## *Reidar Conradi*

Department of Computer and Information Science, Norwegian University of Science
and Technology, NO-7491 Trondheim, Norway.
E-mail: Reidar.Conradi@idi.ntnu.no


## *Torgeir Dingsøyr*

SINTEF Information and Communication Technology, NO-7465 Trondheim, Norway.
E-mail: Torgeir.Dingsoyr@sintef.no


## *Tore Dybå*

SINTEF Information and Communication Technology, NO-7465 Trondheim, Norway.
E-mail: Tore.Dyba@sintef.no


## *Watts S. Humphrey*

Software Engineering Institute, Carnegie Mellon University, 4500 Fifth Avenue,
Pittsburgh, PA 15213, U.S.A.
E-mail: watts@sei.cmu.edu


## *Goel Kahen*

Crown Poly, Inc., 5700 Bickett St., Huntington Park, CA 90255, U.S.A.
E-mail: G_Cohen@crownpoly.com

## Michael D. Konrad

Software Engineering Institute, Carnegie Mellon University, 4500 Fifth Avenue, Pittsburgh, PA 15213, U.S.A.
E-mail: mdk@sei.cmu.edu


## Meir M. Lehman

School of Computing Science, Middlesex University, London, U.K.
E-mail: mml@mdx.ac.uk


## Jacques Lonchamp

LORIA, Campus Scientifique, BP 254, 54500 Vandoeuvre-lès-Nancy, France.
E-mail: jloncham@loria.fr


## Ray Madachy

USC Center for Software Engineering, Department of Computer Science, University of Southern California, Los Angeles, CA 90098-0781, U.S.A.
E-mail: madachy@sunset.usc.edu


## Nils Brede Moe

SINTEF Information and Communication Technology, NO-7465 Trondheim, Norway.
E-mail: Nils.B.Moe@sintef.no


## Deependra Moitra

Infosys Technologies Limited, Bangalore, India.
E-mail: deependra@moitra.com


## Dietmar Pfahl

Fraunhofer Institute Experimental Software Engineering (IESE), Sauerwiesen 6, D-67661 Kaiserslautern, Germany.
E-mail: pfahl@iese.fhg.de

## *Juan F. Ramil*

Computing Department, Faculty of Maths and Computing,
The Open University, Walton Hall, Milton Keynes MK7 7LW, U.K.
E-mail: j.f.ramil@open.ac.uk


## *Walt Scacchi*

Institute for Software Research, Donald Bren School of Information and Computer
Science, University of California, Irvine, Irvine, CA 92697-3425, U.S.A.
E-mail: Wscacchi@uci.edu


## *Patrick Waterson*

Fraunhofer Institute Experimental Software Engineering (IESE), Sauerwiesen 6,
D-67661 Kaiserslautern, Germany.
E-mail: waterson@iese.fhg.de


## *Stephan Weibelzahl*

Fraunhofer Institute Experimental Software Engineering (IESE), Sauerwiesen 6,
D-67661 Kaiserslautern, Germany.
E-mail: weibel@iese.fhg.de


## *Silvia T. Acuña*

Departamento de Ingeniería Informática, Escuela Politécnica Superior, Universidad
Autónoma de Madrid, Avda. Francisco Tomás y Valiente 11,
28049 Madrid, Spain.
E-mail: silvia.acuna@ii.uam.es


## *Natalia Juristo*

Facultad de Informática, Universidad Politécnica de Madrid,
Campus de Montegancedo s/n, 28660 Boadilla del Monte,
Madrid, Spain.
E-mail: natalia@fi.upm.es

# SOFTWARE PROCESS MODELLING:
*A Preface*

Silvia T. ACUÑA[1] and Natalia JURISTO[2]

[1]*Departamento de Ingeniería Informática, Escuela Politécnica Superior, Universidad Autónoma de Madrid, Avda. Francisco Tomás y Valiente 11, 28049 Madrid, Spain,* [2]*Facultad de Informática, Universidad Politécnica de Madrid, Campus de Montegancedo s/n, 28660 Boadilla del Monte, Madrid, Spain. E-mail: silvia.acuna@ii.uam.es ; natalia@fi.upm.es*

## 1. INTRODUCTION

Customers are placing growing demands on the software industry. They are looking for more complex products that are, at the same time, easier to use. Software developer organisations are expected to produce higher quality products and get them to customers faster. In doing so, however, globally distributed development teams have to cope with understaffing and changing technologies. The challenges for the software industry are apparently mounting.

Over the years, a variety of software process models have been designed to structure, describe and prescribe the software systems construction process. Recently, software process modelling is increasingly dealing with new challenges raised by the tests that the software industry has to stand. For example, we have open source development processes that are inherently more dynamic and have a major social component. There are also software development processes that involve assembling off-the-shelf components, where the incorporation of commercial off-the-shelf systems into software processes is often ad hoc and their selection calls for an integral assessment of technical capabilities and human and business issues.

This new context implies innovative modelling approaches and modelling techniques for understanding and improving such processes. These approaches should make provision for open, agile, distributed development processes, where the people play a critical role. Therefore, these new contexts raise unprecedentedly complex challenges for existing software process models that include a range of formalisms for describing or prescribing processes in traditional environments.

This book brings together software process experts to discuss relevant results in software process modelling and give their view of this field. This edited book focuses on new aspects of software process modelling. Specifically, it deals with socio-technological aspects, process modelling for new development types (open source software, dependability applications, etc.) and organisational change management.

In this preface, we first analyse the two main actions that can be taken with respect to the software process: define or model, and evaluate and improve. Then, as the eco-organisational dimension should be just as formalised as the technological dimension in this new software development context, we address the importance of relating social and technical systems in the software process. Finally, we present the chapters that make up this edited book.

## 2.    SOFTWARE PROCESS RESEARCH

The general objective of software process research is to improve software development practice by proposing: a) better ways of designing the developer organisation processes, and b) better ways of improving this organisation at the level of individual processes and the organisation as a whole. To this end, there are two lines of software process research: software process modelling, and software process evaluation and improvement.

### 2.1. Software Process Modelling

The software process is a set of activities undertaken to manage, develop and maintain software systems. In other words, the software process focuses on the construction tasks rather than on the output products. Software process modelling describes the creation of software development process models. Six chapters of the book deal with process modelling. Yet, even today opinion is divided as to exactly what the term "software process" means. Some reject this notion outright, banking on the premise that any task can and will be eventually automated; others believe that engineering processes are best modelled in detail with supporting environment; yet, others tend to think of a process as an executable program whose purpose cannot avoid employing the people's creativity. In their chapter, Dingsøyr,

Moe, Dybå and Conradi suggest that complex and heavy-weight models are not necessary.

There are different types of process modelling. Processes can be modelled at different levels of abstraction (for example, standard models versus tailored models) and they can also be modelled for different purposes (descriptive models versus prescriptive models). Examples of well-known standards are the traditional IEEE STD 1074-1997, ISO/IEC 12207-2002, and the Unified Process. Note that various approaches to process modelling differ primarily as to the understanding of a software process and the original motivations for modelling.

A software process model is an abstract representation of the architecture, design or definition of the software process. Each representation describes, at different detail levels, an organisation of the elements of a finished, ongoing or proposed process, and it provides a definition of the process to be used either as roadmap or for evaluation and improvement.

A process model can be analysed, validated and simulated, if executable. The goal of process simulation is process prediction, which refers to analysing the software process to predict its future behaviour. The chapter by Madachy and Boehm, for example, simulates specific aspects of process dependability that can be predicted, whereas Lehman, Kahen and Ramil simulate the essential activities underlying the software processes to predict process evolution by defining the process feedback loops.

Process models are used mainly to improve process understanding and communication, as well as for software process control (evaluation and improvement) in an organisation. In their respective chapters, Scacchi describes open source software development processes (process analysis) and Lonchamp models these processes (process synthesis). Both use modelling to improve the understanding of this new development type. Lonchamp also pursues process comparison, reuse, and improvement and process enactment support in open source software development modelling. On the other hand, Lehman, Kahen and Ramil aim for the process-modelling goal of supporting process management to pinpoint and control various influences on long-term behaviour. Madachy and Boehm also take up this modelling goal to evaluate dependability strategies.

Each model observes, focuses on or gives priority to particular points of such a complex world as software construction. A model is always an abstraction of reality and, as such, represents a partial and simplified description of reality, that is, a model does not account for all the parts or aspects of the process. Generally, a process model can be divided into several submodels expressing different viewpoints or perspectives. Both Lonchamp and Lehman, Kahen and Ramil adhere to this approach and investigate the processes at a high level of abstraction to rule out complex process models that are difficult to comprehend, validate, utilise or reuse.

Different elements of a process, for example, activities, products (artefacts), resources (personnel and tools) and roles, can be modelled. Traditionally, software process model representations have focused on three elementary process features: the activity, the artefact and the agent (human and computerised). However, other characteristics have been empirically proven to have a big influence on the production process: human competencies, human behaviour, human roles and the organisation of work among human beings. Waterson, Weibelzahl and Pfahl suggest the need for models to address organisational culture and focus on the behavioural capabilities of the people and roles involved in the software process.

## 2.2. Software Process Evaluation and Improvement

Software process evaluation and improvement judges and decides on the quality of the software process of a given organisation, and may propose a process improvement strategy. The efforts of the scientific community in this field have led to quite a number of maturity models and standards, such as ISO 9001, CMMI (Capability Maturity Model Integration) developed by the Software Engineering Institute (SEI) at Carnegie Mellon University, ISO/IEC 15504 and Bootstrap. All these models have two goals: a) to determine the aspects for improvement in a software development organisation; and b) to reach an agreement on what a good process is. This goal stems from the very nature of the evaluation process, as it is essential to use a reference model or yardstick against which to compare the software process of the organisation under evaluation. Therefore, it involves modelling the above process by identifying what sorts of activities have to be carried out by an organisation to assure the quality of the production process and, ultimately, the end product.

Software process evaluation involves analysing the activities carried out in an organisation to produce software. The ultimate goal of process evaluation is to improve software production. Development process evaluation and improvement works under the hypothesis that the quality of the software product is determined by the quality of its development process. This strategy is equivalent to the one implemented in other branches of engineering and in other industries, where the quality of the resulting product is increased by controlling the process used in its production. Software process evaluation and improvement methods introduced innovative concepts that changed the way in which software production activities are perceived. There are two chapters in this book dealing with process improvement.

Software process improvement examines how to improve an organisation's software development practices, once software process evaluation has made clear what the current state of the process is. Software process improvement is not planned as a single step to excellence, but is performed gradually by transitions from one maturity level to another. There are several improvement models and solutions, like the SEI's IDEAL, the Business Improvement Guides (BIGs) developed by the European Software Institute (ESI) or the Process Improvement Guide (PIG) developed by the ISO/IEC 15504 project.

A capable and mature software development organisation institutionalises the improvement effort. In his chapter, Moitra suggests that organisational change management should also be institutionalised for successful software process improvement.

Other evaluation and improvement models focus on organisation and human aspects. For example, People CMM characterises an organisation on the basis of how it manages its workforce. Accordingly, each progressive level of People CMM produces a transformation in the organisational culture of a software organisation in order to improve the development, organisation, motivation and retention of its workforce.

The Personal Software Process (PSP) takes a different approach, albeit also directed at the human aspects of the process. The PSP focuses on individual software engineers' performance. Filling the gap between the CMMI (an organisation-centred approach) and the PSP (an individual-centred approach), the Team Software Process (TSP) came to address the software process improvement problem at the team level. In their chapter, Humphrey and Konrad suggest that the CMMI and People CMM need to be integrated with PSP and TSP to improve organisational performance. Thus, Humphrey and Konrad claim that "the good practices instilled by both CMMI and the People CMM are enhanced by the TSP and PSP, while the PSP and TSP benefit from the integrated technical and people-management environment provided by implementing CMMI and the People CMM".

These two areas (process modelling, and evaluation and improvement) play a central role in software process research. Modelling and evaluation and improvement are, however, closely related. Software development process modelling is one of the key factors for improving software productivity and quality. Modelling, which is the foundation for creating the software process prior to any evaluation or control, that is, designing a good process, is possibly the most critical factor for achieving a quality software production process. The objective therefore is to model the process by identifying what elements there should be at a software developer organisation to assure the quality of the production process and, ultimately, the output product. Large-scale software developer organisations are trying to mature their software development processes on the basis of more precise, integral and formalised descriptions of well-established processes.

## 3.   SOCIO-TECHNICAL ASPECTS OF THE SOFTWARE PROCESS

The two lines of research discussed earlier (software process modelling, and evaluation and improvement) are based on the hypothesis that the process influences product quality. Although leading researchers have suggested that the organisation and people influence software product quality, it is not a subject that the community is researching in depth. For example, back in the 1980s Boehm explicitly mentioned human relations as a key component (alongside adequate resource and program engineering) for achieving a successful software product and conducting a successful software development and maintenance process in his book "Software Engineering Economics". As regards the software process, he claimed that "the human relations goals for the software development and maintenance process have to do with the management of people's activities in a way which satisfies the human needs and fulfils the human potential of the people involved in the process". Additionally, in 1988, Curtis, Krasner and Iscoe reached the conclusion that the "development of large software systems should be dealt with, at least partly, as a process of learning, communication and negotiation". However, few process models today discuss how to organise and manage large development groups to maximise their coordination. This is, nevertheless, just as important as managing the software process.

Software development organisations need to understand that dealing with software problems does not only involve the technical dimensions, like introducing a new tool or selecting a method. The human dimension can be considered even more important than the technical side and, as DeMarco and Lister put it, "most software development projects fail because of failures with the team running them".

The view of software development as a process carried out by teams of people who have to be coordinated and managed within an effective organisational structure helps to identify the different dimensions of software development and the problems that need to be dealt with to establish effective practices. The view is switching from the production and technological dimension to the social and organisational dimension in the understanding that dealing with the problems and questions of software development is not confined to the technological dimension, such as, for example, the introduction of an effective environment or the selection of a suitable life-cycle strategy. These questions are necessary but not sufficient. The organisational dimension, that is, the discipline of organisational and personal behaviour, should also be considered. Moreover, attention should be paid to the complex interrelationship between several organisational, cultural, technological and financial factors within the software development process.

In their respective chapters, both Scacchi and Waterson, Weibelzahl and Pfahl explicitly adopt the approach of analysing software process relationships between social and technical systems and the need to jointly improve and simultaneously design these systems. As we will see later, Waterson, Weibelzahl and Pfahl describe the software process models created using this approach and trace a roadmap of socio-techical systems in the software process. Scacchi describes the evolution of the socio-technical systems approach and characterises this approach for open source software development processes.

Despite all the efforts and progress made in recent years, we are still without:

- A conceptualisation and formalisation of the inclusion of people and the interaction in which they participate and
- A systematic and disciplined process for including organisational aspects in software process modelling.

## 4.   BOOK CONTENT

This edited book deals with four aspects of software process modelling: processes for open source software development (two chapters); behavioural processes (two chapters); socio-technico-organisational processes (three chapters); and software process analysis, definition and evaluation (one chapter).

In the following, we briefly describe the content of each chapter.

Over the last few years, there has been growing and widespread interest in understanding the *processes of open source software development* in both scientific research and the software industry. Two chapters focus on this special type of development. It is important to raise the understanding of the development process in open source software projects. To date there has been no prior model or globally accepted framework that defines how open source software is developed in practice. Hence the importance of the contributions of the following chapters.

The first chapter (Socio-Technical Interaction Networks in Free/Open Source Software Development Processes, Scacchi) deals with the heterogeneity of free/open source software development (F/OSSD) approaches by investigating F/OSSD projects in different and diverse software communities. The second chapter (Open Source Software Development Process Modeling, Lonchamp) investigates the improvement of the open source software process by making this more explicit through process modelling aimed at taking advantage of a common process. Let us look at the content of these two chapters in more detail.

The first chapter of this book aims to present a comprehensive framework for analysing the F/OSSD, which differs in many, interesting ways from traditional development processes. The author proposes socio-technical interaction networks as a conceptual framework for comparatively analysing patterns and networks of interactions among people, products, and processes that are found in a growing base of empirical studies of F/OSSD projects. In "Socio-Technical Interaction Networks in Free/Open Source Software Development Processes", Scacchi proposes four, closely interrelated F/OSSD processes:

a) participating, joining, and contributing, these activities are intra-, inter- and cross-projects and teams;

b) forming alliances and building community through participation, artefacts and tools;

c) projects cooperating, coordinating and controlling, using both software version control tools and virtual project management tools to mobilize, coordinate, control, build, and assure the quality of free/open source software development activities; and

d) co-evolving socio-technical systems for free/open source software, which allows the continued improvement both of the functionality and quality of this type of software systems and of the people and communities involved.

This chapter establishes that F/OSSD processes represent an alternative community-intensive approach for developing software systems and related artefacts, as well as social-cultural (sharing beliefs, values, etc.) relationships. The chapter also presents the limitations and constraints of the approach, considering the four above-mentioned process types. This chapter provides an increased understanding of the development process in free/open source software projects, including an attempt to analyse similarities in the development processes of the range of free/open source software approaches, processes and practices.

The second chapter of this book provides guidelines on how to model the open source software (OSS) process and how to help non-OSS developers to practice OSS, by documenting and facilitating the relevant OSS processes.

In "Open Source Software Development Process Modeling", Lonchamp aims to help improve the OSS process by making these more explicit through process modelling. For this purpose, he presents the Software Process Engineering Meta-model (SPEM) from the Object Management Group (OMG), which he applies to OSS process modelling. SPEM is a complex meta-model of approximately 20 main classes and their relations for defining software engineering process models and their components. This is a three-layered model: definition level and generic level, which specify the common features of all fully-fledged open source projects; and specific level, which describes fine-grained process model fragments characteristic of different open source projects. This application provides new, systematised knowledge of how software is developed in open source projects. This is a significant contribution to the open source research community, again catering for the great variance in OSS approaches and even the variance within concrete OSS projects, as well as for the patterns that Scacchi provides in the earlier chapter for the four F/OSSD process types.

*Software process behaviour modelling and simulation* has come to be a powerful tool for software process improvement. A very comprehensive representation for simulation are the systems dynamics-based models. The model proposed by Abdel-Hamid was the first important application of systems dynamics and of the feedback systems control laws to software process modelling and simulation. Many other proposals have emerged since then. A variety of simulation models have been designed to predict the dynamic process behaviour. But there are few models for evaluating the influence of processes on the attributes of critical applications and optimising the software process. Two chapters deal with this important topic in this book.

In chapter 3, "Software Dependability Applications in Process Modeling", Madachy and Boehm deal with the problem of analysing all the effects of combined strategies on achieving dependability that would be useful for developers as they decide which dependability strategies they should use in a given situation to achieve dependability attributes. This is not an easy problem, since the set should not only reflect the superposition between the opportunities of dependability strategies but also many interpretations in different contexts. Modelling can help determine how much is enough for different situations in order to find the most cost-effective balance of activities. First, the authors present a comprehensive framework for modelling dependability. This framework can be used to model the relationships between the forms for achieving dependability and the dependability attributes. The simulation model will be good for process optimisation, which refers to analysing software process dependability attributes, such as attributes of protection, robustness and quality of service. This analysis allows the selection of strategies for achieving dependability in the development process of critical software systems. These strategies are for defect prevention, finding and fixing defects or for reducing the impact of defects. Additionally, the authors give an overview of analytical and simulation process models that involve dependability in some fashion. They focus on analysing the impact of reliability decisions on these models. Finally, they describe an example that shows how process modelling can be used to optimise a process for dependability.

In chapter 4, "Simulation Process Modelling for Managing Software Evolution", Lehman, Kahen and Ramil describe a systems dynamics model that can serve as a basis of a tool to support decision making regarding the optimal personnel allocation over the systems lifetime. The model is provided as an example of the use of process modelling in order to plan and manage long-term software evolution. The central idea of this research is to demonstrate how the presence of feedback loops in software processes determines the evolution of most of today's computing systems. This model represents the processes at a high level of abstraction and focuses on the long-term issues of the software process. The authors have analysed a lot of software processes from industry from this perspective for comparison and to assist improvements in project planning and progress.

Software development is a conjunction of three worlds: *the organisational environment, the social environment and the technological environment.* The inclusion of these environments will make it possible to output software process models that meet the specified organisational, cultural and technological requirements, providing an exhaustive analysis of the people in the software process, as well as a modelling process and method, which is missing from the models now defined.

In chapter 5, "Software Process Modelling: Socio-Technical Perspectives", Waterson, Weibelzahl and Pfahl report the existence of process models that can all be related to the socio-technical systems (STS) perspective: process simulation models, evaluation models, competency models, maturity models, etc. These authors discuss the fact that STS may include different points of view on process modelling, and there are difficulties in comparing STS and software engineering approaches normally associated with the software process. This chapter covers several important topics of software process studies that have not had enough press in the software engineering literature and particularly work on process models. The final part of this chapter defines a roadmap for future socio-technical studies of the software process.

The importance of people and people motivation in the adoption and use of software processes is widely recognised by the software process scientific community. To date, work on this topic has largely focused on the motivational and people-related issues of the software practitioners themselves. Chapter 6 broadens this focus to examine the motivational issues that govern behaviour of both the developers, their teams, their supported teams, their management and the customers or users of the products developed by the teams and to show how their behaviour can affect the development work. In "Motivation and Process Improvement", Humphrey and Konrad provide several guidelines that organisations may consider to address these people issues and key problems for the software process improvement. Several improvement frameworks such as the Capability Maturity Model (CMM) Integration, People CMM, Personal Software Process, and Team Software Process are characterised to analyse the points and to discuss the benefits that can be achieved by addressing the motivational and behavioural issues at all organisational, engineering and management levels.

In chapter 7, "Managing Organizational Change for Software Process Improvement", Moitra gives an overview of relevant factors that influence the software process improvement process. Although there are several improvement models and solutions, Moitra points out that "the instances of software organisations truly achieving success in their software process improvement efforts are still small in number" and "these efforts mostly fail owing to human issues that have an impact on the organisational change process". Additionally, he presents a model and provides recommendations for managing organisational change for software process improvement.

To round up this book, we have selected a chapter on process definition, that does not follow in the tradition of the classical models and defends the need for lightweight, participatory and comprehensive models.

Chapter 8 considers processes as a set of systematic guidelines arranged in a electronic form. In "A Workshop-Oriented Approach for Defining Electronic Process Guides. A Case Study", Dingsøyr, Moe, Dybå and Conradi describe a workshop-based approach for capturing an existing process using a case study as an example. The approach produces an electronic representation of the process activities that can be used for analysis or communication of the process. The authors discuss the strengths and weaknesses of applying such an approach.

Altogether, the eight chapters not only provide a comprehensive view of the current status of research in software process modelling, but also shed light on the challenges that future research will meet. We hope that readers will therefore find plenty of inspiration from reading this book.

## ACKNOWLEDGEMENTS

We wish to thank all the authors of the submitted chapters, whose research has made this edited book possible, for sharing the product of their work with other people and getting involved in other people's problems. We are also deeply indebted to Angélica de Antonio Jiménez, Reidar Conradi, Torgeir Dingsøyr, Rachel Elliott, Xavier Franch, Jacques Lonchamp, Marta López Fernández, Ray Madachy, Rodion M. Podorozhny, Isabel Ramos Roldán, Mercedes Ruiz, Patrick Waterson and Stephan Weibelzahl for helping us to improve the chapters of this book.

Madrid, SPAIN
*September 2004*

Chapter 1

# SOCIO-TECHNICAL INTERACTION NETWORKS IN FREE/OPEN SOURCE SOFTWARE DEVELOPMENT PROCESSES

Walt SCACCHI
*Institute for Software Research, School of Information and Computer Science,*
*University of California, Irvine, Irvine, CA 92697-3425 U.S.A. E-mail: Wscacchi@uci.edu*

## 1. INTRODUCTION

This chapter explores patterns of social and technological interaction that emerge in free/open source software development (F/OSSD) projects found in different research and development communities. F/OSSD is a relatively new way for building and deploying large software systems on a global basis, and differs in many interesting ways from the principles and practices traditionally advocated for software engineering. Hundreds of F/OSS systems are now in use by thousands to millions of end-users, and some of these F/OSS systems entail hundreds-of-thousands to millions of lines of source code. So what's going on here, and how are F/OSSD processes that are being used to build and sustain these projects different?

One of the more significant features of F/OSSD is the formation and enactment of complex software development processes performed by loosely coordinated software developers and contributors. These people may volunteer their time and skill to such effort, and may only work at their personal discretion rather than as assigned and scheduled. Further, these developers generally provide their own computing resources, and bring their own software development tools with them. Similarly, F/OSS developers work on software projects that do not typically have a corporate owner or management staff to organize, direct, monitor, and improve the software development processes being put into practice on such projects. But how are successful F/OSSD projects and software development processes possible without regularly employed and scheduled software development staff, or without an explicit regime for software engineering project management? Why will software developers participate in F/OSSD projects? Why and how are large F/OSSD projects sustained? How are large F/OSSD projects coordinated, controlled or managed without a traditional project management team? Why and how might these answers to these questions change over time? These are the core research questions that will be addressed in this chapter.

Socio-technical interaction networks (STINs) are an emerging conceptual framework for identifying, organizing, and comparatively analyzing patterns of social interaction, system development, and the configuration of components that constitute an information system. More specifically, a STIN denotes a set of collective relationships among:

> "...people (including organizations), equipment, data, diverse resources (money, skill, status), documents and messages, legal arrangements and enforcement mechanisms, and resource flows. The elements of a STIN are heterogeneous. The network relationships between these elements include social, economic, and political interactions." [Kling 2003].

Subsequently, STINs provide a scheme for examining the networks of people who work together through interrelated social and technical processes that arise to create the complex information systems and products. STINs thus serve as a conceptual framework through which to examine ongoing F/OSSD projects and processes.

STINs may be seen as the conceptual outgrowth of what historically was called "socio-technical systems" (STS) [Emery 1960], informed by "actor network theory". An STS perspective envisions a world of complex organizations that routinely employ technicians/engineers to develop systems for users, where success in developing a system depends on the participation and sustained involvement of the system's users. If people issues in the design, deployment, and evolution of these STS are slighted or ignored, then these systems would be problematic or unsatisfactory to use, else be outright failures. However, understanding this pathology, or intervening to prevent it, is possible through STS practices that can be incorporated into system development processes [Scacchi 2004c]. Historically, STS design approaches prescriptively advocated user involvement and participation in the design and deployment of information systems, and its successors like "participatory design" [Schuler 1993] advocate more up-to-date renditions of STS design. Consequently, STS design was among the earliest approaches to system development that sought to both engage and balance the interests of people (developers, end-users), products (systems, documentation, etc.) and processes (system design and usage) in a manner that focused on participation and involvement of all system stakeholders. Other directions for advancing STS design include its integration with workplace democracy movements [Bjerknes 1995, Ehn 1987] and soft systems approaches [Atkinson 2000], as well as its reconstitution as a customer-driven system design method [Beyer 1997].

Actor-network theory (ANT) [cf. Callon 1986, Latour 1987, Law 1999] on the other hand draws attention to processes by which scientific disputes or technical design alternative become closed and rationalized, ideas accepted, tools and methods adopted, or more simply how decisions are made about what is known. ANT does not assume or encourage prescriptive strategies or motives for why people should participate or be involved in system design. Instead, it draws attention to need for empirical study of what people do in their work, and what tools, resources, and artifacts they produce, use, or consume along the way. Furthermore, ANT draws attention to the relationships that repeatedly emerge in the ways people in different roles and with different resources in overlapping settings articulate scientific research or system development processes through situated work practices.

STINs build on concepts from STS design and ANT by drawing attention to the web of relationships that interlink what people do in the course of their system development work to the resources they engage and to the products (software components, development artifacts, and documents) they create, manipulate, and sustain. STINs thus give us a way to better observe the contexts in which people carry out software development processes and related work practices. In F/OSSD projects, this web is manifest and articulated over the World-Wide Web and associated systems for creating and updating the web, so that it can be observed, navigated, and empirically studied. Introducing and explaining how STINs appear in different F/OSSD projects, is therefore part of the purpose of this chapter. In turn, STINs are then used as a framework to observe and focus on why and how software developers participate in F/OSSD projects, what sustains their interest and communities, how participation and community gives rise to socio-technical conditions that serve to coordinate and control F/OSSD processes and practices, and how and why they evolve over time.

This chapter seeks to explore and develop answers to questions about F/OSSD by examining the patterns and networks of interactions among the people, products, and processes that are found in a growing base of empirical studies of F/OSSD projects. Exhibits from a variety of different F/OSSD projects will be presented and used to empirically ground the analysis and findings to be presented in this chapter.

## 2.    UNDERSTANDING F/OSS DEVELOPMENT PRACTICES AND PROCESSES

There is growing and widespread interest in understanding the practices and processes of F/OSS development. However, there is no prior model or globally accepted framework that defines how F/OSS is developed in practice [Mockus 2002, Scacchi 2002, 2004]. The starting point is thus to investigate F/OSS practices in different communities.

F/OSSD projects are being empirically studied in at least six different and diverse F/OSS communities. These six are centered about the development of software for Internet/Web infrastructure, computer games, electronic business/commerce applications, academic support software, software engineering design systems, and X-ray/deep space astronomy.

Rather than examine F/OSSD practices for a single system (e.g., Linux kernel) which may be interesting but unrepresentative of most F/OSSD projects, or of related systems from the just one community (e.g., Internet infrastructure), the focus here is to identify general F/OSS practices shaped by STINs both within and across these diverse communities. Thus, the F/OSS development practices that are described below have been empirically observed in different projects in each of these communities. Further, data exhibits in the form of screenshots displaying Web site contents from projects across the different F/OSS project communities are used to exemplify the practices, though comparable data from a different selection of F/OSS projects could serve equally well.

From studies to date, there are at least four areas where the formation and activity of STINs is most apparent across F/OSSD projects within and across all six communities. These include (a) participating, joining, and contributing to F/OSS projects; (b) forming alliances and building communities of practice through linked artifacts; (c) coordinating, cooperating, and controlling F/OSSD projects; and (d) co-evolving social and technical systems for F/OSS. Each can be briefly described in turn, though none should be construed as being independent or more important than the others. Furthermore, it appears that each can occur concurrent to one another, rather than as strictly ordered within a traditional life cycle model, or partially ordered in a spiral model.

## 2.1    Participating, joining, and contributing in F/OSS projects

There are complex motivations for why F/OSS developers are willing to allocate their time, skill, and effort by joining a F/OSS project [Hars 2002,

Hertel 2003, von Krogh 2003]. Sometimes they may simply see their effort as something that is fun, personally rewarding, or provides a venue where they can exercise and improve their technical competence in a manner that may not be possible within their current job or line of work. However, people who participate, contribute, and join F/OSS projects tend to act in ways where building trust and reputation [Stewart 2001], achieving "geek fame" [Pavlicek 2000], being creative [Fischer 2001], as well as giving and being generous with one's time, expertise, and source code [Bergquist 2001] are valued traits. In the case of F/OSS for software engineering design systems, participating in such a project is a viable way to maintain or improve software development skills, as indicated in Exhibit 1.

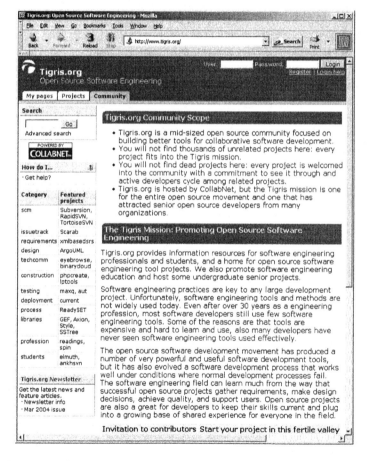

**Exhibit 1: An example near the bottom highlighting career/skill development opportunities arising from participation in F/OSS projects (source: http://www.tigris.org/ , March 2004)**

Becoming a central node in a social network of software developers that interconnects multiple F/OSS projects is also a way to accumulate social capital and recognition from peers. One survey reports that 60% or more F/OSS developers participate in two or more projects, and on the order of 5% participate in 10 or more F/OSS projects [Hars 2002]. In addition, participation in F/OSS projects as a core developer can realize financial rewards in terms of higher salaries for conventional software development jobs [Hann 2002, Lerner 2002]. However, it also enables the merger of independent F/OSS systems into larger composite ones that gain the critical mass of core developers to grow more substantially and attract ever larger user-developer communities [Madey 2004, Scacchi 2004c].

People who participate in F/OSS projects do so within one or more roles. Gacek and Arief [Gacek 2004] provide a common classification of the hierarchy of roles that people take and common tasks they perform when participating in a F/OSS project, as shown in Figure 1. Typically, it appears that people join a project and specialize in a role (or multiple roles) they find personally comfortable and intrinsically motivating [von Krogh 2004]. In contrast to traditional software development projects, there is no explicit assignment of developers to roles, though individual F/OSSD projects often post guidelines or "help wanted here" for what roles for potential contributors are in greatest need.

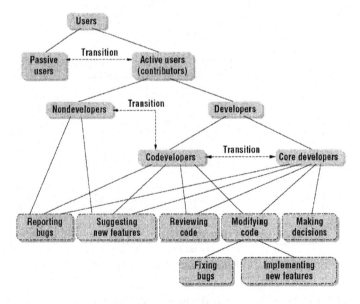

**Figure 1: A classification of roles and associated activities that contributing F/OSS participants can perform [Gacek 2004]**

It is common in F/OSS projects to find end-users becoming contributors or developers, and developers acting as end-users [Mockus 2002, Nakakoji 2002, Scacchi 2002, von Hippel 2002]. As most F/OSS developers are themselves end-users of the software systems they build, they may have an occupational incentive and vested interest in making sure their systems are really useful. However the vast majority of participants probably simply prefer to be users of F/OSS systems, unless or until their usage motivates them to act through some sort of contribution. Avid users with sufficient technical skills may actually work their way through each of the roles and eventually become a core developer, as suggested by Figure 2. As a consequence, participants within F/OSS project often participate in different roles within both technical and social networks [Smith 1999, Preece 2000] in the course of developing, using, and evolving F/OSS systems.

**Figure 2: A layered meritocracy and role hierarchy [cf. Kim 2000]**

Making contributions is often a prerequisite for advancing technically and socially within a community, as is being recognized by other community members as having made substantive contributions [Fielding 1999, Kim 2000]. Most commonly, F/OSS project participants contribute different types of software representations or content (source code, bug reports, design diagrams, execution scripts, code reviews, test case data, Web pages, email comments, online chat, etc.) to Web sites of the F/OSS projects they join. The contribution—the authoring, hypertext linking (when needed), and posting/uploading—of different types of content helps to constitute an ecology [Erickson 2000, Spinuzzi 2000] of software informalisms [Scacchi 2002] that is specific to a F/OSS project, though individual content types are widely used across most F/OSS projects. Similarly, the particular mix of software informalisms employed by participants on a F/OSS project articulates an information infrastructure [Star 1996] for framing and solving problems that arise in the ongoing development, deployment, use, and support of the F/OSS system at the center of a project.

Administrators of open software community Web sites and source code repositories serve as gatekeepers in the choices they make for what information to post, when and where within the site to post it, as well as what not to post [Smith 1999]. Similarly, they may choose to create a site map that constitutes a classification of site and domain content, as well as community structure and boundaries [O'Mahony 2003].

Most frequently, participants in F/OSS projects engage in online discussion forums or threaded email messages as a central way to observe, participate in, and contribute to public discussions of topics of interest to community participants [Yamauchi 2000]. However, these people also engage in private online or offline discussions that do not get posted or publicly disclosed, due to their perceived sensitive content.

Central to the development of F/OSS projects are software extension mechanisms and F/OSS software copyright licenses that insure freedom and/or openness. The extension mechanisms enable modification of the functionality or architecture of software systems via intra-/inter-application scripting or external module plug-in architectures. Copyright licenses, most often derived from the GNU Public License (GPL), are attached to any project developed software, so that it might be further accessed, examined, debated, modified, and redistributed without loss of these rights in the future. These public software licenses stand in contrast to the restricted access found in closed source software systems and end-user license agreements.

Finally, in each of the six communities being examined, participants choose on occasion to author and publish technical reports or scholarly research papers about their software development efforts, which are publicly available for subsequent examination, review, and secondary analysis.

## 2.2    Forming alliances and building community through participation, artifacts, and tools

How does the gathering of individual F/OSS developers give rise to a more persistent project team or self-sustaining community? Through choices that developers make for their participation and contribution to an F/OSSD project, they find that there are like-minded individuals who also choose to participate and contribute to a project. These software developers find and connect with each other through F/OSSD Web sites and online discourse (e.g., threaded email discussions) [Monge 1998], and they find they share many technical competencies, values, and beliefs in common [Crowston

2002, Espinosa 2002, Elliott 2004]. This manifests itself in the emergence of an occupational network of F/OSS developers [Elliott 2003].

Sharing beliefs, values, communications, artifacts and tools among F/OSS developers enables not only cooperation, but also provides a basis for shared experience, camaraderie, and learning [cf. Brown 1991, Fischer 2001, George 1995]. F/OSS developers participate and contribute by choice, rather than by assignment, since they find that conventional software development work provides the experience of working with others who are assigned to a development effort, whether or not they find that share technical approaches, skills, competencies, beliefs or values. As a result, F/OSS developers find they get to work with people that share their many values and beliefs in common, at least as far as software development. Further, the values and beliefs associated with free software or open source software are both signaled and institutionalized in the choice of intellectual property licenses (e.g., GPL) that F/OSSD projects adopt and advocate. These licenses in turn help establish norms for developing free software or open source software, as well as for an alliance with other F/OSSD projects that use the same licenses.

More than half of the 80K F/OSS projects registered at SourceForce.net Web portal employ the GNU General Public License (GPL) for free (as in freedom) software. The GPL seeks to preserve and reiterate the beliefs and practices of sharing, examining, modifying and redistributing F/OSS systems and assets as property rights for collective freedom. A few large F/OSSD project that seek to further protect the collective free/open intellectual property rights do so through the formation of legally constituted non-profit organizations or foundations (e.g., Free Software Foundation, Apache Software Foundation, GNOME Foundation) [O'Mahony 2003]. Other OSS projects, because of the co-mingling of assets that were not created as free property, have adopted variants that relax or strengthen the rights and conditions laid out in the GPL. Dozens of these licenses now exist, with new ones continuing to appear (cf. www.opensource.org). An example of such a variant appears in Exhibit 2. Finally, when OSSD projects seek to engage or receive corporate sponsorship, and the possible co-mingling of corporate/proprietary intellectual property, then some variation of a non-GPL open source license is employed, as a way to signal a "business friendly" OSSD project, and thus to encourage participation by developers who want to work in such a business friendly and career enhancing project [Hann 2002, Sharma 2002].

Developing F/OSS systems is a community and project team building process that must be institutionalized within a community [Sharma 2002, Smith 1999, Preece 2000] for its software informalisms (artifacts) and tools to flourish. Downloading, installing, and using F/OSS systems acquired from other F/OSS Web sites is also part of a community building process [Kim 2000]. Adoption and use of F/OSS project Web sites are a community wide practice for how to publicize and share F/OSS project assets. These Web sites can be built using F/OSS Web site content management systems (e.g., PhP-Nuke) to host project contents that can be served using F/OSS Web servers (Apache), database systems (MySQL) or application servers (JBoss), and increasingly accessed via F/OSS Web browsers (Mozilla). Furthermore, ongoing F/OSS projects may employ dozens of F/OSS development tools, whether as standalone systems like the software version control system CVS, as integrated development environments like NetBeans or Eclipse, or as subsystem components of their own F/OSS application in development. These projects similarly employ asynchronous systems for project communications that are persistent, searchable, traceable, public and globally accessible.

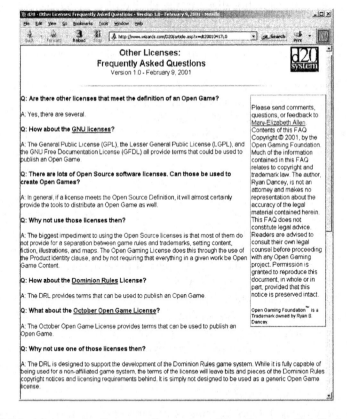

**Exhibit 2: An example of an open license insuring software redistribution and modification freedoms like the GPL, as well as other rights specific to computer games (source: http:www.wizards.com/D20/ , February 2003)**

F/OSS systems, hyperlinked artifacts and tools, and project Web sites serve as venues for socializing, building relationships and trust, sharing and learning with others. "Linchpin developers" [Madey 2004] act as community forming hubs that enable independent small F/OSS projects to come together as a larger social network with the critical mass [Marwell 1993] needed for their independent systems to be merged and experience more growth in size, functionality, and user base. Whether this trend is found in traditional or closed source software projects is unclear. F/OSSD Web sites also serve as hubs that centralize attention for what is happening with the development of the focal F/OSS system, its status, participants and contributors, discourse on pending/future needs, etc. Furthermore, by their very nature, these Web sites (those accessible outside of a corporate firewall) are generally global in reach and accessibility. This means the potential exists for contributors to come from multiple remote sites (geographic dispersion) at different times (24/7), from multiple nations, representing the interests of multiple cultures or ethnicity.

All of these conditions point to new kinds of requirements—for example, community building requirements, community software requirements, and community information sharing system (Web site and interlinked communication channels for email, forums, and chat) requirements. These requirements may entail both functional and non-functional requirements, but they will most typically be expressed using open software informalisms, rather than using formal notations based on some system of mathematical logic.

Community building, alliance forming, and participatory contributing are essential and recurring activities that enable F/OSSD projects to persist without central corporate authority. Figure 3 depicts an example of a social network of 24 F/OSS developers within 5 F/OSS projects that are interconnected through two linchpin developers [Madey 2004]. Thus, linking people, systems, and projects together through shared artifacts and sustained online discourse enables a sustained socio-technical community, information infrastructure [Star 1996], and network of alliances [Kling 2003, Monge 1998] to emerge.

## 2.3 Cooperating, coordinating, and controlling F/OSS projects

Getting software developers to work together, even when they desire to cooperate is not without its challenges for coordinating and controlling who does what when, and to what they do it to. Conflicts arise in both F/OSSD [Elliott 2003, Elliott 2004, Jensen 2004] and traditional software development projects [Sawyer 2001], and finding ways to resolve conflicts becomes part of the cost (in terms of social capital) that must be incurred by F/OSS developers for development progress to occur. Minimizing the occurrence, duration, and invested effort in such conflicts quickly becomes a goal for the core developers in an F/OSSD project. Similarly, finding tools and project organizational forms that minimize or mitigate recurring types of conflicts also becomes a goal for experienced core developers.

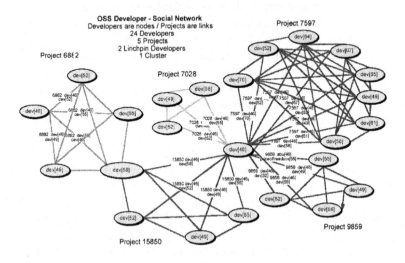

**Figure 3: A social network that links 24 developers in five projects through two key developers into a larger F/OSS project community [cf. Madey 2004]**

Software version control tools such as the concurrent versions system CVS--itself an F/OSS system and document base [Fogel 1999]--have been widely adopted for use within F/OSS projects. Tools like CVS are being used as both a centralized mechanism for coordinating and synchronizing F/OSS development, as well as a venue for mediating control over what software enhancements, extensions, or upgrades will be checked-in and made available for check-out throughout the decentralized community as part of the publicly released version.

Software version control, as part of a software configuration management activity, is a recurring situation that requires coordination but enables stabilization and synchronization of dispersed and somewhat invisible development work [Grinter 1996]. This coordination is required due to the potential tension between centralized decision-making authority of a project's core developers and decentralized work activity of project contributors when two or more autonomously contributed software source code/content updates are made which overlap, conflict with one another, or generate unwanted side-effects [Grinter 2003]. It is also practiced as a way to manage, track, and control both desired and undesired dependencies within the source code [deSouza 2003], as well as among its surrounding informalisms [Scacchi 2002, 2004]. Tools like CVS thus serve to help manage or mitigate conflicts over who gets to modify what, at least as far as what changes or updates get included in the next software release from a project. However, the CVS administrator or configuration control policies provide ultimate authority and control mediated through such systems.

Each project team, or CVS repository administrator in it, must decide what can be checked in, and who will or will not be able to check-in new or modified software source code content. Sometimes these policies are made explicit through a voting scheme [Fielding 1999], while in others they are left informal, implicit, and subject to negotiation. In either situation, version updates must be coordinated in order for a new system build and release to take place. Subsequently, those developers who want to submit updates to the community's shared repository rely extensively on online discussions that are supported using "lean media" such as threaded email messages posted on a Web site [Yamauchi 2000], rather than through onerous system configuration control boards. Thus, software version control, system build and release is a coordination and control process mediated by the joint use of versioning, system building, and communication tools [Erenkrantz 2003].

F/OSSD projects teams can take the organizational form of a *layered meritocracy* [Fielding 1999, Kim 2000] operating as a dynamically organized virtual enterprise [Crowston 2002, Noll 1999]. A layered meritocracy is a hierarchical organizational form that centralizes and concentrates certain kinds of authority, trust, and respect for experience and accomplishment within the team. However, it does not imply a single authority, since decision-making may be shared among core developers who act as peers at the top layer.

Figure 2 illustrates the form of a meritocracy common to many F/OSS projects. In this form, software development work appears to be logically centralized, while being physically distributed in an autonomous and decentralized manner [Noll 1999]. However, it is neither simply a "cathedral" or a "bazaar", as these terms have been used to describe alternative ways of organizing software development projects. Instead, when layered meritocracy operates as a virtual enterprise, it relies on *virtual project management* (VPM) to mobilize, coordinate, control, build, and assure the quality of F/OSS development activities. It may invite or encourage system contributors to come forward and take a shared, individual responsibility that will serve to benefit the F/OSS collective of user-developers. VPM requires multiple people to act in the roles of team leader, sub-system manager, or system module owner in a manner that may be short-term or long-term, based on their skill, accomplishments, availability and belief in community development. This implied requirement for virtual project management can be seen in the text appearing within Exhibit 3.

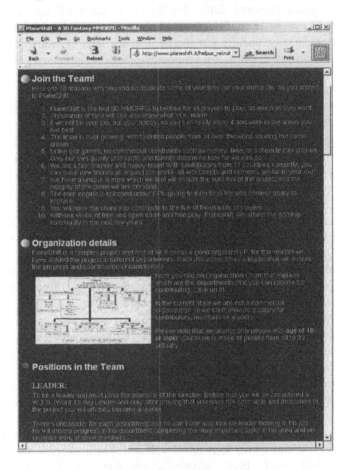

**Exhibit 3: An example statement for how a F/OSS computer game development project seeks to organize and manage itself (source: http://www.planeshift.it/helpus_recruit.html , March 2004)**

Project participants higher up in the meritocracy have greater perceived authority than those lower down. But these relationships are only effective as long as everyone agrees to their makeup and legitimacy. Administrative or coordination conflicts that cannot be resolved may end up either by splitting or forking a new system version with the attendant need to henceforth take responsibility for maintaining that version, by reducing one's stake in the ongoing project, or by simply conceding the position in conflict.

Virtual project management exists within F/OSS communities to enable control via community decision-making, Web site administration, and CVS repository administration in an effective manner. Similarly, VPM exists to mobilize and sustain the use of privately owned resources (e.g., Web servers, network access, site administrator labor, skill and effort) available for shared use or collective reuse by the community.

Traditional software project management stresses planning and control activities. In contrast, Lessig and others [Lessig 1999, Shah 2003] observe that source code is an institution for collective action [O'Mahony 2003, Ostrom 1990] that intentionally or unintentionally realizes a mode of social control on those people who develop or use it. In the case of F/OSS development, Lessig's observation would suggest that the source code controls or constrains end-user and developer interaction, while the code in software development tools, Web sites, and project assets accessible for download controls, constrains, or facilitates developer interaction with the evolving F/OSS system code. CVS is a tool that enables some form of social control. However, the fact that the source code to these systems is available in a free and open source manner offers the opportunity to examine, revise, and redistribute patterns of social control and interaction in ways that favor one form of project organization, system configuration control, and user-developer interaction over others.

Beyond this, the ability for the eyes of many developers to review or look over source code, system build and preliminary test results, and responses to bug reports, also realizes peer review and the potential for embarrassment as a form of indirect social control over the timely actions of contributing F/OSS developers. Thus, F/OSSD allows for this dimension of VPM to be open for manipulation by the core developers, so as to encourage certain patterns of software development and social control, and to discourage others that may not advance the collective needs of F/OSSD project participants. Subsequently, F/OSSD projects are managed, coordinated and controlled, though without the roles for traditional software project managers.

## 2.4 Co-evolving socio-technical systems for F/OSS

Software maintenance, in the form of the addition/subtraction of system functionality, debugging, restructuring, tuning, conversion (e.g., internationalization), and migration across platforms, is a widespread, recurring process in F/OSS development communities. Perhaps this is not surprising since maintenance is generally viewed as *the* major cost activity associated with a software system across its life cycle. However, this traditional characterization of software maintenance does not do justice for what can be observed to occur within different F/OSS communities. Instead, it may be better to characterize the overall evolutionary dynamic of F/OSS as *reinvention*. Reinvention is enabled through the sharing, examination, modification, and redistribution of concepts and techniques that have appeared in closed source systems, research and textbook publications, conferences, and the interaction and discourse between developers and users across multiple F/OSS projects. Thus, reinvention is a continually emerging source of improvement in F/OSS functionality and quality, as well as also a collective approach to organizational learning in F/OSS projects [Brown 1991, Fischer 2001, Huntley 2003, George 1995].

Many of the largest and most popular F/OSS systems like the Linux Kernel [Godfrey 2000, Schach 2002], GNU/Linux distributions [Gonzalez-Barahona 2001, O'Mahony 2003], GNOME user interface [Koch 2002] and others are growing at an exponential rate, as is their internal architectural complexity [Schach 2002]. On the other hand the vast majority of F/OSS projects are small, short-lived, exhibit little/no growth, and often only involve the effort of one developer [Capiluppi 2003, Madey 2004]. In this way, the overall trend derived from samples of 400-40K F/OSS projects registered at the SourceForge.net Web portal reveals a power law distribution common to large self-organizing systems. This means a few large projects have a critical mass of at least 5-15 core F/OSS developers [Mockus 2002] that act in or share project leadership roles [Fielding 1999] that are surrounded by dozens to hundreds of other contributors, and hundreds to millions of end users. These F/OSS projects that attain and sustain such critical mass are those that inevitably garner the most attention, software downloads, and usage. On the other hand, the vast majority of F/OSS projects are small, lacking in critical mass, and thus unlikely to thrive and grow.

The layered meritocracies that arise in F/OSS projects tend to embrace incremental innovations such as evolutionary mutations to an existing software code base over radical innovations. Radical change involves the exploration or adoption of untried or sufficiently different system functionality, architecture, or development methods. Radical software system changes might be advocated by a minority of code contributors who challenge the status quo of the core developers. However, their success in such advocacy usually implies creating and maintaining a separate version of the system, and the potential loss of a critical mass of other F/OSS developers. Thus, incremental mutations tend to win out over time.

F/OSS systems seem to evolve through minor improvements or mutations that are expressed, recombined, and redistributed across many releases with short duration life cycles. End-users of F/OSS systems who act as developers or maintainers continually produce these mutations. These mutations appear initially in daily system builds. These modifications or updates are then expressed as a tentative alpha, beta, release candidate, or stable release versions that may survive redistribution and review, then subsequently be recombined and re-expressed with other new mutations in producing a new stable release version. As a result, these mutations articulate and adapt an F/OSS system to what its developer-users want it to do in the course of evolving and continually reinventing the system.

Last, closed source software systems that were thought to be dead or beyond their useful product life or maintenance period may be *revitalized* through the redistribution and opening of their source code. However, this may only succeed in application domains where there is a devoted community of enthusiastic user-developers who are willing to invest their time and skill to keep the cultural heritage of their former experience with such systems alive. Exhibit 4 provides an example for vintage arcade games now numbering in the thousands that are being revitalized and evolved through F/OSS systems.

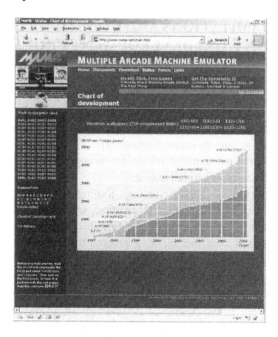

**Exhibit 4: A graphic display depicting sustained growth in the number of vintage arcade ROM sets and games migrated into open source for use on contemporary computer platforms
(source: http://www.mame.net/chart.html , March 2004)**

Overall, F/OSS systems co-evolve with their development communities. This means the evolution of one depends on the evolution of the other. Said differently, an F/OSS project with a small number of developers (most typically one) will not produce and sustain a viable system unless/until the team reaches a larger critical mass of 5-15 core developers. However, if critical mass is achieved, then it may be possible for the F/OSS system to grow in size and complexity at a sustained exponential rate, defying the laws of software evolution that have held for decades [Lehman 1980, Scacchi 2004b]. Furthermore, user-developer communities co-evolve with their systems in a mutually dependent manner [Elliott 2004, Nakakoji 2002, O'Mahony 2003, Scacchi 2002], and system architectures and functionality grow in discontinuous jumps as independent F/OSS projects decide to join forces [Godfrey 2000, Nakakoji 2002, Scacchi 2002b]. Whether this trend is found in traditional or closed source software projects is unclear. But what these findings and trends do indicate is that it appears that the practice of F/OSS development processes is different from the processes traditionally advocated for software engineering.

## 3.    LIMITATIONS AND CONSTRAINTS OF STINs ON F/OSS DEVELOPMENT PROCESSES

F/OSS is certainly not a panacea for developing complex software systems, nor is it simply software engineering done poorly. Instead, it represents an alternative community-intensive approach to develop software systems and related artifacts, as well as social relationships. However, it is not without its limitations and constraints. Thus, we should be able to help see these limits as manifest within or through STINs for each of the four types of processes examined above.

First, in terms of participating, joining, and contributing to F/OSS projects, a developer's interest, motivation, and commitment to a project and its contributors is dynamic and not indefinite. F/OSS developers are loathe to find themselves contributing to a project that is realizing commercial or financial benefits that are not available to all contributors, or that are concentrated to benefit a particular company, again without some share going to the contributors. Some form of reciprocity seems necessary to sustain participation, whereas a perception of exploitation by others can quickly dissolve a participant's commitment to further contribute, or worse to dissuade other participants to abandon an open source project that has gone astray. If linchpin developers lose interest, then unless another contributor comes forward to fill in or take over role and responsibility for the communication and coordination activities of such key developers, then the F/OSS system may quickly become brittle, fragile, and difficult to maintain. Thus, participation, joining, and contributing must become sustained activities on an ongoing basis within F/OSS projects for them to succeed.

Second, in terms of forming alliances and building community through participation, artifacts, and tools points to a growing dependence on other F/OSS projects. The emergence of non-profit foundations that were established to protect the property rights of large multi-component F/OSS project creates a demand to sustain and protect such foundations. If a foundation becomes too bureaucratic as a result to streamline its operations, then this may drive contributors away from a project. So, these foundations need to stay lean, and not become a source of occupational careers, in order to survive and evolve. Similarly, as F/OSS projects give rise to new types of requirements for community building, community software, and community information sharing systems, these requirements need to be addressed and managed by F/OSS project contributors in roles above and beyond those involved in enhancing the source code of a F/OSS project. F/OSS alliances and communities depend on a rich and growing web of socio-technical relations. Thus, if such a web begins to come apart, or if the new requirements cannot be embraced and satisfied, then the F/OSS project community and its alliances will begin to come apart.

Third, in terms of cooperation, coordination, and control, F/OSS projects do not escape conflicts in technical decision-making, or in choices of who gets to work on what, or who gets to modify and update what. As F/OSS projects generally lack traditional project managers, then they must become self-reliant in their ability to mitigate and resolve outstanding conflicts and disagreements. Beliefs and values that shape system design choices, as well as choices over which software tools to use, and which software artifacts to produce or use, are determined through negotiation rather than administrative assignment. Negotiation and conflict management then become part of the cost that F/OSS developers must bear in order for them to have their beliefs and values fulfilled. It is also part of the cost they bear in convincing and negotiating with others often through electronic communications to adopt their beliefs and values. Time, effort, and attention spent in negotiation and conflict management are not spent building and improving source code, but they do represent an investment in building and sustaining a negotiated socio-technical network of dependencies.

Last, in terms of the co-evolution of F/OSS systems and community, as already noted, individual and shared resources of people's time, effort, attention, skill, sentiment (beliefs and values), and computing resources are part of the socio-technical web of F/OSS. Reinventing existing software systems as F/OSS coincides with the emergence or reinvention of a community who seeks to make such system reinvention occur. F/OSS systems are common pool resources [Ostrom 1990] that require collective action for their development, mobilization, use, and evolution. Without the collective action of the F/OSS project community, the common pool will dry up, and without the common pool, the community begins to fragment and disappear, perhaps to search for another pool elsewhere.

## 4.   CONCLUSIONS

Free/open source software development practices are giving rise to a new view of how complex software systems can be constructed, deployed, and evolved on a global basis. F/OSS development does not adhere to the traditional rationality found in the legacy of software engineering life cycle models or prescriptive standards. F/OSS development is inherently a complex web of socio-technical processes, development situations, and dynamically emerging interaction networks. This paper examines and analyzes results from empirical studies that begin to outline some of the socio-technical activities that situate how F/OSS systems are developed in different communities. In particular, examples drawn from different F/OSS project communities reveal how processes and practices for the development and propagation of F/OSS technology are intertwined and mutually situated to the benefit of those motivated to use and contribute to it.

The future of research in the development and use of STINs as a conceptual framework for observing and analyzing F/OSSD processes and practices seems likely to focus attention to the following topics.

First, the focus of software process research is evolving to include attention to socio-technical processes of people, resources, organizational forms, and institutional rules that embed and surround an F/OSS system, as well as how they interact and interface with one another. Such a focus draws attention to the web of socio-technical relations that interlink people in particular settings to a situated configuration of globally available Web-based artifacts and locally available resources (skills, time, effort, computing) that must collectively be mobilized or brought into alignment in order for a useful F/OSS system to be continuously (re)designed to meet evolving user needs.

Second, participation in F/OSS system design, assertion of system requirements, or design decision-making is determined by effort, willingness, and prior public experience in similar situations, rather than by assignment by management or some other administrative authority. Similarly, the openness of the source code/content of a F/OSS system encourages and enables many forms of transparency, access, and ability to customize/localize a system's design to best address user/developer needs in a particular site or installation.

Third, people who participate in the development, deployment, and evolution of F/OSS often do it on a voluntary or self-selected basis. These people quickly recognize the need to find ways to cooperate and collaborate in order to minimize individual effort and conflict while maximizing collective accomplishment. This is most easily observed in the online (or Web-based) communications, shared source code files and directories, application invocation or system configuration scripts, Web pages and embedded hyperlinks, and other textual artifacts that people in free/open source software project communities employ as the media, content, and (hyperlinked) context of system design and evolution. However, there is a continually emerging need to minimize and mitigate conflicts that arise in F/OSSD projects due to the absence of a traditional project management regime that might otherwise act to competently resolve (or to incompetently bungle) such software development conflicts. As a result, F/OSSD projects have adapted or evolved the use of tools, interlinked artifacts, and organizational forms that effectively create a project management capability and socio-technical control framework without (traditional) project managers.

Fourth, the world of F/OSSD is different in many interesting ways and means when compared to the world of software engineering within corporate or centralized enterprise settings. Knowing and understanding one does not provide a sufficient basis for assuming an understanding of the other, yet both worlds develop complex software systems and artifacts using development processes that may (or may not) be well understood. This analysis of the socio-technical interaction networks that facilitate and constrain F/OSSD processes and practices points to new concepts, situations, events, and data for understanding how large software systems are developed, deployed, and evolved within F/OSSD communities of practice. Each merits further study, articulation, and refinement.

Last, the four preceding research directions collectively begin to draw attention to matters beyond software development processes, as traditionally addressed. Instead, future STIN and software process research can employ Web analyses [Kling 1982, Kling 2003], ethnographic methods [Elliott 2004, Scacchi 2002, Viller 2000] and contemporary socio-technical system design techniques [Scacchi 2004c] to study and model how people accomplish software development processes and practices in an organizational setting using F/OSS systems, artifacts, tools, people, and circumstances at hand. Understanding the F/OSS system or interaction network will need to include understanding the workplace, interorganizational networks, social worlds and cultural milieu that embed and situate how people interact with and through the F/OSS systems at hand in the course of their work and workflows. Similarly, there is a basic need to discover new ways and means that enable traditional software developers to understand and become users of F/OSSD practices so as to empower and sustain both traditional and F/OSS developers in their collective effort to continuously improve their software development skills, practices, and processes. This chapter therefore represents a step in this direction.

## ACKNOWLEDGEMENTS

The research described in this chapter is supported by grants #ITR-0083075, #ITR-0205679, #ITR-0205724, and #ITR-0350754 from the U.S. National Science Foundation. No endorsement implied. Mark Ackerman at University of Michigan, Ann Arbor; Les Gasser at University of Illinois, Urbana-Champaign; John Noll at Santa Clara University; and Margaret Elliott and Chris Jensen at the UCI Institute for Software Research are collaborators on the research described in this chapter.

## REFERENCES

Atkinson, C.J., Socio-Technical and Soft Approaches to Information Requirements Elicitation in the Post-Methodology Era, *Requirements Engineering*, 5, 67-73, 2000.

Bjerknes, G. and Bratteteig, T., User Participation and Democracy. A Discussion of Scandinavian Research on System Development, *Scandinavian Journal of Information Systems*, 7(1), 73-98, 1995.

Bergquist, M. and Ljungberg, J., The Power of Gifts: Organizing Social Relationships in Open Source Communities, *Info. Systems J.*, 11, 305-320, 2001.

Beyer, H. and Holtzblatt, K., *Contextual Design: A Customer-Centered Approach to Systems Designs*, Morgan Kaufmann Publishers, San Francisco, CA, 1997.

Brown, J.S. and Duguid, P., Organizational Learning and Communities-of-Practice: Toward a Unified View of Working, Learning, and Innovation, *Organization Science*, 2(1), 40-57, 1991.

Callon, M., Law, J. and Rip, J., (eds.), *Mapping the Dynamics of Science and Technology: Sociology of Science in the Real World*, Macmillan Press, London, 1986.

Capilupppi, A., Lago, P. and Morisio, M., Evidences in the Evolution of OS Projects through Changelog Analyses, *Proc. 3rd Workshop on Open Source Software Engineering*, Portland, OR, May 2003.

Crowston, K., Annabi, H. and Howison, J., Defining Open Source Software Project Success, *Proc. 24th Intern. Conf. Information Systems* (ICIS-2003), December 2003.

Crowston, K. and Scozzi, B., Open Source Software Projects as Virtual Organizations: Competency Rallying for Software Development, *IEE Proceedings–Software*, 149(1), 3-17, 2002.

Ehn, P. and Kyng, M., The Collective Resource Approach to System Design, in G. Bjerknes, P. Ehn, and M. Kyng (eds.), *Computers and Democracy—a Scandinavian Challenge*, Avebury, Aldershot, 1987.

Emery, F.E. and Trist, E.L., Socio-Technical Systems, in C.W. Churchman & M. Verhurst (eds.), *Management Science, Models and Techniques*, Vol. 2, 83-97, Pergamon Press, London, 1960.

Elliott, M. and Scacchi, W., Free Software Developers as an Occupational Community: Resolving Conflicts and Fostering Collaboration, *Proc. ACM Intern. Conf. Supporting Group Work*, 21-30, Sanibel Island, FL, November 2003.

Elliott, M. and Scacchi, W., Free Software Development: Cooperation and Conflict in A Virtual Organizational Culture, in S. Koch (ed.), *Free/Open Source Software Development*, Idea Publishing, to appear, 2004.

Erenkrantz, J., Release Management within Open Source Projects, *Proc. 3rd. Workshop on Open Source Software Engineering*, 25th. Intern. Conf. Software Engineering, Portland, OR, May 2003.

Erickson, T., Making Sense of Computer-Mediated Communication (CMC): CMC Systems as Genre Ecologies, *Proc. 33rd Hawaii Intern. Conf. Systems Sciences*, IEEE Press, 1-10, January 2000.

Espinosa, J. A., Kraut, R.E., Slaughter, S. A., Lerch, J. F., Herbsleb, J. D. and Mockus, A., Shared Mental Models, Familiarity, and Coordination: A Multi-Method Study of Distributed Software Teams, *Intern. Conf. Information Systems*, 425-433, Barcelona, Spain, December 2002.

Fielding, R.T., Shared Leadership in the Apache Project, *Communications ACM*, 42(4), 42-43, 1999.

Fischer, G., External and Shareable Artifacts as Opportunities for Social Creativity in Communities of Interest, in J. S. Gero and M. L. Maher (eds.), *Proc. Computational and Cognitive Models of Creative Design*, 67-89, Heron Island, Australia, December 2001.

Fogel, K., *Open Source Development with CVS*, Coriolis Press, Scottsdale, AZ, 1999.

Gacek, C. and Arief, B., The Many Meanings of Open Source, *IEEE Software*, 21(1), 34-40, January/February 2004.

George, J.F., Iacono, S. and Kling, R., Learning in Context: Extensively Computerized Work Groups as Communities-of-Practice, *Accounting, Management and Information Technology*, 5(3/4), 185-202, 1995.

Godfrey, M.W. and Tu, Q., Evolution in Open Source Software: A Case Study, *Proc. 2000 Intern. Conf. Software Maintenance* (ICSM-00), San Jose, CA, October 2000.

Gonzalez-Barahona, J.M., Ortuno Perez, M.A., de las Heras Quiros, P., Centeno Gonzalez, J. and Matellan Olivera, V., Counting Potatoes: The Size of Debian 2.2, *Upgrade Magazine*, II(6), 60-66, December 2001.

Grinter, R.E., Supporting Articulation Work Using Software Configuration Management Systems, *Computer Supported Cooperative Work*, 5(4), 447-465, 1996.

Grinter, R.E., Recomposition: Coordinating a Web of Software Dependencies, *Computer Supported Cooperative Work*, 12(3), 297-327, 2003.

Hann, I-H., Roberts, J., Slaughter, S. and Fielding, R., Economic Incentives for Participating in Open Source Software Projects, *Proc. Twenty-Third Intern. Conf. Information Systems*, 365-372, December 2002.

Hars, A. and Ou, S., Working for Free? Motivations for participating in open source projects, *Intern. J. Electronic Commerce*, 6(3), 2002.

Hertel, G., Neidner, S. and Hermann, S., Motivation of software developers in Open Source projects: an Internet-based survey of contributors to the Linux kernel, *Research Policy*, 32(7), 1159-1177, July 2003.

Huntley, C.L., Organizational Learning in Open-Source Software Projects: An Analysis of Debugging Data, *IEEE Trans. Engineering Management*, 50(4), 485-493, 2003.

Jensen, C. and Scacchi, W., Collaboration, Leadership, and Conflict Negotiation in the NetBeans.org Community, *Proc. 4th Workshop on Open Source Software Engineering*, Edinburgh, UK, May 2004.

Kim, A.J., *Community-Building on the Web: Secret Strategies for Successful Online Communities*, Peachpit Press, 2000.

Kling, R., Kim, G. and King, R., A Bit More to IT: Scholarly Communication Forums as Socio-Technical Interaction Networks, *Journal American Society for Information Science and Technology*, 54(1), 47-67, 2003.

Kling, R. and Scacchi, W. The Web of Computing: Computer Technology as Social Organization, in A. Yovits (ed.), *Advances in Computers*, 21, Academic Press, 3-85, 1982.

Koch, S. and Schneider, G., Effort, Co-operation and Co-ordination in an Open Source Software Project: GNOME, *Info. Sys. J.*, 12(1), 27-42, 2002.

Latour, B., *Science in Action*, Harvard University Press, Cambridge, MA, 1987.

Law, J. and Hassard, J., (eds.), *Actor Network Theory and After*, Blackwell Publishers, 1999.

Lehman, M.M., Programs, Life Cycles, and Laws of Software Evolution, *Proc. IEEE*, 68, 1060-1078, 1980.

Lerner, J. and Tirole, J., Some Simple Economics of Open Source, *J. Industrial Economics*, 50(2), 197-234, 2002.

Lessig, L., *CODE and Other Laws of Cyberspace*, Basic Books, New York, 1999.

Madey, G., Freeh, V. and Tynan, R., Modeling the F/OSS Community: A Quantative Investigation, in Koch, S., (ed.), *Free/Open Source Software Development*, Idea Publishing, to appear, 2004.

Marwell, G. and Oliver, P., *The Critical Mass in Collective Action: A Micro-Social Theory*. Cambridge University Press, 1993.

Mockus, A., Fielding, R. and Herbsleb, J.D., Two Case Studies of Open Source Software Development: Apache and Mozilla, *ACM Transactions on Software Engineering and Methodology*, 11(3), 309-346, 2002.

Monge, P.R., Fulk, J., Kalman, M.E., Flanagin, A.J., Parnassa, C. and Rumsey, S., Production of Collective Action in Alliance-Based Interorganizational Communication and Information Systems, *Organization Science*, 9(3), 411-433, 1998.

Nakakoji, K., Yamamoto, Y., Nishinaka, Y., Kishida, K. and Ye,Y., Evolution Patterns of Open-Source Software Systems and Communities, *Proc. 2002 Intern. Workshop Principles of Software Evolution*, 76-85, 2002.

Noll, J. and Scacchi, W., Supporting Software Development in Virtual Enterprises, *J. Digital Information*, 1(4), February 1999.

O'Mahony, S., Guarding the Commons: How community managed software projects protect their work, *Research Policy*, 32(7), 1179-1198, July 2003.

O'Mahony, S., Developing Community Software in a Commodity World, in M. Fisher and G. Downey (eds.), *Frontiers of Capital: Ethnographic Reflections on the New Economy*, Social Science Research Council, to appear, 2004.

Ostrom, E., Calvert, R. and T. Eggertsson (eds.), *Governing the Commons: The Evolution of Institutions for Collective Action*, Cambridge University Press, 1990.

Paulson, J.W., Succi, G. and Eberlein, A., An Empirical Study of Open-Source and Closed-Source Software Products, *IEEE Trans. Software Engineering*, 30(4), 246-256, April 2004.

Pavelicek, R., *Embracing Insanity: Open Source Software Development*, SAMS Publishing, Indianapolis, IN, 2000.

Preece, J., *Online Communities: Designing Usability, Supporting Sociability*, John Wiley & Sons, Chichester, UK, 2000.

Sawyer, S., Effects of intra-group conflict on packaged software development team performance, *Information Systems J.*, 11, 155-178, 2001.

Scacchi, W., Understanding the Requirements for Developing Open Source Software Systems, *IEE Proceedings–Software*, 149(1), 24-39, February 2002.

Scacchi, W., Free/Open Source Software Development Practices in the Computer Game Community, *IEEE Software*, 21(1), 59-67, January/February 2004a.

Scacchi, W., Understanding Free/Open Source Software Evolution, in N.H. Madhavji, M.M. Lehman, J.F. Ramil and D. Perry (eds.), *Software Evolution*, John Wiley and Sons Inc, New York, to appear, 2004b.

Scacchi, W., Socio-Technical Design, to appear in W. S. Bainbridge (ed.), *The Encyclopedia of Human-Computer Interaction*, Berkshire Publishing Group, 2004c.

Schuler, D. and Namioka, A.E., *Participatory Design: Principles and Practices*, Mahwah, NJ, Lawrence Erlbaum Associates, 1993.

Schach, S.R., Jin, B., Wright, D.R., Heller, G.Z. and Offutt, A.J., Maintainability of the Linux Kernel, *IEE Proceedings–Software*, 149(1), 18-23, February 2002.

Shah, R.C. and Kesan, J.P., Manipulating the governance characteristics of code, *Info*, 5(4), 3-9, 2003.

Sharma, S., Sugumaran and Rajagopalan, B., A Framework for Creating Hybrid Open-Source Software Communities, *Information Systems J.*, 12(1), 7-25, 2002.

Sim, S.E. and Holt, R.C., The Ramp-Up Problem in Software Projects: A Case Study of How Software Immigrants Naturalize, *Proc. 20th Intern. Conf. Software Engineering*, Kyoto, Japan, 361-370, 19-25 April, 1998.

Smith, M. and Kollock, P. (eds.), *Communities in Cyberspace*, Routledge, London, 1999.

Spinuzzi, C. and Zachry, M., Genre Ecologies: An open-system approach to understanding and constructing documentation, *J. Computer Documentation*, 24(3), 169-181, 2000.

de Souza, C.R.B., Redmiles, D., Mark, G., Penix, J. and Sierhuis, M., Management of interdependencies in collaborative software development, *Proc. 2003 Intern. Symp. Empirical Software Engineering* (ISESE 2003), IEEE Computer Society, 294–303, 2003.

Star, S.L. and Ruhleder, K., Steps Toward an Ecology of Infrastructure: Design and Access for Large Information Spaces, *Information Systems Research*, 7(1), 111-134, March 1996.

Stewart, K.J. and Gosain, S., An Exploratory Study of Ideology and Trust in Open Source Development Groups, *Proc. 22nd Intern. Conf. Information Systems* (ICIS-2001), in New Orleans, LA. 2001.

Truex, D., Baskerville, R. and Klein, H., Growing Systems in an Emergent Organization, *Communications ACM*, 42(8), 117-123, 1999.

Viller, S. and Sommerville, I., Ethnographically informed analysis for software engineers, *Intern. J. Human-Computer Studies*, 53, 169-196, 2000.

von Hippel, E. and Katz, R., Shifting Innovation to Users via Toolkits, *Management Science*, 48(7), 821-833, July 2002.

von Krogh, G., Spaeth, S. and Lakhani, K., Community, Joining, and Specialization in Open Source Software Innovation: A Case Study, *Research Policy*, 32(7), 1217-1241, July 2003.

Yamauchi, Y., Yokozawa, M., Shinohara, T. and Ishida, T., Collaboration with Lean Media: How Open-Source Software Succeeds, *Proc. Computer Supported Cooperative Work Conf.* (CSCW'00), 329-338, Philadelphia, PA, ACM Press, December 2000.

# Chapter 2

# OPEN SOURCE SOFTWARE DEVELOPMENT PROCESS MODELING

Jacques LONCHAMP

*LORIA, BP 254, 54500 Vandoeuvre-les-Nancy, France. E-mail: jloncham@loria.fr*

**Abstract**:    This chapter draws attention to software process modeling for open source software development. It proposes a three-layered open source software development process model. Its 'definitional' and 'generic' levels specify the common features of all fully-fledged open source projects. Its 'specific' level allows to describe fine-grained process model fragments characteristic of different open source projects. In this chapter, the specific level is exemplified with the release management process of NetBeans IDE and Apache HTTP Server projects. The underlying modeling approach is SPEM (Software Process Engineering Meta-model) from the OMG. The paper closes with a discussion of the interest of explicit software process models for (1) process understanding and communication, (2) process comparison, reuse, and improvement, (3) process enactment support.

**Key words**:    Open source software development process modeling; open source software development; open source software; SPEM; software process modeling.

## 1.    INTRODUCTION

In the last ten years, open source software (OSS) has attracted the attention of not only the practitioner, but also the business and the research communities. In short, OSS is a software whose source code may be freely modified and redistributed with few restrictions, and which is produced by loosely organized, ad-hoc communities consisting of contributors from all over the world who seldom if ever meet face-to-face, and who share a strong sense of commitment [1]. The basic principle for the OSS development process (OSSDP) is that by sharing source code, developers cooperate under a model of systematic peer-review, and take advantage of parallel debugging that leads to innovation and rapid advancement [2]. Today, Linux and Apache Server are used in respectively 30% and 60% of the Internet's public servers. This demonstrates that OSSDP can produce software of high quality and functionality. Other success stories include Perl, Tcl, Python and PHP programming languages, sendmail mail handler, Mozilla browser, MySQL database server, Eclipse and NetBeans Java integrated development environments. Recently, many organizations have started to look towards OSS and OSSDP as a way to minimize their development efforts by reusing open source code and to provide greater flexibility in their development practices [3].

Two factors may impede this growing interest in OSSDP. First, neither Apache, Mozilla, NetBeans, or any other OSS projects, provide documents on their Web portals that explicitly and precisely describe what development processes are employed. OSS projects do not typically provide explicit process models, prescriptions, or schemes other than what may be implicit in the use of certain development tools for version control and source code compilation. Secondly, most studies that report on OSS projects like Apache and Mozilla [4, 5, 6] provide only informal narrative descriptions of the overall software development process. Such narrative descriptions cannot be easily analyzed, compared, visualized, enacted, and transferred for reuse in other projects. Consequently, developers who want to join an OSS project must discover its underlying development process by using public information sources on the Web. These sources include process enactment information such as informal task prescriptions, community and information structure, work roles, project and product development histories, electronic messages and communications patterns among project participants. Such a discovery approach is very tedious and the variability in development process performance across iterations can blur its results. Similarly, software engineers wanting to start a new OSS project, cannot reuse explicit descriptions or models of the software processes and must discover them through ad hoc trial-and-error. Finally, government agencies, academic institutions and industrial firms which begin to consider OSSDP seek to find what are the best processes or development practices to follow [7]. Explicit modeling of these processes in forms that can be shared, reviewed, modified, and redistributed could be an important contribution to their dissemination and continuous improvement.

The lack of interest in software process modeling techniques observed within and outside of the open source community can be attributed to several reasons. First, it could be argued that OSS projects are ingrained in the hacker culture and represents the antithesis of software engineering [8], with a 'bazaar' [9] or 'development in the wild' style. Just as there is no single development model for proprietary software, neither is there only one detailed model in the OSS world. However, many observations show that at least a set of common features (roles, activities, tools, etc.) are shared by many fully-fledged OSS projects, i.e., it exists a kind of high level generic software process model that we will try to specify. Secondly, it could be objected that OSS development practices are continuously evolving in these communities whose members operate with a high degree of autonomy. Therefore, modeling such processes at the risk of freezing them could be counterproductive. Our observations suggest that most of these evolutions stay at a very detailed level. Other observations relate evolutions to the infancy of OSS projects and to temporary crisis periods [10]. The most important process fragments of a mature project seem rather stable and often core participants make efforts in order to stabilize and standardize them. Lastly, process model formalisms are often criticized: they would be too complex, too low level and fine-grained and not easy to use and share. We will show that the Software Process Engineering Meta-model (SPEM) [11] from the Object Management Group (OMG) can constitute a good candidate for OSSDP modeling because of two main reasons: first, it provides a minimal set of modeling elements, allowing both structural and behavioral descriptions at different levels of formality and granularity, and second, it uses UML [12] as a notation.

This chapter is organized around four themes. First, some definitions about open source projects are given and the consequences of their diversity from the process modeling perspective are discussed. Second, the SPEM meta model that we use for modeling OSSDPs is presented. Third, our three-layered model proposal with its 'definitional', 'generic', and 'specific' levels is described and illustrated. Finally, the interest of software process modeling of OSS projects for (1) process understanding and communication, (2) process comparison, reuse and improvement, (3) process enactment support, is discussed.

## 2. OPEN SOURCE PROJECTS

It is frequent to make a distinction between the terms 'free software' and 'open source software'. Free software refers not to price but to liberty to modify and redistribute source code. The Free Software Foundation [13], founded by Richard Stallman, advocates the use of its GNU General Public License (GPL) as a copyright license which creates and promotes freedom. He writes "to understand the concept, you should think of free speech, not free beer" [14]. The term 'open source' was coined by a group of people concerned that the term 'free software' was anathema to businesses. This resulted in the creation of the Open Source Initiative (OSI) [15]. We use the acronym OSS for both movements for the sake of simplicity and because both movements share most of their practical goals and follow similar development processes. The OSI definition [16] includes the following criteria:

- *free redistribution*: the license shall not restrict any party from selling or giving away the software as a component of an aggregate software distribution; no royalty or fee is required for such sale,
- *source code*: the program must include source code,
- *derived works*: modifications and derived works are allowed, not necessarily subject to the same license as the original work,
- *integrity of author's source code*: derived works must carry different names or version numbers than the original work,
- *no discrimination against persons or groups*,
- *no discrimination against fields of endeavor*,
- *distribution of license*: no need of any additional license,
- *license must not be specific to a product*,
- *license must not restrict other software*,
- *license must be technology-neutral.*

GNU GPL, BSD, Apache, MPL (Mozilla) and Artistic (Perl) licenses are all examples of licenses that conform the OSI definition, unlike Sun Community Source License [8].

Another distinction can be drawn between OSS projects that result from the initiative of a given individual or group of individuals, and OSS projects that are supported by, or organized within, industrial software companies. Examples here include the NetBeans [17] and Eclipse [18] OSS projects that are both developing Java-based interactive development environments, based in part on the corporate support respectively from SUN and IBM. The consequences are noticeable in the way these projects are managed (e.g. composition of the steering committee, decision-making processes) and through the existence of peripheral processes under the exclusive responsibility of the company which backs the project (mainly quality insurance processes). But as will be shown in section 4.3.1 the release process of NetBeans is not deeply impacted by such a corporate support.

OSS projects can also be classified into communities of interest, centered about the production of software for different application domains, such as games, Internet infrastructure, software system design, astronomy, etc. This factor has a low impact on how the software is produced [19].

At the opposite, the project community size is important. Below some critical mass, in terms of active developers, OSSDPs do not match our generic description, as for instance the extreme case of the 'solo work, internal patches' scenario of [20]. The definitional level of our model specifies what a 'fully-fledged' OSS project is, roughly corresponding to the 'team work, external patches' scenario [20].

## 3.  SPEM META MODEL DESCRIPTION

This section presents the Software Process Engineering Meta-model (SPEM) defined by the OMG. SPEM is a meta-model for defining software engineering process models and their components [11]. A tool based on SPEM would be a tool for process model authoring and customizing. The actual enactment of processes, i.e. planning and executing a project using a process model described with SPEM, is not in the scope of this process modeling approach.

The modeling approach is object-oriented and uses UML as a notation [12]. The SPEM specification is structured as a UML profile, i.e. a set of stereotypes, tags and constraints added to the UML standard semantics, and provides also a complete MOF-based meta-model [21]. SPEM is built from the SPEM_Foundation package, which is a subset of UML 1.4, and the SPEM_Extensions package, which adds the constructs and semantics required for software process engineering. Such an approach facilitates exchange with both UML tools and Meta Object Facility (MOF) based tools or repositories. Figure 1 shows the four-layered architecture of modeling as defined by the OMG.

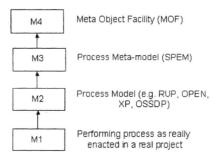

**Figure 1: The OMG modeling architecture**

At the core of SPEM is the idea that a software development process is a collaboration between abstract active entities, called '*Process Roles*', that perform operations, called '*Activities*', on concrete, tangible entities, called '*Work Products*'. More precisely (see Figure 2), a process model definition is built out of *Model Elements*. Each *Model Element* describes one aspect of a software engineering process, and can be associated to an *External*

*Description* in some natural language, suitable for a reader of the process model. A *Dependency* is a process-specific relationship between process *Model Elements*. For instance, a 'precedes' dependency acts from one *Activity* (or *Work Definition*) to another to indicate start-start, finish-start or finish-finish dependencies between the work described, depending on the value of the 'kind' attribute. *Guidance* is a *Model Element* associated with the major *Model Elements*, which contains additional descriptions for practitioners such as techniques, guidelines and UML profiles, procedures, standards, templates of work products, examples of work products, definitions, and so on.

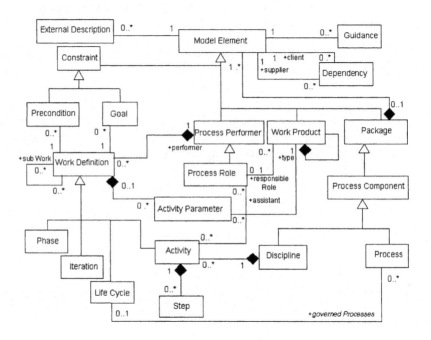

**Figure 2: SPEM main classes**

A *Work Product* is a description of a piece of information or physical entity produced or used by the *Activities* of the software engineering process. Examples of *Work Products* include models, plans, code, executables, documents, databases, and so on.

A *Work Definition* is a *Model Element* describing the execution, the operations performed, and the transformations enacted on the *Work Products* by the *Process Roles*. *Activity*, *Iteration*, *Phase*, and *Lifecycle* are kinds of *Work Definition*. Any *Work Definition* can be associated with *Preconditions* and with *Goals*. They are both *Constraints*, expressed in terms of the states of the *Work Products* that are *Activity Parameters* to this *Work Definition*. The *Precondition* defines what *Work Products* are needed and in which state they must be to allow the work definition to start. *Activities* are the main element of work. A *Step* is an atomic and fine-grained *Model Element* used to decompose *Activities*. *Activities* are partially ordered sets of *Steps*. The *Life Cycle* associated to a *Process* is a *Work Definition* containing all the work to be done in a software engineering process. This *Lifecycle* can be decomposed into *Phases* and/or *Iterations*. A *Phase* is a high-level work definition, bounded by a milestone that can be expressed in terms of *Goals*: which *Work Products* and in which state they must be completed. An *Iteration* is a large-grained *Work Definition* that represents a set of *Work Definitions* focusing on a portion of the *Process* that results in a release (internal or external).

A *Process Performer* is a *Model Element* describing the owner of *Work Definitions*. *Process Performer* is used for work definitions that cannot be associated with individual *Process Roles*, such as a *Lifecycle* or a *Phase*. A *Process Role* describes the responsibilities and competencies of an individual carrying out *Activities* within a *Process*, and responsible for certain *Work Products*.

Process packages allow any arbitrary (and overlapping) groupings of process Definition Elements. A Process Component is a package that has some internal consistency, and that is used for structuring a large Process. A Process is a complete description of a software engineering process, in term of Process Performers, Process Roles, Work Definitions, Work Products, and associated *Guidance*. A *Discipline* is a *Process Package* organized from the perspective of one of the software engineering disciplines: configuration management, analysis and design, test, and so forth.

Being a UML Profile, the SPEM benefits of UML diagrams to present different perspectives of a software process model: in particular, class diagram, package diagram, activity diagram and use case diagram. The SPEM notation suggests alternate representations for most frequently used concrete classes of the meta-model: these icons are depicted in Figure 3.

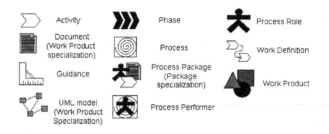

**Figure 3: SPEM icons**

SPEM standard aims at accommodating a large range of existing and described software development processes, and not excluding them by having too many features or constraints [11].

## 4.    OSSDP MODELING

### 4.1   The definitional level

Our first highly abstract model is shown in Figure 4. The whole OSSDP is described as a single SPEM *Process Package* with two *Disciplines*: 'Software development processes' and 'Community processes'. This prescriptive model indicates that a fully-fledged OSSDP *requires the implication of a wide and organized community of distributed volunteer contributors.*

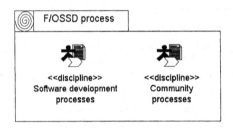

**Figure 4: The definitional model**

Most OSS projects are actually designed and developed by individuals, not communities: 57% have one or two developers [22] (34% according to [23]), and only 15% of them have more than 10 developers [22] (19% according to [23]). In the first category, these very small OSS projects are directed by a single 'lead developer' – usually the software's original author – who assumes all the responsibilities and interacts with a small community of end users.

Our model focuses on the latter category, roughly corresponding to the 'team work, external patches' scenario of [20], and which includes the most successful OSS projects.

For some authors, small OSS projects are projects still in infancy, and large projects are mature ones [20]. For instance, Stephano Mazzocchi's 'Stellar Model' [24] compares these stages and lifecycles to the ones of stars and gravitational systems in general: expansion, fragmentation, contraction. In our model, we are describing mature OSS projects.

## 4.2 The generic level

Our second level defines a generic model of OSSDP, resulting from a synthesis of many studies that report on OSS projects, and a survey of a number of OSS Web portals. It is divided in two parts: the global view and the use case view.

### 4.2.1 The global view

Each *Discipline* of the definitional level is first described as a set of *Model Elements*: *Process Roles* with the *Work Definitions* they perform (*Activities* or complex *Work Definitions*), *Work Products* (*Documents*) and *Guidance* entities mainly describing *tool usage* (see Figures 5 and 6).

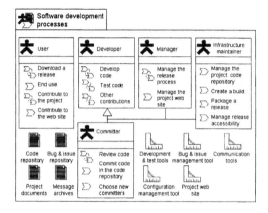

**Figure 5: The Software Development Discipline**

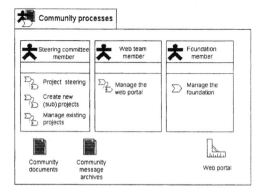

**Figure 6: The Community Development Discipline**

*Process Roles* reflect the different levels of participation which exist in all OSS projects. They "simply reflect a natural gradient of interest, competence and commitment" (E. Raymond, cited in [8]).

Our model can abstract different concrete development organizations. For instance, in projects with a closed 'inner circle', all Developers are also Committers who are granted write access rights to the project code repository. In some projects, the Steering Committee is an elected governing board (e.g. Apache Group), while other projects have a single project owner (or 'benevolent-dictator' [25]). When the number of participants grows, secondary leaders emerge. Rather than project owners, they normally act as managers (e.g., release managers) or maintainers (e.g., module or infrastructure maintainers). More generally, leaders are also Developers which is a radical difference from traditional development models. Most projects operate as meritocraties [8]: the more someone participates, the more merit or trust they earn from their peers, and the more they are allowed to do. When the size of the software becomes too large, new functionalities are added by means of ancillary (sub) projects. By this way, development teams are kept small so that coordination can be handled by simple and often implicit mechanisms.

Our model also emphasizes that tool mediation is the norm for OSS projects: all policies such as authentication or regulation of commit privileges are enforced by the tools on the project server. Most tools are open source software and similar across projects, lowering the entry barrier for participation. CVS and Subversion (version management), Bugzilla and GNATS (bug and issue tracking), Hypermail (mailbox to HTML transformer) are some examples of popular tools in open source communities. Communication is predominantly asynchronous through private mail and public or semi public mailing lists.

### 4.2.2  The use case view

The complex *Work Definitions* of both *Disciplines* are refined with SPEM use case diagrams which in turn recursively define *Activities* or simpler *Work Definitions*. Use cases allow to specify that several *Process Roles* are collaborating within a complex *Work Definition*. These graphical descriptions are easy to understand and can be further clarified with SPEM *External Descriptions*.

Figure 7 shows the User-oriented use case diagrams refining 'Download a release' and 'Contribute to the project' *Work Definitions*. These diagrams emphasize the fact that the most important participants in OSSDP are the people who use the software. Users contribute to the project by providing feedback to developers in the form of bug reports and feature suggestions, and by participating in various issue discussions. Peer review is implicit in OSS projects: source code is available to every user, and technical communication is conducted in public. Most developers start out as users and therefore guide their development efforts from the user's perspective.

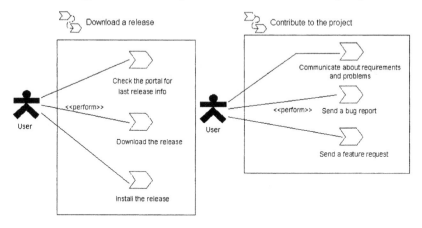

**Figure 7: The User-oriented use cases**

In general, OSS projects have a small, elite team of capable developers, all of whom are granted write access to the source code repository ('Committers'). This core group creates the vast majority of new functionality. A much larger group mainly provides bug fixes ('Developers'). Small increments (bug fix or enhancement) and rapid iteration typify all OSS projects. Figure 8 shows the Developer and Committer-oriented use case diagrams refining 'Develop code', 'Test code', 'Review code', and 'Other contributions' *Work Definitions*.

As we can see in Figures 7 and 8, there is no formal requirements process: requirements are determined implicitly, as whatever the developers actually build. Since developers are also end users and domain experts, they should understand the requirements in a deep way.

Design activities are also missing from Figure 8. Design takes place at the very beginning of the project when an early version of the product is produced by an individual or a small closed group (see the 'Provide Initial Code' *Activity* in Figure 10). This early version is sometimes built from scratch, or more often, it reuses and extends an existing product. For instance, Apache was based on the NSCA HTTPD server and Mozilla was derived from the Netscape Communicator code base.

In OSS projects, there are no distinct phases: participants work concurrently on whatever task (code, test, discuss, etc.) they find interesting.

A good modular design of the product under construction makes such division of labor and parallelism easier.

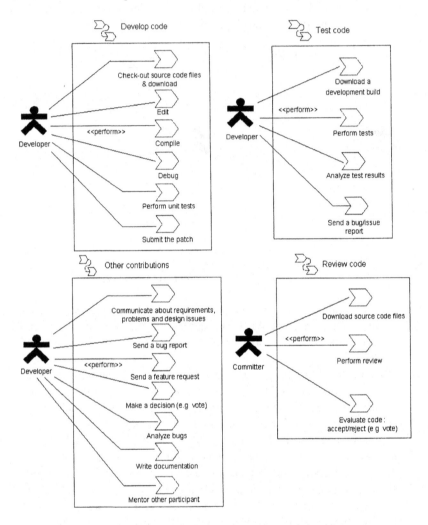

**Figure 8: The Developer and Committer-oriented use cases**

To synchronize change, at some point, all important changes are merged into a new release. Developers must contribute their finalized code for the new release. Release cycles overlap, with release $_{i+1}$ development starting in parallel with release $_i$ reviewing and debugging. At the highest level of parallelism, some OSS projects also maintain parallel code branches: one for ongoing development and the other for stability and widespread use. Linux is a well known example of this approach, where the middle number of the version identifier characterizes the release: odd numbers are for development kernels and even numbers for stable ones. Figure 9 depicts the Manager-oriented use cases related to the release management process.

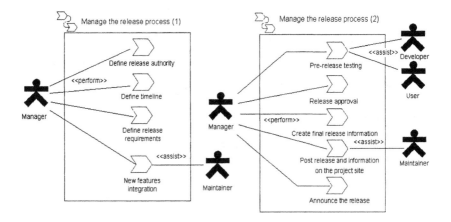

**Figure 9: The Manager-oriented use cases**

Most activities at the community level (see Figure 10) are oriented for making easier participation and communication, such as Web portal management.

Open source development is much more informal than usual software engineering projects: there are typically no plans or schedules. Some projects have a brief vision summary and a development roadmap, produced by the Steering Committee Members (see Figure 10) and describing for instance the milestone schedule for the next year (in the Mozilla project). But, as participants are volunteers there is no real commitment to deliver something within a fixed timeframe.

### 4.2.3 Discussion

Our prescriptive model is consistent with Scacchi's generic OSSDP model [26] (Figure 11) or Gilliam's model [27] (Figure 12). It has a larger scope and encompasses all the basic aspects of software development, in terms of Roles, Tools, Documents, and Activities. In a different way, Scacchi and Gilliam models emphasize the cyclic nature of the overall process and the central role of experience sharing. Our model can also be compared with textual descriptive process models or frameworks, such as [8] and [28]. Unlike all these informal descriptions, our model can be refined until it provides a precise and description of specific existing OSSDPs, amenable to systematic analysis, comparison, and re-use. This point will be discussed and exemplified in the next sections.

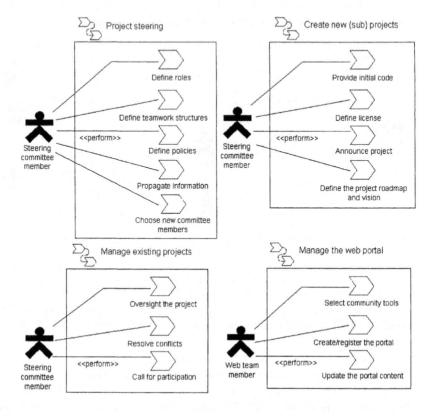

**Figure 10: Community-oriented use cases**

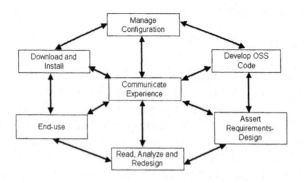

**Figure 11: Scacchi's generic OSSDP model**

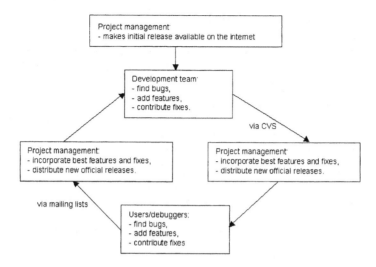

**Figure 12: Gilliam's model of OSSDP**

Eric Raymond principles ([29]) stay at a more abstract level, but many of them have a direct counterpart in terms of the process model:

- every good work of software starts by scratching a developer's personal itch,
- good programmers know what to write; great ones know what to rewrite (and reuse),
- if you have the right attitude (i.e. code sharing), interesting problems will find you,
- treating your users as co-developers is your least-hassle route to rapid code improvement and effective debugging,
- release early; release often; and listen to yours customers,
- given a large enough beta-tester and co-developer base, almost every problem will be characterized quickly and the fix obvious to someone,
- if you treat your beta-testers as if they are your most valuable resource, they will respond by becoming your most valuable resource,
- the next best thing to having good ideas is recognizing good ideas from your users; sometimes the latter is better,
- perfection (in design) is achieved not when there is nothing to add, but rather when there is nothing more to take away,
- to solve an interesting problem, start by finding a problem that is interesting to you,
- provided the development coordinator has a medium at least as good as the Internet, and knows how to lead without coercion, many heads are inevitably better than one.

## 4.3    The specific level

At this level, our model describes the specific features discovered by analyzing the project shared information spaces on the Web. Each OSS project defines its own *Process Roles, Documents, Guidance,* and more or less detailed procedural behaviors that we translate into SPEM activity diagrams. In the next two subsections we exemplify the approach with the release management process of the NetBeans IDE project and the Apache HTTP Server project. We have chosen these projects because of several reasons: their rich information space, the availability of many studies that report on them ([30, 4, 10, 31, 32]), their release management process, since it reflects much of the underlying philosophy of OSS projects [33].

### 4.3.1  The NetBeans IDE release management process

In a first step, we specialize the concepts of the generic process model. Figure 13 exemplifies some specializations of the generic *Process Roles* and *Documents* entities.

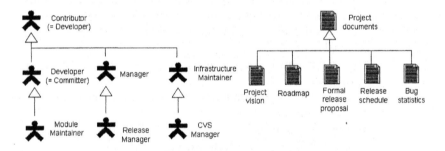

**Figure 13: Generic concept specializations**

In NetBeans, Contributors do not have write-access to the source tree managed by CVS (Concurrent Versions System). Committers are called Developers, and have CVS write-access for some individual modules. Each module has one Module Maintainer who has check-in permissions (for that module or global), and who manages a group of Developers. All Managers and Maintainers are also Contributors. A number of project *Documents* play a central role for coordinating the participants during the release process.

The informal description of the release process found on the Web portal is a mail posted by the current Release Manager to the developers mailing list (nbdev). The description of the process may slightly evolve from one release to another. We give below an excerpt of two successive versions of that informal description (Figures 14 and 15).

NETBEANS RELEASE PROCESS – PROPOSAL    **[NB 3.1 nbdev mailing list 20/9/2000]**
---------------------------------------------------

* when we want to make a new release of NetBeans IDE some volunteer will be chosen to be a release manager (RM)  The RM's role is to coordinate all the release efforts
* module owners will agree upon a code freeze date. The RM will announce this date on nbdev.
* developers are expected to finish their work on new features before the code freeze date
* when the code freeze happens, a new branch is made off the CVS trunk, the convention is to name the branch 'releaseXY' where X.Y is the version number of the new release
* branch releaseXY will be built nightly and tested by developers. Bugs will be filed in Bugzilla. If there are no Blocker and Critical bugs for five days, we can declare the release has reached the beta stage. README, INSTALL, release notes, list of changes will be completed. Announcement will be posted on nbannounce and nbusers. Users are welcome to download the software, and beta test it
* users will file found bugs in Bugzilla, developers will (try to) fix them. The release becomes stable when there is no Blocker, Critical, Major bugs for at least 10 days.
* during that process the RM will post the bug statistics daily on nbdev, to keep all parties informed
* when the release becomes stabled, zip, tarball will be created and put on website. The final download, install test will be done. Wait for one day and an official announcement will be posted.
* parties will be thrown at different places around the globe

**Figure 14: NetBeans release process description for version 3.1**

NetBeans Release Process    **[NB 3.2 nbdev mailing list 11/2/2001]**
---------------------------------

* we do release once per three months, it means four releases each year. This is the goal.
* although the general schedule is one release per three months, the exact dates must be set for each release
* the release schedule consists of the feature freeze, the first and second release candidate and the final release.
* feature freeze is the date after which only code changes due to bug fixes are allowed to be checked in CVS
* after feature freeze UI changes should be minimal, i.e  feature freeze implies UI freeze  Any UI changes must be communicated in advance and should be carried out only because of bug fixes
* at the feature freeze a side branch in CVS will be created for fixing bugs and finalizing documentations. The naming convention for a CVS branch is releaseXY where X.Y is the version number of the release
* during the stabilization phase the binaries are marked as NB X.Y beta, daily built is made available for download and all users are invited to test the software. Developers are expected to promptly respond to bug reports. Bug reports are of course preferably filed in the bug database, but the developers should also monitor the nbusers mailing list and reply to users' feedbacks posted there.
* at the end of the stabilization phase a series of builds will be declared as release candidates. If no serious issues are found the last release candidate automatically becomes the final release. There must be at least one week between the last release candidate and the final release.
* after the first release candidate is made all code changes must be negotiated in advance by posting requests on nbdev
* during the stabilization phase the README and release notes are being put together. The first drafts of these two critical documents should rather be made earlier than later.

**Figure 15: NetBeans release process description for version 3.2**

On the basis of these textual descriptions, we have devised a multi layered SPEM activity diagram. At the first level, Figure 16 specifies the sequence of all *Activities* of the generic use case model that was depicted by

Figure 9. Some *Activities* are then decomposed into smaller *Steps*. 'Define release requirements', 'Define release authority', 'Define timeline', and 'Pre release testing' *Activities* are taken below as examples of such refinements (see Figures 18, 20, 22, 23). For each refined *Step*, we give excerpts of documents, mainly emails from the developers mailing list, as their rationale or illustration. At this level, we are starting to devise process model fragments from process enactment instances discovered in the project information space, instead of formalizing process descriptions written by core participants as previously. The reliability of these model fragments is more questionable but can be strengthened by the frequency of the observed pattern in the project history. Some researchers propose to automatically extract these model fragments from the artifacts (source code files, messages in public discussion forums, Web pages), the artifact update events (version release announcements, Web page updates, message postings), and the work contexts (roadmap for software version releases, Web site architecture, communications systems in use ) [34, 35].

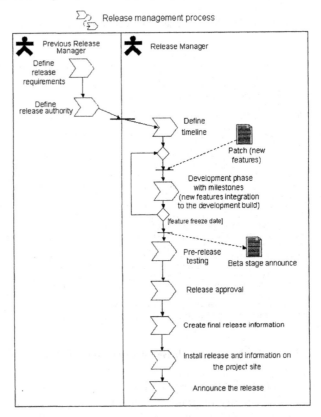

**Figure 16: NetBeans release management process**

Figure 17 shows a release proposal (a mail from nbdev mailing list) and Figure 18 explains how it has been constructed.

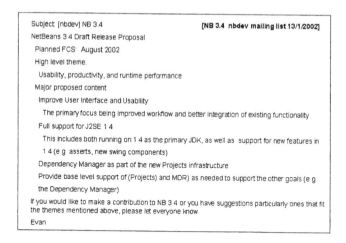

Subject: [nbdev] NB 3.4        **[NB 3.4 nbdev mailing list 13/1/2002]**

NetBeans 3 4 Draft Release Proposal

Planned FCS: August 2002

High level theme.

Usability, productivity, and runtime performance

Major proposed content

Improve User Interface and Usability

The primary focus being improved workflow and better integration of existing functionality

Full support for J2SE 1 4

This includes both running on 1 4 as the primary JDK, as well as support for new features in

1 4 (e g asserts, new swing components)

Dependency Manager as part of the new Projects infrastructure

Provide base level support of (Projects) and MDR as needed to support the other goals (e g

the Dependency Manager)

If you would like to make a contribution to NB 3 4 or you have suggestions particularly ones that fit the themes mentioned above, please let everyone know

Evan

**Figure 17: A release proposal part of 'Define release requirements' activity**

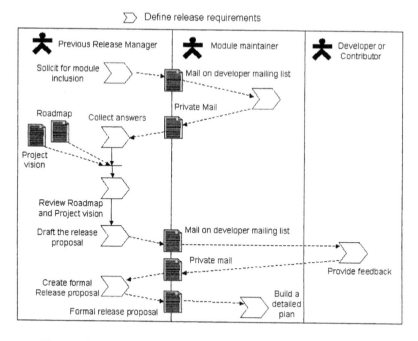

**Figure 18: 'Define release requirements' refined activity diagram**

The 'Define release authority' *Activity* includes a public call for the designation of a new Release Manager (see the mails in Figure 19).

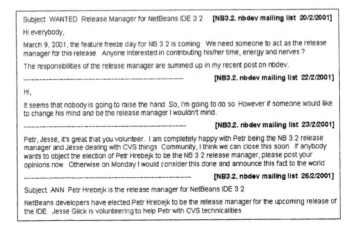

**Figure 19: Mails related to the 'Define release authority' activity**

The process for defining the release authority can slightly change from one iteration to the next. Figure 20 defines a kind of 'standard practice' with candidacy announcements and consensus establishment.

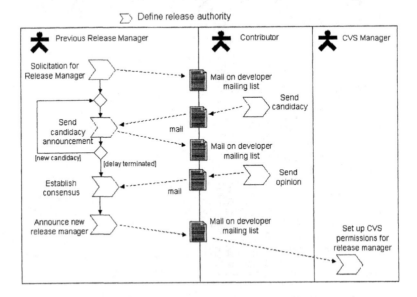

**Figure 20: 'Define release authority' refined activity diagram**

Projects regularly enforce feature freeze (and/or code freeze). During NetBeans feature freeze, no new functionality can be added to the code base, however bug fixes are permitted. The 'Define timeline' *Activity* (Figure 22) produces a release schedule specifying all milestones (Figure 21).

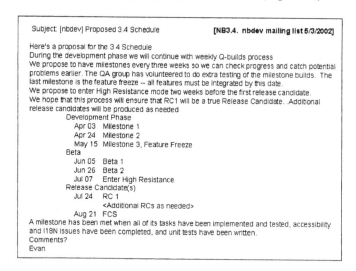

Figure 21: A release schedule proposal part of 'Define timeline' activity

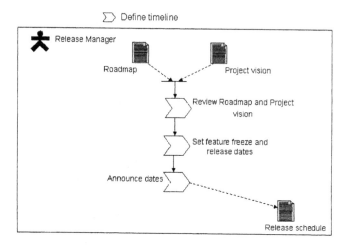

Figure 22: 'Define timeline' refined activity diagram

The 'Pre-release testing' *Step* of Figure 16, which constitutes the core of the release process, is refined twice. The first refinement (Figure 23) shows the 'stabilization phase' followed by a sequence of release candidates (RC).

The 'high resistance mode' ensures that lead programmers review code changes. Every RC build is created when there is no known critical bug. If any critical bug is discovered within one week after RC is built, the bug has to be fixed and a new RC is created. If no critical bug is discovered within one week in RC, this build will become the final (stable) release.

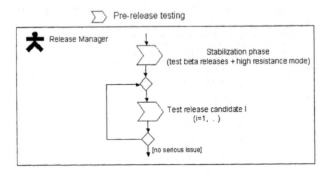

**Figure 23: 'Pre-release testing' first refinement**

The second refinement (Figure 24) gives more details about the 'Stabilization phase' during which Developers and Contributors propose bug fixes to the beta release which is daily built.

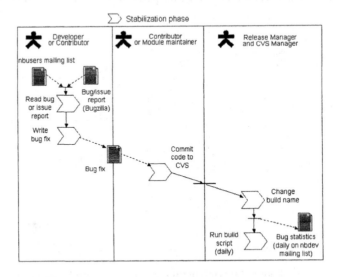

**Figure 24: 'Pre-release testing' second refinement**

In addition, several *Activities* implemented by Sun's Quality Assurance team, responsible for the commercial product SunONE Studio which extends

NetBeans, come with the open source release process such as weekly Q-builds, for ensuring an assured level of quality, and extra testing of the milestone builds during the stabilization phase. This close relationship with a 'commercial process' has no deep impact on NetBeans OSSDP.

### 4.3.2 The Apache Server release management process

On the Apache Server Web portal a document informally describes the release process (see Figure 25).

This document describes the general release policies used by the Apache HTTP Server Project. As described herein, this policy is not set in stone and may be adjusted by the Release Manager.

Who can make a release? Technically, any one can make a release of the source code due to the Apache Software License. However, only members of the Apache HTTP Server Project (committers) to project can make a release designated with Apache. Other people must call their release something other than "Apache" unless they obtain written permission from the Apache Software Foundation

Who is in charge of a release? The release is coordinated by the Release Manager (hereafter, abbreviated as RM). Since this job requires coordination of the development community (and access to CVS), only committers to the project can be RM. However, there is no set RM. Any committer may perform a release at any time. In order to facilitate communication, it is deemed nice to alert the community with your planned release schedule before executing the release.

Who may make a good candidate for RM? Someone with lots of time to kill. Being an RM is a very important job in our community because it takes a fair amount of time to produce a stable release

When do I know if it is a good time to release? It is our convention to indicate showstoppers in the STATUS file in the repository. A showstopper entry does not automatically imply that a release can not be made. As the RM has final authority on what makes it into a release, they can choose to ignore the entries. An item being denoted as a showstopper indicates that the group has come to a consensus that no further releases can be made until the entry is resolved. These items may be bugs, outstanding vetos that have not yet been resolved, or enhancements that must make it into the release

What power does the RM yield? Regarding what makes it into a release, the RM is the unquestioned authority. No one can contest what makes it into the release

How can an RM be confident in a release? The RM may perform sanity checks on release candidates. One highly recommended suggestion is to run the httpd-test suite against the candidate. The release candidate should pass all of the relevant tests before making it official. Another good idea is to coordinate running a candidate on apache.org for a period of time. This will require coordination with the current maintainers of apache org's httpd instance. In the past, the group has liked to see approximately 48-72 hours of usage in production to certify that the release is functional in the real world.

What can I call this release? At this point, the release is an alpha. The Apache HTTP Server Project has three classifications for its releases: Alpha Beta General Availability (GA). Alpha indicates that the release is not meant for mainstream usage or may have serious problems that prohibits its use. When a release is initially created, it automatically becomes alpha quality. Beta indicates that at least three committers have voted positively for beta status

and there were more positive than negative votes for beta designation. This indicates that it is expected to compile and perform basic tasks. However, there may be problems with this release that prohibit its widespread adoption. General Availability (GA) indicates that at least three committers have voted positively for GA status and that there were more positive than negative votes for GA designation. This release is recommended for production usage.

Who can vote? Non-committers may cast a vote for a release's quality. In fact, this is extremely encouraged as it provides much-needed feedback to the community about the release's quality. However, only binding votes casted by committers count towards the designation. Note that no one may veto a release

How do we make it public? Once the release has reached the highest-available designation (as deemed by the RM), the release can be moved to the httpd distribution directory on apache.org. Approximately 24 to 48 hours after the files have been moved, a public announcement can be made. We wait this period so that the mirrors can receive the new release before the announcement. An email can then be sent to the announcements lists (announce@apache.org, announce@httpd apache org). Drafts of the announcement are usually posted on the development list before sending the announcement to let the community clarify any issues that we feel should be addressed in the announcement

Should the announcement wait for binaries? In short, no. The only files that are required for a public release are the source tarballs (.tar Z, .tar gz). Volunteers can provide the Win32 source distribution and binaries, and other esoteric binaries

**Figure 25: Informal release process description**

Some examples of specialization of the generic *Process Roles* are shown in Figure 26. All Apache projects (HTTP Server, Jakarta, XML, etc.) are managed using a collaborative, consensus-based process. Apache is a meritocracy where the rights and responsibilities follow from the skills and contributions of participants. The Project Management Committee (PMC) is a group of Committers who take responsibility for the long-term direction of the projects in their area. Members of the PMC are self-selected Committers. There is a single PMC for each parent project which is commissioned directly by the Apache Software Foundation Board of Directors. The Board of Directors ultimately has the final decision making power on any project. They delegate this responsibility to the PMC of each project. Although the Release Manager has the ultimate say in what goes into the final release, the PMC can make suggestions. The PMC is in turn responsible for many sub-projects, each of which with its own group of Committers.

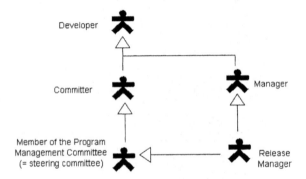

**Figure 26: Some Apache Server process roles**

The high level activity diagram that can be devised from the informal process description is similar to the diagram drawn for the NetBeans process (see Figure 16). Differences stay at a more detailed level. For instance, the 'Define Release authority' *Activity* just includes the self designation from a Member of the PMC who accepts to act as the Release Manager, instead of the public call for candidates in the NetBeans process. Other specific *Activities* are described with more details below.

It should be noted that all important information about the release (its definition, timeline, status, changes, expected new features, and so on) is recorded within the repository STATUS file (see Figure 27). The STATUS file defines in particular 'showstoppers', which are issues that require a fix before the next release. They are defined by 'lazy consensus': a showstopper is valid if no Committer disputes the issue by sending a negative vote or a veto vote.

Each of the Apache Project's active source code repositories contain a file called "STATUS" which is used to keep track of the agenda and plans for work within that repository. The active STATUS files are automatically posted to the mailing list each week

Many issues will be encountered by the project, each resulting in zero or more proposed action items Action items must be raised on the mailing list and added to the relevant STATUS file All action items may be voted on, but not all of them will require a formal vote. Types of Action Items :

- long Term Plans : are simply announcements that group members are working on particular issues related to the Apache software These are not voted on

- short Term Plans are announcements that a developer is working on a particular set of documentation or code files, with the implication that other developers should avoid them or try to coordinate their changes. This is a good way to proactively avoid conflict and possible duplication of work.

- release Plan is used to keep all the developers aware of when a release is desired, who will be the release manager, when the repository will be frozen in order to create the release, and assorted other trivia to keep us from tripping over ourselves during the final moments Lazy majority decides each issue in the release plan.

- release Testing after a new release is built, colloquially termed a tarball, it must be tested before being released to the public. Majority approval is required before the tarball can be publically released.

- showstoppers are issues that require a fix be in place before the next public release. They are listed in the STATUS file in order to focus special attention on the problem. An issue becomes a showstopper when it is listed as such in STATUS and remains so by lazy consensus

-product Changes : changes to the Apache products, including code and documentation, will appear as action items under several categories corresponding to the change status

    - concept/plan : an idea or plan for a change. These are usually only listed in STATUS when the change is substantial, significantly impacts the API, or is likely to be controversial. Votes are being requested early so as to uncover conflicts before too much work is done.

    - proposed patch. a specific set of changes to the current product in the form of input to the patch command (a diff output)

    - committed change : a one-line summary of a change that has been committed to the repository since the last public release.

**Figure 27: Description of the STATUS file**

This organization makes the 'Define Release requirements' and 'Define timeline' process fragments quite simple with a simple update of the STATUS file (see Figure 28).

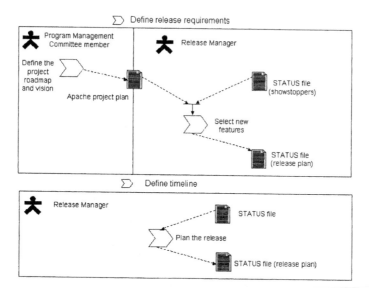

**Figure 28: 'Define release requirements' and 'Define timeline' refinements**

'Pre release testing', which constitutes the core of the release process, is different from its NetBeans counterpart due to the democratic and distributed style of management of the Apache project, and to different quality insurance procedures.

First, transitions from the alpha stage (i.e., a release which may have serious problems that prohibits its use) to the beta stage (i.e., a release expected to compile and to perform basic tasks) and from the beta stage to the final stage (i.e., a release recommended for production usage) are collective decisions taken after a vote (see Figure 29) with a majority consensus rule: at least three Committers should have voted positively for the new status and the number of positive votes for that designation should exceed the number of negative votes.

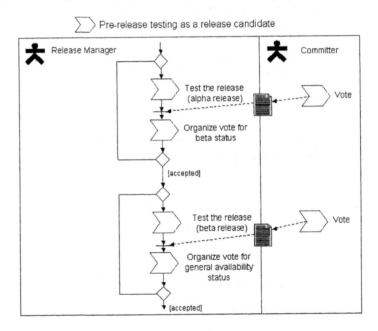

**Figure 29: Pre-release testing**

Secondly, to ensure a high level of quality, different prescriptions should be satisfied:

- the regression test suite should be run against the release candidate; Figure 30 shows that new test cases are expected from Committers each time they fix a bug,
- each release candidate should be used in production (i.e., for running the main apache.org Web server) for a given period of two or three days (see Figure 31).

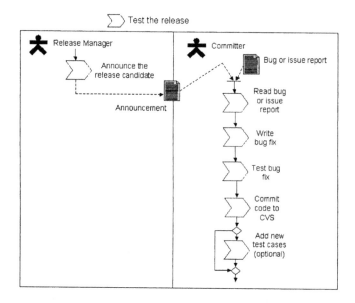

**Figure 30: First refinement of pre-release testing**

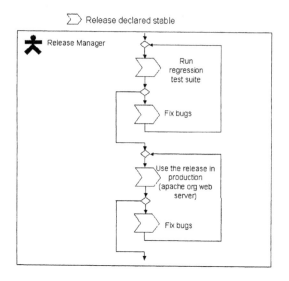

**Figure 31: Second refinement of pre-release testing**

According to the informal process description (see Figure 25), these policies "are not set in stone and may be adjusted by the Release Manager" under the circumstances. It is worth noting that no process-oriented proposals or discussions can be found within recent Apache Server mailing list archives while many of them can be found within NetBeans archives: debates about the Board election process, the Q-build process, the criteria and process a module has to pass to be marked as stable, and so on. Surprisingly, NetBeans process is more a collective construction than Apache process, while NetBeans is a project supported by an industrial software company. The reason could be the level of maturity of the process, higher in Apache than in NetBeans. Another study of the Apache project reports many process discussions during its early stages (in 1995) about the vote and patch system, show stopper bugs and code freeze [10].

## 5.   DISCUSSION

Three main goals and benefits can be attached to the modeling of software processes [36], [37]: (1) process understanding and communication, (2) process comparison, reuse, and improvement, (3) process enactment support. We discuss these three aspects in the case of OSS development modeling in general, and in the case of using SPEM in particular.

### 5.1   Process understanding and communication

OSSDPs can be described as a network of (largely social) processes arranged in a highly dynamic topology [38]. Besides the release process that we have studied in depth in the previous section, other process fragments include testing, work coordination, critiquing, suggesting, tool-building, bug triage, negotiation, evaluation, etc.

Generally, models of specific process fragments with ad hoc implicit notations, such as the 'life cycle of changes' in FreeBSD project [39] (Figure 32), stay at a very abstract level. A detailed process fragment description should at least specify the main relationships between people (roles), products and activities.

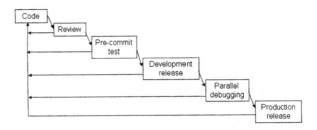

**Figure 32: The life cycle of changes in FreeBSD project**

It has been partly done for different process fragments of the FreeBSD project in a following paper [40] with a more precise notation including roles and decision points (Figure 33).

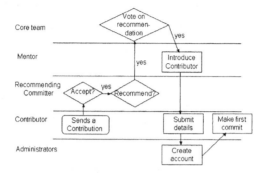

**Figure 33: 'Adding a new Committer' process model fragment in FreeBSD project**

Many software process modeling formalisms are designed for describing the relatively 'linear with feedback loops' structure of classical software development processes. It is the case, for instance, of Petri net based formalisms [41, 42]. At the opposite, SPEM allows to describe different perspectives of a software process model through all basic UML diagrams. In this chapter we used nested package diagrams for defining the main *Model Elements*, use case diagrams for showing the relationship between *Process Roles* and the main *Work Definitions*, and activity diagrams for presenting the sequencing of *Activities* with their input and output *Work Products*. We could also use Class diagrams for representing the structure, decomposition, and dependencies of *Work Products,* and Statechart diagrams for specifying the behavior of SPEM *Model Elements,* and therefore all the remaining concepts of the SPEM meta model. For OSS communities, which are basically communities of developers, UML diagrams should be easier to understand and accept than any other process modeling formalism and a valuable alternative to informal textual descriptions. This could be the first step for promoting the use of software process models in the OSS community for process understanding and communication.

The main weakness of SPEM is its approach for modeling tools. Unlike many other software process meta models (e.g. [43, 44]), tools are not first class concepts. We have represented them within *Disciplines* by using the more general *Guidance* concept, because one possible kind of guidance is tool usage specification (called '*Tool Mentor*'). This solution is not fully satisfactory: no specific notation exists for specifying the relationships between tools and *Work Definitions*, *Work Products* and *Process Roles*. It would be interesting to have more precise and systematic notations for specifying how tools mediate the development process because it constitutes a fundamental characteristics of all OSSDPs (see section 4.2.1).

## 5.2   Process comparison, reuse and improvement

OSSDPs mainly differ in their decision-making style, their coordination style, and their quality insurance procedures. All these aspects can be precisely documented through process modeling techniques, and the SPEM approach in particular.

For instance, Apache adopts an approach to coordination well suited to small projects. The server itself is kept small (77 kSLOC). Any functionality beyond the basic server is added by means of ancillary projects that interact with Apache only through Apache's well-defined interface. The coordination is successfully handled by a small core team (10-15 persons) using primarily implicit mechanisms: a knowledge of who has expertise in what area, general communication about what is going on, and who is doing what and when. There is no waiting for approvals, permission, and so forth. This highly implicit coordination style is exemplified by Figure 30 concerning bug fixing during the release process. The larger NetBeans project (758 kSLOC) includes more formal means of coordinating the work, such as module owners (Module Maintainer *Process Role*) who approve and perform changes to the modules. This more disciplined coordination style is exemplified by Figure 24 for the same bug fixing activity.

By codifying OSSDPs as formal models, the OSS community could share their 'best practices' as open source software process models [7]. Empirically, a process is good because people freely accept to follow it: participants 'are voting with their feet' [10]. New projects could start with such 'approved procedures' instead of reinventing everything through trial and errors. The high modularity of the SPEM approach could favor reuse of model fragments corresponding to loosely articulated sub process and therefore incremental process reuse and improvement.

Our multi level approach allows to analyze if a given project complies with our generic level and at which level of details it differs from other projects. The use of a well defined meta model with a sufficient expressive power is important. For instance, it is not easy to compare the release engineering process model fragment of FreeBSD as depicted by Figure 34 [40] with the corresponding model fragments from the Apache and NetBeans projects because many questions have no answer: who build the release schedule? when? how? which activities can take place after the feature freeze and after the code freeze? how the release is stabilized? who is in charge of the deployment? which tools are used?

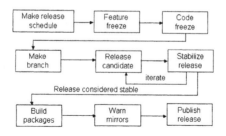

**Figure 34: FreeBSD release engineering process model fragment**

## 5.3 Process enactment support

Software process performers (developers, managers) can receive indirect support through guidance information, which helps them to perform their work, such as determining the current status of the process, the appropriate next steps to be executed, the decision points and their meanings, etc. Guidance is provided through manual or mechanical interpretation of software process models simultaneously and synchronously with the actual process performance [36]. Software process performers can also receive direct support through enactable software process models which are mechanically interpreted by process engines within process-aware tools, in order to orchestrate the performance of the actual development and to automate it as far as possible [36, 43].

Very few experiments aim at applying mechanical support to OSSDPs. Jensen and Scacchi describe a prototype for enacting formal models written in the PML language in order to simulate them [30]. Use of the GENESIS platform, a process-aware toolkit for supporting distributed software development, is discussed in the context of OSS projects [45]. The broader idea of 'workflow support' is sometimes mentioned, for specific process fragments [46], such as routing proposed changes by non Committers to Committers, notifying all developers that have recently checked-in changes to a group of code that its documentation has been updated, tracking and communicating workflow progress to project leaders. It is worth noting that the actual enactment of processes is not in the scope of SPEM [11].

Some OSS developers do not like the idea of specifying process models "I am opposed to a long rule-book as that satisfies lawyer-tendencies, and is counter to the technocentricity that the project so badly needs" (email reported in [40]). Process enactment support for development tasks would certainly be rejected by most of the OSS developers. However, tasks that are not development related, should be automated so that the Committers can do what they do the best and enjoy the most: develop software [40].

## 6.   CONCLUSION

Today, software engineering offers a spectrum of approaches with process intensive methodologies such as the Capability Maturity Model [47] at one extreme and lightweight methodologies such as open source or agile methodologies [48] at the other. Lightweight methodologies emphasize the fact that software development is fundamentally a human activity. Some approaches which combine control with some flexibility, like Rational's Unified Process [49] are positioned in the middle.

Open source development is not a silver bullet [50] but just an alternative approach showing how the Internet can change the way software is constructed, deployed, and evolved. Open source development 'offers useful information about common problems as well as some possible solutions for globally distributed product development' [8]. Process modeling gives a great opportunity to analyze, compare, visualize, and transfer for reuse these possible solutions.

This chapter defines a multi level modeling approach for describing in a common framework both the generic characteristics of OSSDPs and the special features of specific projects. The chapter contrasts NetBeans and Apache release management processes, and discusses the strengths and weaknesses of the approach and the SPEM notation. This work is a first step towards the systematic description and analysis of OSSDPs. We aim at characterizing different families of OSSDPs by showing that each family share a larger set of common properties than those of the generic level.

It is tempting to suggest that closed source development and open source development could be hybridized [51]. The general opinion recognizes the interest of reusing some principles and solutions of OSSDP in other contexts for developing specific software products, such as tools and platforms [51], and more generally all applications faced by developers [3]. Our approach could help such hybridization by providing a common framework for analysis and discussion of all the processes by which a group of people can produce high quality software with a cooperative style of development departing from the traditional hierarchical and management driven style.

# REFERENCES

[1] *An Introduction to Open Source Communities*, E.E. Kim, Blue Oxen Associates, Technical report, BOA-00007, 2003.

[2] *Results from Software Engineering Research into Open Source Development Projects Using Public Data*, S. Koch, and G. Schneider, Diskussionspapiere zum Tätigkeitsfeld Informationsverarbeitung und Informationswirtschaft, Hansen, H.,R., and Janko, W., 22, Wirtschaftsuniversität Wien, Austria, 2000.

[3] *Reusing Open-Source Software and Practices: The Impact of Open-Source on Commercial Vendors*, A. W. Brown, and G. Booch, ICSR-7, LNCS 2319, Springer-Verlag, 2002, pp. 123-136.

[4] *A Case Study of Open Source Software Development: The Apache Server*, A. Mockus, R.T. Fielding, and J. Herbsleb, 21st International Conference on Software Engineering (ICSE), Los Angeles, CA, 1999, pp. 263-272.

[5] *Two case studies of open source software development: Apache and Mozilla*, A. Mockus, R.T. Fielding, and J. Herbsleb, ACM Transactions on Software Engineering and Methodology, 11(3), ACM, 2002, pp. 309-346.

[6] *An Overview of the Software Engineering Process and Tools in Mozilla Project*, C.R. Reis, and R. Pontin de Mattos Fortes, Workshop on OSS Development, Newcastle upon Tyne, UK, 2002, pp. 162-182.

[7] *Issues and Experiences in Modeling Open Source Software Development Processes*, W. Scacchi, 3rd Workshop on Open Source Software Engineering, ICSE'03, Portland, Oregon 2003, pp. 121-126.

[8] *A Descriptive Process Model for Open-Source Software Development*, Johnson, K., Master Thesis, Univ. Calgary, Alberta, 2001.

[9] *The Cathedral & the Bazaar - Musings on Linux and Open Source by an Accidental Revolutionary*, E.S. Raymond, O'Reilly & Associates Inc., Sebastopol, 1999.

[10] *The-User Developer Convergence: Innovation and Software Systems Development in the Apache Project*, Osterlie, T., Master Thesis, Norwegian Univ. of Science and Technology, 2003.

[11] *Software Process Engineering Metamodel Specification, version 1.0*, OMG Document formal/02-11-14, 2002.

[12] *Unified Modeling Language Specification, version 1.5*, OMG Document formal/2003-03-01, 2003.

[13] *Free Software Foundation Web site*, http://www.gnu.org.

[14] *The Free Software Definition* (on line), Stallman, R.,
http://www.fsf.org/philosophy/free-sw.html, 1999.

[15] *Open Source Initiative Web site*, http://www.opensource.org.

[16] *The Open Source Definition, Version 1.9* (on line), OSI, http://www.opensource.org, 2003.

[17] *Netbeans Project Web site*, http://www.netbeans.org.

[18] *Eclipse Project Web site*, http://www.eclipse.org.

[19] *Software Development Practices in Open Software Development Communities: A Comparative Case Study*, W. Scacchi, First Workshop on Open Source Software Engineering, ICSE'01, Toronto, Ontario, Canada, 2001.

[20] *Characterizing the OSS process*, A. Capiluppi, P. Lago, and M. Morisio, 1st Workshop on Open Source Software Engineering, ICSE'01, Toronto, Canada, 2001.

[21] *Meta Object Facility Specification, version 1.4*, OMG Document formal/02-04-03, 2003.

[22] *Evidences in the evolution of OS projects through Changelog Analyses*, A. Capiluppi, P. Lago, and M. Morisio, 3rd Workshop on Open Source Software Engineering, ICSE'03, Portland, Oregon 2003, pp. 19-24.

[23] *Cave or Community? An Empirical Examination of 100 Mature Open Source Projects*, S. Krishnamurthy, First Monday, 7 (6), 2002.

[24] *The stellar model of open source, Version 0.1* (on line), S. Mazzocchi, Java Apache Project, http://bioinformatics.weizmann.ac.il/software/apache/java/framework/stellar.html, 1999.

[25] *Homesteading the noosphere, Version 3.0* (on line), Raymond, E.S.,
http://www.catb.org/~esr/writings/homesteading/, 2000.

[26] *Open Source Software Development Processes, Version 2.5* (on line), W. Scacchi,
http://www.ics.uci.edu/~wscacchi/Software-Process/Open-Software-Process-Models/Open
-Source-Software-Development-Processes.ppt, 2002.

[27] *Improving the Open Source Software Model with UML Case Tools*, J.O. Gilliam, Linux Gazette, 67, June 2001.

[28] *A Framework for Open Source Projects*, Rothfuss, G.J., Master Thesis, Department of Information technology, University of Zurich, 2002.

[29] *The Cathedral and the Bazaar, Version 3.0* (on line), Raymond, E.S.,
http://www.catb.org/~esr/cathedral-bazaar/cathedral-bazaar/, 2000.

[30] *Simulating an Automated Approach to Discovery and Modeling of Open Source Software Development Processes*, C. Jensen, and W. Scacchi, ProSim'03 Workshop on Software Process Simulation and Modeling, Portland, Oregon, 2003.

[31] *Open Source Software Development Processes in the Apache Software Foundation* (on line), Ata, C., Gasca, V., Georgas, J., Lam, K., and Rousseau, M., http://www.ics.uci.edu/~michele/SP/final.doc, 2002.

[32] *A First Look at the NetBeans Requirements and Release Process* (on line), Oza, M., Nistor, E., Hu, S., Jensen, C., and Scacchi, W., http://www.ics.uci.edu/~cjensen/papers/FirstLookNetBeans/, 2002.

[33] *Release Management Within Open Source Projects*, J.R. Erenkrantz, 3rd Workshop on Open Source Software Engineering, ICSE'03, Portland, Oregon 2003, pp. 51-56.

[34] *Automating the Discovery and Modeling of Open Source Software Development Processes*, C. Jensen, and W. Scacchi, 3rd Workshop on Open Source Software Engineering, ICSE'03, Portland, Oregon 2003, pp. 75-78.

[35] *Distributed Collective Practices and Free/Open-Source Software Problem Management: Perspectives and Methods*, L. Gasser, and G. Ripoche, CITE'03, 2003, pp. 349-365.

[36] *A Structured Conceptual and Terminological Framework for Software Process Engineering*, J. Lonchamp, Second Int. Conf. On the Software Process (ICSP2), Berlin, RFA, IEEE Computer Society Press, 1993, pp. 41-53.

[37] *A field study of the software design process for large systems*, B. Curtis, H. Krasner, and N. Iscoe, Communications of the ACM 31(11), 1988, pp. 1268-1287.

[38] *Understanding Continuous Design in F/OSS Projects*, L. Gasser, G. Ripoche, W. Scacchi, and B. Pennel, ICSSEA, Paris, France, 2003.

[39] *Putting it all in the trunk: Incremental software development in the FreeBSD open source project*, N. Jorgensen, Information Systems Journal, 11, 2001, pp. 321-326.

[40] *A Project Model for the FreeBSD Project*, Saers, N., Master Thesis, University of Oslo, 2003.

[41] *SPADE: An Environment for Software Process Analysis, Design, and Enactment*, In Software Process Modelling and Technology, chapter 9, Research Studies Press, 1994, pp. 223-247.

[42] *Software process analysis based on FUNSOFT nets*, W. Deiters, and V. Gruhn, Systems Analysis Modelling Simulation 8 (4-5), 1991, pp. 315-325.

[43] *Software Process: Principles, Methodology, Technology*, J.C. Derniame, B.A. Kaba, and D.G. Wastell (Eds.), Lecture Notes in Computer Science 1500, Springer Verlag, 1999.

[44] *Towards a Reference Framework for Process Concepts*, R. Conradi, C. Fernstrom, A. Fuggetta, and R. Snowdon, Software Process Technology - Proceedings of the 2nd European Software Process Modeling Workshop, Trondheim, Norway, Springer Verlag LNCS 635, 1992, pp. 3-17.

[45] *Open-Source Development Processes and Tools*, C. Boldyreff, J. Lavery, D. Nutter, and S. Rank, 3rd Workshop on Open Source Software Engineering, ICSE'03, Portland, Oregon 2003, pp. 15-18.

[46] *Beyond Code – Content Management and The Open Source Development portal* (position paper), T.J. Halloran, W.L. Scherlis, and J.R. Erenkrantz, 3rd Workshop on Open Source Software Engineering, ICSE'03, Portland, Oregon 2003, pp. 69-74.

[47] *Capability Maturity Model Version 1.1.*, M.C. Paulk, B. Curtis, M.B. Chrissis, and C.V. Weber, IEEE Software, 10, 4, 1993, pp. 18-27.

[48] *Is Open Source Software Development Essentially an Agile Method?*, J. Warsta, and P. Abrahamsson, 3rd Workshop on Open Source Software Engineering, ICSE'03, Portland, Oregon 2003, pp. 143-147.

[49] *The Rational Unified Process – an Introduction*, P. Kruchten, Addison-Wesley, 1998.

[50] *When is Free/Open Source Software Development Faster, Better, and Cheaper than Software Engineering?*, W. Scacchi, Working Paper, Institute for Software Research, UC Irvine, 2003.

[51] *Why Not Improve Coordination in Distributed Software Development by Stealing Good Ideas from Open Source?*, A. Mockus, and J.D. Herbsleb, 2nd Workshop on Open Source Software Engineering, ICSE'02, Orlando, Florida, 2002.

# Chapter 3

# SOFTWARE DEPENDABILITY APPLICATIONS IN PROCESS MODELING

Ray MADACHY and Barry BOEHM
*USC Center for Software Engineering, Department of Computer Science,*
*University of Southern California, Los Angeles, CA 90098-0781 U.S.A.*
*E-mail: {madachy, boehm}@sunset.usc.edu*

**Abstract:** Software process modeling can be used to reason about strategies for attaining software dependability. The impact of different processes and technologies on dependability attributes can be evaluated through modeling and simulation. Strategies may have overlapping capabilities, and process modeling is useful for assessing mixed strategies. Dependability has many facets, and there is no single software dependability metric that fits all situations. A stakeholder value-based approach is useful for determining relevant dependability measures for different contexts. Analytical models and simulation techniques including continuous systems and discrete event modeling approaches can be applied to dependability. Continuous systems modeling is easier for aggregate analyses. Discrete event has some advantages for dependability applications because multiple attributes related to dependability measures can be attached to system entities, particularly when those same attributes are represented in empirical data. Combined approaches using the advantages of both are attractive for dependability applications. Two primary processes can be modeled to investigate dependability phenomena. Development process models mainly address software defect introduction and removal rates. Operational process models address the probability of various classes of failure: race conditions, deadlocks, missing real-time deadlines. An overview of sample applications is presented. An elaborated example shows how modeling can be used to optimize a process for dependability. There have been relatively few dependability modeling applications to-date, and the field is rich for exploration.

**Key words:** Software process modeling; software dependability; system dynamics; discrete event modeling.

## 1.   INTRODUCTION

Software process modeling can be used to reason about software dependability decisions. The impact of different processes and technologies on dependability attributes can be evaluated through modeling and simulation. Strategies may have overlapping capabilities, and process modeling is useful for assessing mixed strategies. Another complication is that investments in software dependability compete for resources. Modeling can help find the right balance of activities that contribute to dependability with other constraints such as cost and schedule.

There are some analytical models dealing with dependability attributes, particularly exponential reliability growth models. However, analytical models have limitations and they don't model the impact of methods for achieving dependability. The software process has many interacting elements, and is too complex to model with closed-form analytical solutions. Process modeling can provide an integrated view of the software process including system feedback, tradeoffs and sensitivity to changing operational scenarios. Executable simulation models allow for understanding, communication, training and decision support. They are ideally suited for running low-cost experiments in lieu of field experiments.

Important modeling applications to address are process improvement goals with respect to dependability. Encapsulating knowledge of complex software process interactions in models allows one to improve processes. Defect prevention is a highly relevant area related to dependability that process modeling can specifically address. It is a high maturity key process area in process improvement frameworks including the Software Capability Maturity Model (CMM) and CMM-Integrated (CMM-I).

A simulation model can be used to optimize processes with respect to dependability by running it at various parameter values and evaluating the outputs after the proper experimental design. In particular simulation can be used to answer the question "how much is enough?" Efficient software processes require a careful balance. Typically there are counteracting effects at work. Cost or risk may rise due to one aspect of a process policy, but due to another aspect they will decrease along the same direction. Optima are found by adding the effects together. Examples of this are described later.

## 2. BACKGROUND

This section will address the definitions of dependability and strategies for achieving dependability attributes. It will then describe common modeling approaches that can be applied for dependability.

### 2.1 Software dependability overview

Dependability has many interpretations when considered from different perspectives. Assessing processes that contribute to dependability requires one or more evaluation criteria or metrics that enable quantitative comparisons of candidate process solutions. In practice, a one-size-fits-all metric is unachievable. Different systems have different success-critical stakeholders, and these stakeholders depend on the system in different ways.

An important step in understanding the nature of software dependability is to identify the major classes of system stakeholders, and to characterize the relative strengths of their dependencies on various attributes of a given information system. A universal attribute to be optimized on software systems cannot be defined. Different systems may have multiple stakeholders with different dependencies on the system. Thus, a value-based approach that considers stakeholder value propositions can be used to determine relevant dependability measures for given system scenarios.

Several questions need to be answered in order to understand dependability concerns and characterize the dependencies of different stakeholders. This involves identifying the system attributes that stakeholders depend on, the different classes of stakeholders with unique dependency patterns, and the strength of their dependencies for each attribute. With this information the value propositions can be balanced for a given system.

Dependability attributes are not always independent and the relationship between technologies for achieving dependability and resultant dependability measures is not easy to model. Table 1 lists some representative dependability attributes and their definitions. The table is not exhaustive but does show the primary dependability attributes of concern we have identified. See [Boehm et al. 2004a], [Boehm et al. 2004b] for further details and discussion of the attributes.

Three generic strategies of achieving dependability are to avoid problems (defect prevention), eliminate problems (finding and fixing defects) or to reduce the impact of problems. Table 2 shows each of these strategies broken down into some specific opportunities for achieving dependability (the list is also not completely exhaustive but shows some major strategies).

This structure is also called an opportunity tree; a hierarchical taxonomy of opportunities for achieving objectives.

Table 1: Representative dependability attributes

| Dependability Attribute | Definition |
|---|---|
| Protection | |
| Safety | A system provides safety to the extent that it minimizes stakeholders' expected loss of value due to death, injury, illness, or damage to equipment, property, or the environment. |
| Security | A system provides security_to the extent that it minimizes stakeholders' expected loss of value from unauthorized access, use, disclosure, disruption, modification, or destruction of information assets, including financial losses and loss of value due to death, injury, illness, or damage to equipment, property, or the environment. |
| Privacy | A system provides privacy to the extent that it minimizes stakeholders' expected loss of value from authorized or unauthorized access, use, disclose, or modification of stakeholders' personal information, including financial losses and loss of reputation. |
| Robustness | |
| Reliability | A system provides reliability to the extent that it maximizes the probability that the system will provide stakeholder-desired levels of service (liveness, accuracy, performance, others) with respect to a system's operational profile (probability distributions of transaction frequencies, task complexities, workload volumes, others) over a given period of time. |
| Availability | A system provides availability to the extent that it maximizes the fraction of time that the system will provide stakeholder-desired levels of service with respect to a system's operational profile. |
| Survivability | A system provides survivability to the extent that it maximizes the total expected value obtained from achieving stakeholder-desired levels of service and from reduced levels of service when the desired levels of service are unachievable. |

Table 1: Representative dependability attributes (cont'd)

| Dependability Attribute | Definition |
|---|---|
| Quality of Service | |
| Performance | A system provides performance to the extent that it maximizes the value of processed information achievable within the available resources (i.e., processors, storage devices, communication bandwidth, etc.) being used to process the system's workload (the volume and distribution of requested services/functions over a given time period). For information utilities in which value cannot be determined, an alternate definition is that a system provides performance to the extent that it provides stakeholders with their desired information with minimum utilization of limited resources and response time. |
| Accuracy, Consistency | A system provides accuracy to the extent that it minimizes the difference between delivered computational results and the real world quantity that they represent. |
| Usability | A system provides usability to the extent that it maximizes the value of a user community's ability to benefit from a system's capabilities with respect to the system's operational profile (probability distributions of transaction frequencies, task complexities, workload volumes, others). |
| Evolvability | A system provides evolvability to the extent that it maximizes the added value achievable in modifying the system or component in desired/valued directions within a given time period. |
| Interoperability | A system provides interoperability to the extent that it maximizes the value of exchanging information or coordinating control across co-dependent systems. |
| Correctness | A system provides correctness to the extent that its implementation precisely satisfies its requirements and/or design specifications. |
| Affordability (Cost) | A system provides affordability to the extent that it maximizes the value added by developing new capabilities within a given budget. |
| Timeliness (Schedule) | A system provides timeliness to the extent that it maximizes the value added by developing new capabilities within a given delivery time. On the other hand, if the set of desired capabilities is fixed, an alternate definition is that a system provides timeliness to the extent that it minimizes the calendar time required to deliver the set of capabilities. |
| Reusability | A system provides reusability to the extent that it maximizes the return on investment of reusing system capabilities in other products. |

Table 2: Dependability strategies opportunity tree

| Generic Strategies | Specific Strategies | |
|---|---|---|
| defect prevention | root cause analysis | fishbone diagrams |
| | | brainstorming meetings |
| | defect analysis | defect categorization (e.g. ODC) |
| | | defect prioritization |
| | | defect tracking |
| | | six sigma |
| | | Pareto analysis |
| | formal methods | mathematical proofs |
| | | cleanroom technique |
| | traditional implementation methods | architecture technology |
| | | requirements methods |
| | | design/code methods |
| defect detection and removal | reviews | peer reviews, inspections |
| | | project reviews |
| | | pair programming |
| | automated analysis | completeness checking |
| | | consistency checking |
| | | traceability testing |
| | | compliance testing |
| | testing | requirements and design |
| | | structural |
| | | operational profile |
| | | alpha and beta usage |
| | | regression |
| | | value/risk-based |
| | | test automation |
| | | unit/function |
| defect impact reduction | fault tolerance | |
| | decrease effect of downtime | |
| | decrease effect of failure | |
| | N-version programming | |

### 2.1.1  Dependability modeling framework

A framework for the contribution of process modeling to dependability is evaluating the effectiveness of the strategy opportunities in Table 2 against specific dependability goals in Table 1. Much of the difficulty lies in modeling connections between the strategies, intermediate quantities, and desired dependability attributes.

With this framework, modeling can investigate the effects of combined strategies on achieving dependability. Since there is much overlap between the opportunities, modeling can help determine how much is enough for different situations in order to find the most cost-effective balance of activities. The decision-maker can choose any combination of the assessment techniques to attain desired attributes. The decisions regard where and how many resources should be applied, and models are used to examine the impact on dependability attributes.

## 2.2 Modeling approaches

Two primary modeling approaches for software dependability are analytical modeling and process simulation modeling (herein referred to as process modeling). These approaches and their tradeoffs are summarized in the following sections.

### 2.2.1 Analytical models

The most common analytical models for dependability applications are reliability growth models. In contrast to a Rayleigh function that models defect patterns during development, reliability growth models typically use data from the formal testing phases. They are based on the rationale that defect arrival and failure patterns during testing are good indicators of fielded product reliability. After development when formal testing occurs, it is assumed that software becomes more stable and thus reliability grows over time.

The reliability growth models are most often used for reliability projection before software is shipped and when development is complete. They can also be used to model the failure pattern or defect arrival pattern in the field.

The exponential distribution is the most important distribution in reliability studies, and is often the basis for many reliability growth models. It models the defect arrival pattern in the final testing phases, and is easily used to fit defect arrival data over time that comes from testing.

Two major classes of software reliability growth models are time between failure models and fault count models. For both types, the most important assumption is effective testing. Examples of different reliability growth models are provided in [Kan 1995].

Not many reliability growth models have been verified in environments with real industrial data and few are in continued use. Their focuses are typically narrow and rarely include related factors outside of dependability. They are scenario-independent and assume stable operational profiles, which is often not the case.

### 2.2.2 Process modeling and simulation

The most common approaches to process (simulation) modeling are continuous systems modeling (e.g. system dynamics) and discrete-event modeling. Either method can be used for dependability applications. Whether a system is represented as continuous or discrete depends on the specific objectives of a study. A continuous approach assumes system entities can be treated as homogeneous; a discrete approach assumes individual characteristics are of importance. Some discrete systems can be assumed to be continuous for easy representation. Much difficulty will be avoided if each entity does not need to be traced individually.

In general, system dynamics is easier to use and a more powerful technique to model long term trends and external system descriptions [Madachy-Tarbet 2000]. Discrete approaches are normally better to handle short-term analysis for discrete, small process steps. System dynamics provides a global perspective (e.g for strategic analyses) while discrete approaches focus on low-level details (resource utilization, queuing, etc.).

Discrete-event modeling has some advantages for dependability analysis. In particular, different attributes can be attached to entities like defects. The attributes may change when system events occur during the simulation (such as a defect detection or fixing event). Defects can be characterized by their type, severity, detection effort, removal effort, etc. The advantage of assigning detailed attributes is a primary reason that companies addressing defect prevention resort to discrete event or combined modeling. Such attributes would be very difficult to model with traditional system dynamics. Some system dynamics modeling tools allow arrays, which may also be used to assign attributes.

Discrete models contain entities that move through activities carrying attributes. They can capture the development process in rich detail. Because these models advance time in discrete or event-based increments, they do not capture the effect of continuously varying factors.

Systems dynamics models capture the dynamic behavior of project variables. Significantly, the interaction and feedback among continuous variables can be observed. System dynamics approaches have modeled defect levels with no provision to assign attributes to individual defects. That is because the technique treats flowing entities as homogeneous quantities. However, systems dynamics models do not capture process steps easily. See [Kellner-Madachy-Raffo 1999] for a more detailed comparison of process modeling approaches.

A hybrid approach combining continuous and discrete-event modeling is very attractive for dependability applications. A combined approach is advantageous because it can model the creation of artifacts with attributes, modify those attributes based on system variables, and allow system variables to vary continuously. Some aspects of the software process can be described easily with continuous systems structures, where applicable, and others can be represented with discrete-event modeling when detailed entity attributes are advantageous. See [Martin-Raffo 2000], [Lakey 2003] for information on hybrid software process modeling.

## 2.3 Process model constructs

Any modeling approach has to have provisions for representing defects since latent software defects may impact a system with respect to dependability attributes. The number of defects is generally considered a rough measure of overall quality, but is most closely tied to the dependability attribute *correctness* (depending on the stakeholder perspective). To ascertain tradeoffs with respect to dependability decisions, modeling the resources (e.g. effort and schedule) expended to achieve dependability are also necessary. Thus the defects should be found and fixed to achieve dependability. Modeling the resources expended on defect detection and removal supports tradeoff decisions to achieve dependability goals.

Both continuous systems and discrete approaches can easily model defects and effort expenditure. Reusable defect modeling constructs using system dynamics are provided in [Madachy 2004]. Also provided are structures that link defects with other process factors.

Feedback within the process is handled much easier with system dynamics. As stated previously, discrete approaches are advantageous when attributes for specific entities like defects or software units are to be represented.

A way to model different defect severities using system dynamics is to have separate flow chains for different severity levels. One flow chain could be for minor defects and another for major defects, for example. But this approach quickly breaks down as the number of severity levels increases. It could get quite laborious to create multitudinous flow chains representing all the desired attribute values, and a continuous range of values for the attributes is not feasible.

The outputs of a simulation can include defects and expended effort. The number of remaining defects in a software system will provide an indication of dependability. The cumulative effort represents the cost to achieve the degree of dependability.

Discrete event approaches provide the assigning of attributes to entities like defects. The attributes change value when system events occur. Orthogonal Defect Classification (ODC) is a simple example where attributes can be aligned with empirical process data. The standard ODC attributes are phase found, activity, trigger, impact, target, type, qualifier and source. Each of the ODC attributes has a number of available descriptive values. These attributes may overlap with empirical dependability measures. A model that partially implements the ODC attribute set is referenced in [Rus 2002].

## 3. SAMPLE APPLICATIONS

This section overviews some major process modeling efforts that involve dependability in some fashion. Many past applications handled defects as part of an integrated process model, and only a few have focused on dependability and its impact for stakeholders. The vast majority that represented defects examined defect levels and their effect on cost and schedule to find and fix them.

Many have evaluated the impact of reviews, quality assurance, test processes and other assessment techniques on quality (as measured by defect levels). Some of these have modeled the quality tradeoffs with respect to cost and schedule.

### 3.1 Integrated project modeling

The first major software process model was developed by Abdel-Hamid [Abdel-Hamid-Madnick 1991]. It integrated various facets of a software project including software production, quality assurance, planning, control and monitoring. System dynamics was used to model defect flows and interventions including quality assurance and testing. It had provisions for defects that pass through phases and other defects that get multiplied.

The flow chains in Figure 1 were used to model the generation, detection and correction of errors during development. The chains are simplified and only show the connections to adjacent model elements. There are two types of errors in the model called passive and active. Active errors can multiply into more errors. All design errors are considered active since they could result in coding errors, erroneous documentation, test plans, etc. Coding errors may be either active or passive.

There is a positive feedback loop between the undetected active errors and the active error regeneration rate. Potentially detectable errors are fed by an error generation rate. The errors committed per task is defined as a function against the percent of job worked. The workforce mix and schedule pressure also affect the error generation rates. The model addresses both the growth of undetected errors as escaped errors and bad fixes that generate more errors, and the detection/correction of those errors. Figure 2 shows a graph of some of the important quantities for a representative simulation run.

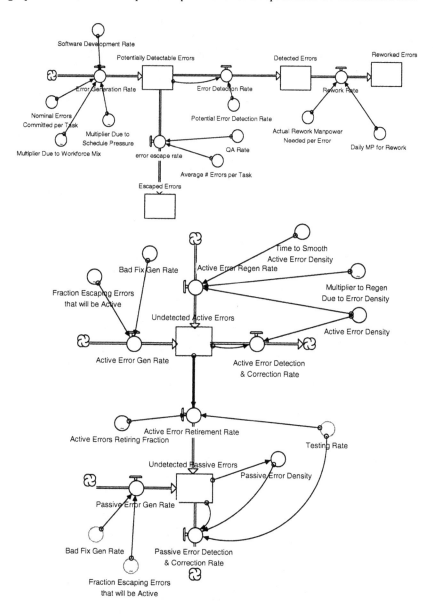

**Figure 1: Integrated project model defect flow chains**

*Software Dependability Applications in Process Modeling*

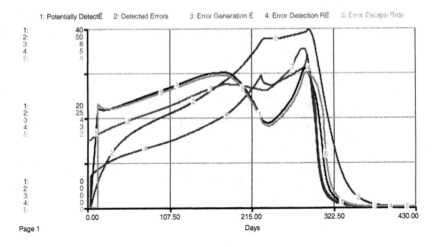

**Figure 2: Integrated project model defect dynamics**

The error detection rate is a function of how much effort is spent on QA. It is assumed that easy, obvious errors are detected first, and that subsequent errors are more expensive and subtle to find.

System testing is assumed to find all errors escaped from the QA process and bad fixes resulting from faulty rework. Any remaining errors could be found in maintenance, but is not included in the model.

A representative example of determining "how much is enough" was provided by the model. The optimal amount of quality assurance activities was experimentally determined to address the attributes of *affordability* and *timeliness*. The tradeoffs are shown in Figure 3.

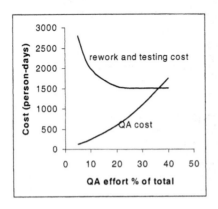 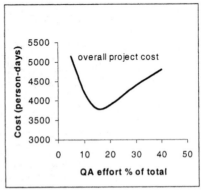

**Figure 3: Quality assurance tradeoffs**

Too much quality assurance can be wasteful, yet not enough will impact the effort and schedule adversely because defects will get through. The key is to run a simulation at applicable values across the spectrum and determine the optimum strategy, or sweet spot of the process. Based on their assumptions of a project environment, about 15% of the total project effort was the optimal amount to dedicate to quality assurance. For further information, this model is reviewed in substantial detail in [Madachy 2004].

## 3.2 Modeling peer review effects on quality

A number of extensive modeling efforts have focused on peer reviews as a means to finding and fixing defects including process tradeoffs. Several researchers have used system dynamics to investigate the cost, schedule and quality impact of using formal inspections and other peer reviews on work products [Madachy 1996], [Tvedt 1996], and others have used discrete event modeling [Raffo 1995], [Eickelmann et al. 2002].

In [Madachy 1996], a process model examined the effects of inspection practices on cost, schedule and quality (defect levels) throughout the lifecycle. It used system dynamics to model the interrelated flows of tasks, errors and personnel throughout different lifecycle phases and was calibrated to industrial data. It demonstrated the effects of performing inspections or not, the effectiveness of varied inspection policies, and the effects of other managerial policies such as manpower allocation.

Figure 4 shows a portion of the defect model associated with design errors. Not shown are connections with other elements of the model. Errors are generated in conjunction with software design, according to an error density. The proportion of errors caught in inspection depends on the inspection efficiency (percent of errors found), also called yield. Those errors found are reworked. The effort expenditures associated with doing inspections and fixing errors are also modeled. The undetected design errors enter the coding phase, and the model includes error multiplication between phases. Errors that remain until system testing are eventually found and fixed at a higher cost. Figure 5 shows the design defect dynamics from a typical run.

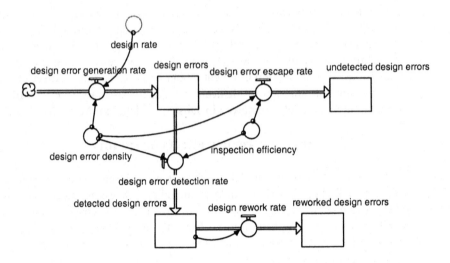

**Figure 4: Design defect structure from inspection model**

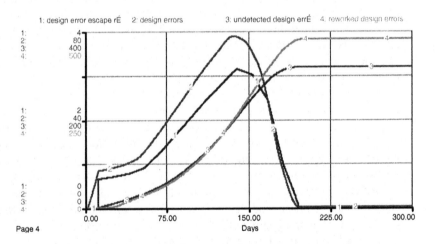

**Figure 5: Design defect dynamics from inspection model**

Analysis from the model showed several inspection policy tradeoffs. One result showed diminishing returns from inspections as a function of error generation rates per Figure 6. The implication for process planning is that if other methods for achieving low defect levels are used (such as a cleanroom technique), then inspections are not always warranted. They could negatively impact *affordability* and *timeliness* while not achieving significantly higher *correctness* or other attributes of concern.

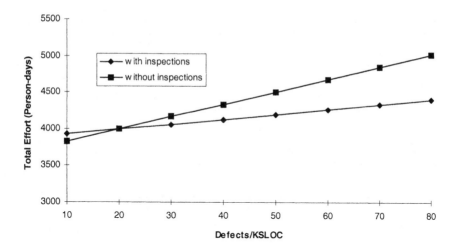

**Figure 6: Diminishing returns from inspections**

Another result was that code inspections were not always warranted. When the design was thoroughly inspected, code inspections were not as cost effective. A dynamic cost driver for use of inspections was derived. See [Madachy 1996] for more details of the model and quality tradeoffs.

A discrete event model for analyzing the effect of inspections was developed in [Raffo 1995]. The quantitative cost/quality tradeoffs for performing inspections were very close to those derived from [Madachy 1996] at the top-level. Both studies support the contention that even though inspections may increase effort early on, the overall development costs and schedule are reduced. Dependability improves on all fronts when using inspections within the assumptions of the models.

The [Tvedt 1996] model allows one to evaluate the impact of process improvements on cycle time. It specifically addresses concurrent incremental software development to assess the impact of software inspections. The model enables controlled experiments to answer such as "What kind of cycle time reduction can I expect to see if I implement inspections?" or "How much time should I spend on inspections?" It modeled the specific activities within the inspection process so that one can experiment with effort dedicated to preparation, inspection, rework, etc.

## 3.3   Modeling reliability

Rus and colleagues have developed process models to evaluate strategies for achieving reliability [Rus 1998], [Rus-Collofello 2001], [Rus-Collofello-Lakey 1999]. The objective of the research in [Rus 1998] was to model software engineering practices for achieving specified software quality factors, and the impact of applying the practices on cost, schedule and software quality. Quality factors are those identified in the non-functional requirements of the product such as reliability and usability. The best practices for achieving the desired value of each factor was identified.

In [Rus-Collofello 2001], a prototype system dynamics simulator was developed to predict the reliability of a software product in addition to cost and schedule. The impact of different reliability practices was modeled considering the dynamics of defect evolution and the factors that influence it. A defect evolves through the stages of introduction, detection and removal. In the simulator, existing reliability prediction and growth models are integrated to relate defects to failure occurrences in system testing. The tool can be used to support decisions with respect to reliability strategies, and simulated projects showed that allocating more effort earlier in development eventually saves effort and time.

A combined process model to evaluate reliability strategies was applied to a large industry project in [Rus-Collofello-Lakey 1999]. Factors that affect reliability and their relationships with other project parameters were included, and it was shown that reliability cannot be divorced from cost or schedule. The appropriate combination of strategies was selected in the model based on individual project characteristics.

ODC was used for reliability modeling in [Rus 2002]. Defect data collected using the ODC scheme could be used to calibrate a model with ODC attributes. For example, process data on the effectiveness of different testing techniques for different types of defects would be useful to represent in the model. ODC within itself doesn't capture everything that might be applicable to dependability. One such attribute is defect severity [Rus 2002], which is commonly recorded. Figure 7 from this study shows a sample profile of defects and their contribution to the dependability properties *reliability* and *security*.

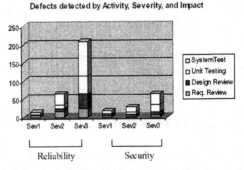

Defects detected by Activity, Severity, and Impact

**Figure 7: Profile of detected defects and their contribution to dependability properties [Rus 2002]**

## 3.4 Defect prevention

A number of organizations are using process modeling as a preventive measure. These efforts contribute to achieving high process maturity levels per the CMM and CMM-I. One example is Motorola, who has been modeling defect generation and prevention as part of their overall efforts to improve software processes [Eickelmann et al. 2002]. They have used combined approaches that use discrete aspects to tie a variety of attributes to defects including different severity levels and corresponding defect finding effectiveness values. They have recently started using ODC attributes in their process modeling.

## 3.5 Example: Analyzing impact of reliability decisions

This example derived from [Madachy 2004] addresses the dependability attributes *reliability*, *affordability* and *timeliness* in a commercial market context. The stakeholder business value being optimized is profit, and the goal is to maximize profit from investing in processes that contribute to reliability. The dependability of a product is a primary factor in sales. Achieving revenue from a reliable product is balanced against its affordability and timeliness of delivery. The model demonstrates a value-based framework for decision analysis by modeling dependability impact on costs and profit of achieving different reliability levels.

The value-based product model is described in detail in [Madachy 2004]. It supports software business decision-making by experimenting with product strategies and development practices. The model relates the interactions between product development investments, software reliability practices, market share, license retention, pricing and revenue generation for a commercial software enterprise. Risk consequence will be used to find the reliability sweet spot.

For simplification, software reliability as defined in the COCOMO II cost model [Boehm et al. 2000] is used to model the tradeoff between reliability and development cost. There are four different settings of reliability from low to very high that correspond to four development options. Expert consensus was used to relate Mean Time Between Failure (MTBF) values to the ratings scales. Regression analysis of 161 project data points was used to determine relative cost.

The tradeoff modeled in the reliability cost driver is increased cost for increased reliability; the increased cost also results in longer development time. The resulting reliability will modulate the actual sales relative to the highest potential. A less reliable product will be done quicker; it will be available on the market sooner but sales will suffer from poor reliability. A

Delphi poll of software marketing experts was conducted to quantify the relative sales impact of different reliability levels.

Table 3 shows a mapping between reliability, notional values for the traditional Mean Time Between Failure (MTBF) measurement, and the relative impact to sales used in the model. The percent of potential sales relative to the highest reliability captures the stakeholder value of reliability.

Table 3: Reliability ratings and impacts

| Reliability Rating | Defect Impact | Mean Time Between Failure (Hours) | Relative Cost | Percent of Potential Sales Captured Relative to Highest Reliability |
|---|---|---|---|---|
| Low | Small, recoverable losses | 10 | .92 | 30% |
| Nominal | Moderate, recoverable losses | 300 | 1.00 | 65% |
| High | Large, unrecoverable losses | 10,000 | 1.10 | 95% |
| Very High | Human life | 300,000 | 1.26 | 100% |

The following analysis steps are performed to find the reliability sweet spot:

- vary reliability across runs
- assess the consequences of opposing trends: market delays and bad reliability losses
- sum market losses and development costs
- calculate resulting net revenue to find process optimum.

The consequences are calculated for the different options. Only point estimates are used for the sake of this example. A more comprehensive risk analysis would consider probability distributions to obtain a range of results. Probability is considered constant for each case shown here to determine the costs (or losses). A set of runs is performed that simulate the development and market release of a new product. The product can potentially increase market share by 30%, but the actual gains depend on the level of reliability. Only the highest reliability will attain the full 30%. Other market parameterizations are an initial total market size equals $64M annual revenue, the vendor has 15% initial market share, and the overall market doubles in 5 years.

Figure 8 shows the experimental results for an 80 KSLOC product, fully compressed development schedules and a 3-year revenue timeframe for different reliability options. The resultant sweet spot corresponds to reliability being high. The total cost consisting of delay losses, reliability losses and development cost is minimum at that setting for a 3-year time horizon. Details of the intermediate calculations for the loss components are provided in [Madachy 2004].

The sweet spot depends on the applicable time horizon, among other things. The horizon may vary due for several reasons such as another planned major upgrade or new release, other upcoming changes in the business model, or because investors mandate a specific timeframe to make their return.

The experiment was re-run for typical time horizons of 2, 3 and 5 years using a profit view (the cost view is transformed into a profit maximization view by accounting for revenues). The results in Figure 9 illustrate that the sweet spot moves from reliability equals low to high to very high. It is evident that the optimal reliability depends on the time window. A short-lived product (a prototype is an extreme example) does not need to be developed to as stringent reliability as one that will live in the field longer.

This work shows how software business decision-making can improve with information gained from simulation experiments. It also illustrates that commercial process sweet spots with respect to reliability are a balance between market delay losses and reliability losses. Reliability does impact the bottom line. Business policies operate within a multi-attribute decision space though, and there are other dimensions besides time horizon that can be varied. Other considerations for the model include pricing scheme impacts, varying market assumptions, periodic upgrades of greater or lesser reliability, and feedback from the user base to incorporate new features.

## 4.    SUMMARY AND CONCLUSIONS

Process modeling is ideally suited for evaluating dependability strategies. But dependability has many dimensions and specific attribute measures need to be defined before modeling starts. We recommend a stakeholder value-based approach for doing so.

Different modeling paradigms can be used in a dependability context including analytical models, continuous systems modeling, discrete-event simulation and hybrid modeling. Process modeling can address a wider variety of phenomena. Hybrid modeling in particular has great potential for complex dependability applications, because it combines the advantages of both continuous systems and discrete-event modeling.

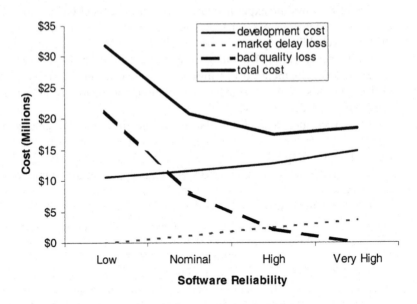

**Figure 8: Calculating reliability sweet spot (3-year timeframe)**

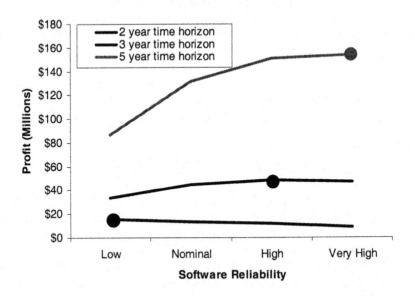

**Figure 9: Reliability sweet spot as a function of time horizon**

Generalized results from an array of process models indicate that effort should be put up front in the lifecycle in order to achieve dependability in the most cost-effective manner. Largely this is because the cost to fix defects increases over the lifecycle span. Typically the up-front effort is on software assessment activities such as reviews and quality assurance.

Quality should be built-in rather than the result of repeated testing. Testing later in the software lifecycle incurs greater costs to find and fix defects. But there are always diminishing returns for dependability strategies, and the effort should be carefully applied without waste. Process modeling was shown to be handy for finding the process sweet spots.

Overall, modeling the relationships between ways to achieve dependability and dependability attributes is difficult. The problem is exacerbated due to the fact that dependability has so many interpretations in different contexts. Therefore there have been relatively few dependability applications to-date considering the numerous potentials, and the field is ripe for exploration.

## REFERENCES

[Abdel-Hamid-Madnick 1991] Abdel-Hamid T, Madnick S, *Software Project Dynamics*, Englewood Cliffs, NJ, Prentice-Hall, 1991

[Boehm et al. 2000] B. Boehm, C. Abts, W. Brown, S. Chulani, B. Clark, E. Horowitz, R. Madachy, D. Reifer, B. Steece, *Software Cost Estimation with COCOMO II*, Prentice-Hall, 2000

[Boehm et al. 2004a] B. Boehm, L. Huang, A. Jain, R. Madachy, "The Nature of Information System Dependability: A Stakeholder/Value Approach", University of Southern California Center for Software Engineering working report, 2004

[Boehm et al. 2004b] B. Boehm, L. Huang, A. Jain, R. Madachy, "Reasoning about the ROI of Software Dependability: The iDAVE Model", *IEEE Software*, to-be published

[Eickelmann et al. 2002] N. Eickelmann, A. Anant, J. Baik, S. Hyun, "Quantitative Control of Process Changes Through Modeling Simulation and Benchmarking", Proceedings of the 17th International Forum on COCOMO and Software Cost Modeling, USC, Los Angeles, CA, October 2002

[Kan 1995] S. Kan, *Metrics and Models in Software Quality Engineering*, Addison-Wesley, 1995

[Kellner-Madachy-Raffo 1999] M. Kellner, R. Madachy, D. Raffo, "Software Process Simulation Modeling: Why? What? How?", *Journal of Systems and Software*, Spring 1999

[Lakey 2003] P. Lakey, "A Hybrid Software Process Simulation Model for Project Management", Proceedings of ProSim'03, Portland OR, 2003

[Madachy 1996] R. Madachy, "System Dynamics Modeling of an Inspection-Based Process", Proceedings of the Eighteenth International Conference on Software Engineering, IEEE Computer Society Press, Berlin, Germany, March 1996

[Madachy 2004] R. Madachy, *Software Process Dynamics*, IEEE Computer Society Press, Washington D.C., to-be published, 2004

[Madachy-Tarbet 2000] R. Madachy, D. Tarbet, "Case Studies in Software Process Modeling with System Dynamics", *Software Process Improvement and Practice*, Spring 2000

[Martin-Raffo 2000] R. Martin, D. Raffo, "A Model of the Software Development Process Using Both Continuous and Discrete Models", *Journal of Systems and Software*, Vol. 46, 2000

[Raffo 1995] D. Raffo, Modeling Software Processes Quantitatively and Assessing the Impact of Potential Process Changes on Process Performance, Ph.D. Dissertation, Graduate School of Industrial Administration, Carnegie Mellon University, Pittsburgh, PA, 1995

[Rus 1998] I. Rus, "Modeling the Impact on Project Cost and Schedule of Software Engineering Practices for Achieving and Assessing Software Quality Factors", Ph.D. Dissertation, Arizona State University, 1998

[Rus 2002] I. Rus, "Combining Process Simulation and Orthogonal Defect Classification for Improving Software Dependability", Proceedings of Thirteenth International Symposium on Software Reliability Engineering, 2002

[Rus-Collofello 2001] I. Rus, J. Collofello, "Integrating Process Simulation and Reliability Models", *Crosstalk*, January 2001

[Rus-Collofello-Lakey 1999] I. Rus, J. Collofello, P. Lakey, "Software Process Simulation for Reliability Management," *Journal of Systems and Software*, vol. 46, no. 2/3, pp. 173-182, April 1999

[Tvedt 1996] J. Tvedt, "An Extensible Model for Evaluating the Impact of Process Improvements on Software Development Cycle Time", Ph.D. Dissertation, Arizona State University, 1996

# Chapter 4

# SIMULATION PROCESS MODELLING FOR MANAGING SOFTWARE EVOLUTION[*]

Meir M. LEHMAN[1], Goel KAHEN[2] and Juan F. RAMIL[3]

[1]*School of Computing Science, Middlesex University, London, U.K., [2]Crown Poly, Inc., 5700 Bickett St., Huntington Park, CA 90255, U.S.A., [3]Computing Department, Faculty of Maths and Computing, The Open University, U.K.*
*E-mail: mml@mdx.ac.uk ; G_Cohen@crownpoly.com ; j.f.ramil@open.ac.uk*

**Abstract:**   Software that is regularly used for real world problem solving or addressing a real world application must be continually adapted and enhanced to maintain its fitness to an ever changing real world, its applications and application domains. This adaptation and enhancement activities are termed *progressive*. As progressive activity is undertaken, the complexity (e.g., functional, structural) of the evolving system is likely to increase unless work, termed *anti-regressive*, is also undertaken in order to control and even reduce complexity. However, with progressive and anti-regressive work naturally competing for the same pool of resources, management will benefit from means to estimate the amount of work and resources to be applied to each of the two types. After providing a necessary background, this chapter describes a systems dynamics model that can serve as a basis of a tool to support decision making regarding the optimal personnel allocation over the system lifetime. The model is provided as an example of the use of process modelling in order to plan and manage long-term software evolution.

**Key words:**   Complexity; feedback; laws of software evolution; process improvement; resource estimation; System Dynamics.

[*] This book chapter is a revised version (revision carried out by J.F. Ramil) of a paper published as Lehman M.M., Kahen G. and Ramil J.F., Behavioural Modelling of Long lived Evolution Processes–Some Issues and an Example, J. of Software Maintenance and Evolution, vol. 14, 2002, pp. 335–351.

## 1.  INTRODUCTION

Real world software must be progressively fixed, adapted and enhanced, that is, *evolved*, if it is to remain satisfactory to its stakeholders, as evidenced by the universally experienced need for continual software maintenance [1]. The investigation of software evolution includes the complementary concerns relating to the achievement of evolution, the *how*, and the nature of the evolution phenomenon, *what* it is and *why* it occurs. Interest in the *how* is concerned with *methods*, *tools* and *techniques* changing functional, performance and other characteristics of the software in a controlled, disciplined, reliable, fast, cost-effective manner. Interest in the *what/why*, on the other hand, focuses on *understanding* software evolution and its underlying drivers. The following exemplify the type of questions investigated under the what/why viewpoint:

- why does software evolution occur?
- why is it inevitable?
- what are identifiable characteristics and attributes of the software evolution phenomenon?
- what, if any, common patterns are displayed by different evolving software systems and evolution processes?
- do such patterns relate, in any way, to system *size*, the nature of applications, operational domain, organisational domains and the software engineering paradigm being followed?
- what is the impact of the software evolution phenomenon on, for example, the software itself, the software process, the application and the domains in which the software is used?
- what are the implications of such impact on the management of the evolution process?

In a world increasingly dependent on computers and software both views, the *how* and the *what/why*, represent concerns that must be addressed to achieve mastery of the software process and its technology. The *how* view has been widely adopted but only a small number of researchers world-wide [e.g. 2, 3, 4, 5] have taken the *what/why* view and addressed the above and related questions.

The groups adopting and focussing on the *how* have concentrated their attention on the formal description of evolving software artefacts such as specifications, architectures, programs and so on.

Formal process modelling has been missing from the second, the *what/why*, view. This absence may be justified on the basis that its premature adoption is possibly counterproductive. Early formalisation may limit creativity and the search for adequate understanding of the evolution phenomenon and for means for its mastery [6, 7]. Instead, since the late 60s [8] such studies have adopted an approach based on observation of the evolutionary behaviour of various industrially evolved software systems, collection and analysis of empirical data, development of isolated models, their phenomenological interpretation and formulation of hypotheses to be tested directly or indirectly. This approach has largely followed an investigative method, based on repeated observation of empirical data, abstraction of observation so that the focus is on high level characteristics, followed by identification of regularities and its interpretation. This has led to results that include the *SPE* program classification schema [1], the *laws* of software evolution [1, 5, 9, 10], and a principle of software uncertainty [11]. More recent results include recognition of the implications of the feedback nature of the total evolution process [12] and the presence of distinguishable *stages* in evolutionary trends of software systems. The accumulated of results provide inputs to the development of a theory of software evolution [13]. Achieving a theory of software evolution will provide a systematic basis for the study of software evolution and its management. However, even before such a theory is fully achieved one can exploit the practical potential of the existing results for the planning, management and control of industrial evolution process improvement. This chapter illustrates this by presenting a process model which is consistent with the above results and that can be used to inform decisions related to software evolution management. The presented model will require adaptation, a more comprehensive empirical quantitative validation before it can be used for decision making. The emphasis in this chapter is on the modelling procedure and the level of abstraction at which a model is constructed rather than in the model itself or its output. This chapter is structured as follows: section 2 justifies the use of system dynamics models, section 3 presents the modelling approach, section 4 presents and discusses a simulation process model and the results obtained, section 5 indicates areas for further work in this topic, section 6 provides pointers to related work and section 7 ends the chapter with some final remarks.

## 2.    SOFTWARE PROCESS MODELLING USING SYSTEM DYNAMICS

Managers and designers of software processes could frequently benefit from reasoned exploration of behavioural issues but in general lack the tools to do so. Only a tiny minority of software organisations around the world have reported the use of process simulation, with the vast majority focused on shorter-term process issue rather than in long term evolution. In a given domain, (or more technically in a *universe of discourse*), the use of formalisms and techniques such as simulation facilitates precise reasoning in that domain. This also applies to the what/why topics in general and to what we term *behavioural* process modelling in particular.

Formalisms to facilitate reasoning about various aspects of software maintenance and development, system evolution, have emerged over the last 15 years or so from, for example, the work in process modelling languages [14, 15, 16, 17]. The emphasis of that work has been primarily on process *prescription*, with models intended to reflect and explore elements such as processes workflow controls, sub-process activation conditions and properties of the process seen as a program (deadlock avoidance, etc.).

Process *behaviour* and properties such as the economic feasibility of a process or aspects of performance, however measured are, in general, as relevant as *prescription*. Success of a project and survival of the organisation that undertakes it depends in many businesses, on economic viability of long-term evolution and/or timely replacement of a legacy system. Thus the argument in favour of process simulation accords with a recent call for software engineering research to abandon the flatland of purely *technological* issues and to proceed to address other dimensions such as cost and value [18]. For this reason the study of process *behaviour* is considered of relevance in the present context. Of course, with the limitation that, given that people play a fundamental role in the software process, behavioural modelling and forecasting will, at best, be limited to representation of the process at an aggregated level.

Behavioural process modelling may be based on *black-* and *white-box* views. Black box views are exemplified by performing a linear fit or by fitting other mathematical function to empirical data. In general, the resultant black box models cannot help much when one wishes to identify potential process improvements. In this case one requires white box views that seek to reflect mechanisms inside the process, provide explanation for the observed behaviour and offer means for the identification of potential process improvements. The white-box view is illustrated by the models developed by the software process simulation community [19].

It has been recognised that an industrial software process involves many feedback loops which pass information and commands from and to different process participants and stakeholders and their activities [5, 7, 10, 12]. Feedback loop behaviour has been identified as one of the sources of uncertainty and counterintuitive behaviour in projects and organisations. One particular white box simulation modelling approach, termed *system dynamics* (SD) [20, 21, 22], is of particular interest here because of its natural provision for representing feedback loops. SD enables the disciplined study of such feedback loops and their impact on process performance. It has been applied, for example, at the software project level [23]. In our research we use SD to explore and achieve understanding of the total software evolution process for long-lived software, the focus of the SD model presented in this chapter.

System dynamics, and tools such as *Vensim*® [24] supporting it, were developed to study the time behaviour (dynamics) of complex systems in industry and other domains. Many of the available tools enable building and simulation of the models using graphical interfaces and incorporate numerical methods needed for the simulation. The semantics and syntax of SD models, procedures to build and validate them and guidelines for interpretation of simulation outputs have been discussed, for example, in [20, 21, 22, 24].

## 3.    A PROCESS MODELLING APPROACH

In order to increase its effectiveness, a modelling approach should be accompanied by procedures and guidelines to support its use. The approach followed here to behavioural process modelling includes the following activities:

i    identification of specific questions to be answered, that is, the modelling requirements

ii    identification of a set of attributes representing the process at a high level of abstraction, by means, for example, of a high level description of the process to be modelled

iii    gathering of historical data which reflecting the attributes of interest

iv    identification of *reference modes* [22], that is, trajectories, patterns and regularities observed in attributes of interest. These provide inputs for characterisation of relationships between attributes and for model validation

v    construction of an initial model that reflects only essential elements, keeping detail to the minimum necessary

vi    calibration and validation of the model output against real world behaviour

vii    iteration, refinement and validation until an appropriate level of detail is reached.

The need for the above activities follows from several observations. A system dynamics model can, for example, reflect a system at many levels. It is, therefore, important to identify an appropriate starting level of abstraction or aggregation. Subsequent refinement must lead, in a disciplined fashion, to a model that appears appropriate for the purpose for which it is being constructed. In doing this, one tries to conform, when possible, to a top-down development process of successive refinement [25, 26] and its further elaboration in 1984 in the LST formal development paradigm [27]. Starting at a high-level of abstraction, the model is further elaborated by a sequence of refinements driven by observation and experimentation of the developing model, successive transformations and validation steps. In general, the output of each transformation step provided the input to the next. The process terminates when a model reflecting the desired level granularity and precision is achieved in, for example, the context of policies or improvements to be assessed.

In model building and refinement, the recommendation is to aggregate or even exclude some of the real world detail. In particular those elements believed to be constant or of second order may initially be omitted. In general, in the first instance, only influences that may change significantly over system lifetime need be reflected in the model.

## 4.    A BEHAVIOURAL PROCESS MODEL EXAMPLE

### 4.1    Progressive and anti-regressive work

A need for continual enhancement of functional power is one of the inevitable pressures that emerge when evolving software that addresses real world problems or automates real world activities [1]. Human resources and budgets and for evolution of a software system will, in general, be determined at least one, often several, years ahead. The resources available over some predetermined period or for the development of a new release will be primarily intended for *progressive* [28] activity. This represents activity that adds functionality to the system, enhances performance and, in general, adds capability to the system as perceived by users and by marketing organisations.

In the long-term evolution context, a further underlying fact of life must be accepted. As successive versions of a real world software system emerge, source code is augmented, system size increases and fixes, adaptations, functional and non-functional enhancements get implemented which are ever more remote from the originally conceived. The consequence of all these and, in particular, of the superposition of change upon change upon change is that the software system *complexity*, however it is defined or measured, is likely to increase as the system is evolved [9]. This may bring with it a decline in the *functional growth rate*, as observed in plots of system growth over releases e.g., [5]. If this issue is not promptly recognised and addressed, it is likely to lead to decreasing evolvability, increasing maintenance and evolution costs and even stagnation.

The satisfaction of new or changed needs must not conflict with the need to ensure that the software remains evolvable. The latter is achieved by executing activities such as, for example, re-structuring [29], *refactoring* [30] and documentation, termed, in general, *anti-regressive* activities [9]. They neutralise or reverse system degradation due, for example, to growing structural, functional and operational complexity. Given commercial, competitive marketplace pressures, such work is not regarded, in general, as of high priority, but it has long-term impact and, therefore, long-term justification. However, the anti-regressive activity is in competition with the progressive since both have to draw, in general, on the same resource pool.

The allocation decision confronts a trade-off. If the main focus is on progressive and the anti-regressive work is neglected or understaffed, system structure and complexity will degrade with the enumerated consequences. A solution to achieve a more disciplined and predictable evolution is to apply anti-regressive effort, so reducing the level of progressive activity. In general, there will be no clear measure or other indicator of how much anti-regressive effort is required, how the required level may be determined or how to determine the impact and effectiveness of any given level. Whatever level of resource is applied will detract from that available for system evolution so reducing the *rate of evolution* and paying the price in a competitive market place. It is for management, with the help, for example, of models as the one presented here, to decide the appropriate level to invest to control or overcome system aging to ensure future evolvability. In the limit, if all resources are devoted to anti-regressive activity, system evolution, once again, comes to a halt.

These extreme situations spell the effective death of the system. Between them there must be a division of progressive and anti-regressive levels of investment that achieves the best balance between immediate added functional capability and system evolution potential and longevity. One requires methods and mechanisms to support systematic determination of an appropriate division of resources. Behavioural process modelling provides means and a support tool for resolving the management conflict that has been outlined. The system dynamics approach is illustrated by description of a simple model and some results obtained from it. Even this simple model provides a tool for separation of concerns between progressive and anti-regressive work.

The model is of remarkable simplicity considering, for example, that it is intended to decide how much effort should be applied to the control of complexity at the total system level.

Instead of using direct measures of complexity [31], the model presented here assumes that each unit of progressive work requires a minimum number of anti-regressive work units to forestall accumulation of an anti-regressive deficit [32]. As the required but neglected anti regressive effort accumulates over time, its impact on productivity begins to be noticeable. Only restoration to an adequate level can reverse the growth trend and restore productivity. The model provides a tool to determine what is adequate under those assumptions.

## 4.2   Top-down modelling viewed in a sequence

*Level-rate* diagrams are one of the graphical representations used in SD modelling. A level-rate diagram is a graph that consists of two connected sub-graphs: the *stock and flow* and the *information* network. The former resembles a hydraulic system with icons that suggest tanks, pipes and valves. Levels (or stocks) are represented by variables within the boxes. The variables on the valve icons represent *flow variables* or *rates*. The double-line arrows represent *flows*. The remainder of the model, represented by single line arrows and variables connected by them constitutes the information network. Single lines indicate that the variable being pointed is calculated as a function of the variable at the arrow's origin.

To make the model easier to understand it is presented here in a sequence of increasing detail comprising a series of four increasingly detailed level-rate diagrams. These reflect the process of successive refinement. An initial top-level view is provided by Figure 1. It shows the arrival and implementation or rejection of work requests, their validation, and delivery of the product to the field. It is visualised as a process that addresses a continuing flow of work in the form of changes in requirements, functional adaptation, enhancements and so on. The colour grey and the "<...>" in the variable *Time* indicate that it is somehow special: its values are not controlled by the model builder, but assigned directly by the simulation engine.

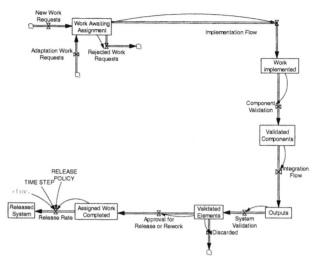

**Figure 1: The initial representation**

Figure 2 presents a first refinement of the model, making provision for delaying output of the validation step and for the authorisation of rework. Figure 3 refines the model still further to include the assignment of resources to progressive work. Finally, the full model in Figure 4 includes the sub-graph for the splitting the effort between progressive and anti-regressive work.

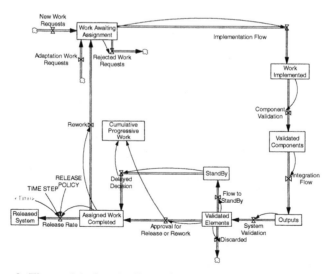

**Figure 2: The model after the first refinement: some part of output held, rejected or recycled**

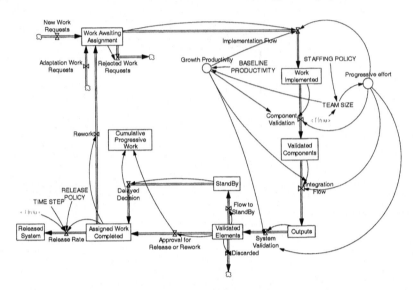

**Figure 3: Second refinement: resources allocated in order to implement new functionality**

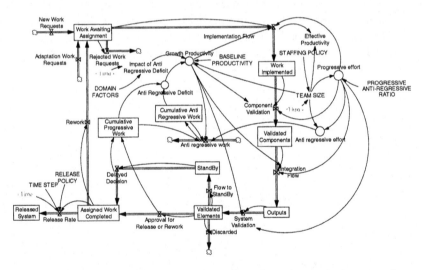

**Figure 4: Third refinement: resource allocation for complexity control**

The diagrammatic representation in Figures 1-4 can provide, at best only, a high level understanding. Limitations of space prevent presentation of the various expressions relating its variables. These expressions included in the executable model in Vensim language are available upon request from the present authors.

As already stressed, an essential part of the approach being described is that the model be empirically validated at the appropriate level of detail after each refinement. One possible way of achieving this is by calibrating the model, comparing predictive model output with actual behaviour of a software system.

## 4.3 Model calibration

Before discussing the attempts made at model calibration and the various virtual experiments performed based on the model, a note is required. The model presented in this chapter is offered primarily as an example of a high level approach to behavioural modelling of the process and of the type of outputs one may expect. The emphasis is not in the particular model being presented. Its use of the latter as a decision making aid in an actual evolution process must be preceded by its calibration to that process and empirical validation, following procedures such as those described in [20, 21, 22, 23, 24]. The sections on calibration and validation in this chapter address only some of the aspects involved. The interested reader is referred to the references for a fuller discussion.

What follows are some remarks on model calibration. The latter may start by exposing the model to available data so that confidence in the model increases progressively. Such increases will, generally, be accompanied by growing understanding of the process being modelled. As a first step in the calibration process, parameters must be set to be consistent with the process being modelled. This implies measurement of real world attributes represented in the model. Once those values are obtained, one sets model parameters to reflect real values. In practice, some of these may not be readily available, as for example when, as in the present case, one is modelling long term behaviour that spans over several years, even decades. It may, therefore, be necessary to, identify ranges of parameters that produce specific behaviours. In doing so, the model builders start to identify which parameters are critical in determining specific behaviours. Then one proceeds to check with process experts and/or by using documentary sources the possible values in the real process, thereby, building confidence in the model. Of course, this only yields a partial calibration. A full calibration requires that all model parameters reflect real world measures. On the other hand, validation requires that the model is shown to *predict* real world behaviour not observed during model building or calibration and remains accurate over time. Hence, calibration and validation must be continual activities as long as the model is intended to be used.

In some cases, non availability of direct measures forces one to use attribute surrogates. For example, to calibrate the present model to a collaborator's system, the level of effort applied, represented by the variable *STAFFING POLICY*, was assumed to be roughly proportional to the count of *modules handled* [1] per month, an indicator of work-rate, that, in a later study [5], was found to be correlated with estimates of the effort applied. Other parameters were found to have no visible impact on growth trend within a range of values. This suggested that the mechanism to which they related had no major impact on growth trend at the present level of detail; that it was not a candidate for calibration adjustments in the current setting. The inflexion point at around month 96 was hypothesised as - and modelled by - a step change in the value of *Impact of Anti-regressive Deficit*. Alternative explanations to discontinuity points have been put forward, for example in [33]. They may reflect a switch of process stages in the sense of other researchers [7].

By fixing the known - or estimated - parameters and exploring the impact of changes in the others on model's output, one establishes the sensitivity of the output to all model parameters. For example, in the present model, it was evident that the value of parameters representing the flows feeding to *Work Awaiting Assignment* were relatively unimportant with respect to the rest of the model as long as there was "enough work waiting". This was, in fact, accepted as an appropriate property of the model since it implements common experience in real world evolution processes that the work waiting queue tends never to be empty.

Having described the partial calibration process follows, it is, nevertheless, interesting to note that a relatively simple model - by comparison other that involve tens or even hundreds of variables [23] - such as the one presented in Figures 1-4 closely approximate real world patterns of behaviour. Figure 5 shows how closely the model reproduces the growth trend of one software system - an information system - over 176 months of its lifetime.

As illustrated by Figure 5, the model is able to replicate actual trends despite the fact that, in general, only a small sub-set of the model parameters were known. Note that in order to de-emphasise their role no numerical values are shown attached to the ordinate of Figure 5 and subsequent figures in this chapter. Numeric detail may change depending, for example, on the specific process being modelled and the measures selected to represent the various attributes.

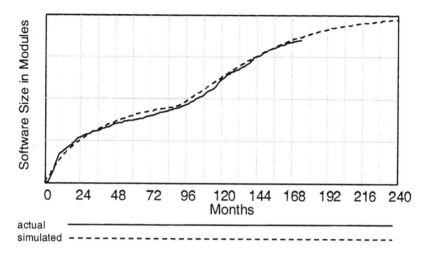

**Figure 5: Simulated model output vs actual growth trend (in number of modules) for an information system**

Model parameters whose value could not be readily ascertained were set to values that minimised the difference between the actual growth trend and model outputs. Of course, the validity of values obtained in this way to advance, for example, understanding of the process and its model representation, depends on confirmation of its validity by, for example, successful behavioural prediction. If one were to use the model as a decision-making tool, one would have to pursue the next stage of model refinement by determining actual values of the data related to the parameters and recalibrating. However, the model as presented here suffices to exemplify the approach and to perform some virtual experiments as shown below.

## 4.4 Virtual experiments

Experiments performed using a process model such as the one presented here are termed virtual because they are not performed in the real world of software organisations and processes. By their very nature this technique must be used when policies such as, for example, alternative long-term evolution strategies are being evaluated. These can, generally, not be investigated *in vivo* since the latter would require measurement and evaluation of alternative evolution processes based on different policies. Instead one relies on virtual experiments with models that, to some degree, represent the observed phenomena. With adequate care, the conclusions can then be applied in the real world.

The specific experiment to be described concerns the long-term consequences of different levels of anti-regressive activity on system growth rate. Figure 6 represents the simulated model output for 3 values of anti regressive work, expressed in percentage of total resources.

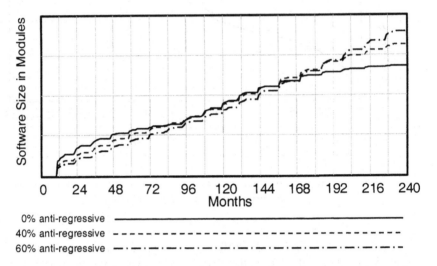

**Figure 6: Simulated model output for several values of anti regressive work. The anti-regressive work is expressed in percentage of total human resources available for the evolution of the system**

The trends reflected in Figure 6 include, however, temporal variations in effort applied and an inflexion point. All these made difficult to interpret the impact of changes in the level of anti-regressive work. To simplify interpretation, one can investigate the impact of parameter changes, one parameter at the time. This is illustrated in Figures 7 and 8 where, to isolate the inflexion point issue from this analysis, the model was fitted to the first growth segment only. Execution of the resultant model permits a clearer visualisation of the effect of different anti-regressive policies. This is illustrated in Figures 7 and 8, which presents the results of model execution, permitting visualisation of the effect of different anti-regressive policies.

Figure 7 shows several simulated trajectories resulting from alternative fixed allocation strategies. Their features include several cross-over points. For the lowest level of anti-regressive work one achieves the highest *initial* accomplishment rates, suggesting initially low anti-regressive activity, to maximise initial growth rate.

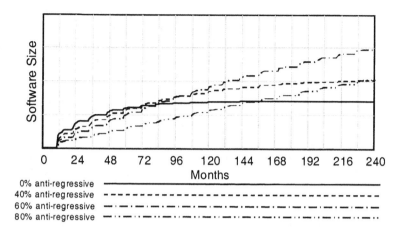

**Figure 7: Growth trends under different levels of anti-regressive work**

Figure 8 indicates the impact of different levels of a fixed anti regressive work on growth-productivity, that is, the number of elements created per unit of *total* effort applied. Total means adding both progressive and anti-regressive work.

Together the two illustrated experiments suggest that a constant a level, in this case approximately 60 percent of resources allocated to anti regressive work maximises long-term growth capability. *This number will vary from process to process. What is important here is that anti regressive work in excess of some level, constitutes, at least in the context of the present model, resource wastage.*

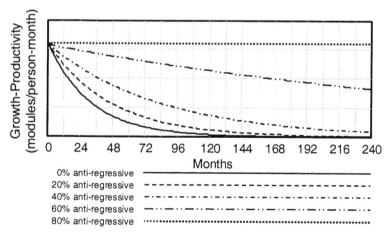

**Figure 8: Growth-productivity under different policies**

Direct interpretation of the results suggests that trajectories should be switched at cross-over points, to maintain a progressive/anti-regressive ratio that's exploits the trajectory with the highest growth rate. This is, however, unachievable by simply increasing the anti-regressive/progressive work ratio since the inertial effect of the accumulated anti-regressive work deficit is difficult to overcome. Other strategies such as those involving system re-structuring or even partial system replacement may be required to achieve a visible recovery in growth rate [33]. To some extent this illustrates the counterintuitive behaviour of feedback systems. In any event, whether restructuring occurs or not, the virtual experiments suggest that as a system ages one may seek to maintain system growth rate or, equivalently, minimise total effort required to achieve the desired evolution rate, and hence productivity, by adjusting the level of anti-regressive activity.

## 4.5   Model validation

It is hoped that the model presented and its discussion has sufficed to illustrate the approach, the contribution to software process modelling and process management.

Before its active use as a decision-making tool, for example, it is important that a behavioural model be calibrated and empirically validated at the appropriate level of detail, ideally after each refinement. Successful calibration requires that at least those parameters that are critical in determining model output reflect real values. The experimentation process must include observations that identify critical attributes one needs to measure based on indications of the sensitivity of model outputs to changes in parameter values. For these illustrations, such critical parameters include those, for example the *Impact of Anti-regressive Deficit* (Figures 1-4), that determines the progressive/anti-regressive ratio and, ultimately, productivity. These are likely to vary between organisations from time to time, artefact to artefact, product to product, process to process and even from stage to stage [4] in the evolution of a system. Hence, calibration and validation must be ongoing activities. Validation involves assessment of predictive power of the model by comparison of its output to actual behaviour. This requires, *inter alia* that the model can be shown to *predict* real world behaviour not taken into consideration during model building and calibration. The initial model will be based on available data. As additional data is obtained from experimentation, interpretation of the results of model execution and real world observation, confidence in the model increases progressively as will understanding of the process being modelled.

## 5.    FURTHER WORK

One of the main assumptions upon which the presented model is based is that each unit of progressive work will require a given number of anti-regressive work units in order to counteract the effects of progressive work in system complexity. More empirical analysis is needed in order to understand the quantitative relationship between progressive and anti-regressive work and to determine how such relationship may itself evolve as a result of, for example, process improvements.

The optimal level of anti-regressive work is likely to vary from process to process. It is also likely to vary over the operational life of a long-lived software system. During initial development and the early evolutionary phases anti-regressive effort is unlikely to be effective. That will, however change, as changes and additions to the system become ever more orthogonal to initial functional and architectural concepts and system structure. Eventually the desirable level of anti-regressive effort will stabilise in a way that still permits the allocation of sufficient resources to ensure further effective system evolution. This is one of the aspects that may need to be considered in further refinements of the model.

More detailed policies and mechanisms such as the inclusion of a management feedback control loop that changes the degree of anti-regressive activity over time in response to some simulated circumstance should only require minor model modification for impact exploration.

For wider application, the model presented will need to be refined to accommodate, for example, allocation of work to a wider variety of concerns than anti-regressive and progressive work. A procedure to classify maintenance and evolution activity may serve this purpose [34]. One could further address the split between the other categories of effort, though in principle it appears that anti-regressive effort provides *a major contributor* to sustain evolution process effectiveness over the entire application lifetime. Extension to more general paradigms, such as component-based and reuse-based processes, and customisation of the model to specific process instances is likely to raise issues not considered here. These would likely include the need for measures of stakeholder satisfaction and system value [18].

The high level modelling approach presented can be complemented by measurement at a lower level of the complexity of a module or a function [31]. Once the level of effort for anti-regressive work has been decided, one could use detailed measurement of the complexity of modules or functions in order to identify which modules or functions of the system should be *refactored* [30] before others for maximum impact on system evolvability.

Considerable benefits to software process improvement can emerge from the use of process simulation models at any level of process maturity, with the benefits varying from level to level [40]. For example, a simulation model that has been empirically calibrated and empirically validated with respect to data from a given organisation can be used as a baseline model [35]: the impact of future process changes and other relevant management decisions can be assessed against the model. That is, one can use such model to assess whether future process adjustments are in fact measurable improvements. Other benefits are indicated in [35]. One needs to consider, however, that assessing the level of maturity of a process involves other aspects [36] than those typically reflected in a simulation model. A process simulation model is not a substitute of process maturity assessment methods, but it can support and complement them.

## 6.    RELATED WORK

In contrast to the general trend of software process simulation modelling [19] which address individual *ab initio* projects, the present work focuses on the total evolution process and long-term behaviour [1, 32, 37, 38, 39, 40, 41]. A related characteristic of the work presented here, also recognised by others [42], is process representation at a high level of abstraction. This contrasts with wider efforts that investigated processes at a low level of abstraction [e.g. 23], which can lead to large (e.g. more than 100 variables) simulation models which present challenges if one wishes to achieve understanding, calibration, validation, use or reuse of such models.

The process simulation model reported here is inspired in the understanding reflected by the laws of software evolution. Hence, the understanding of the laws of software evolution and, in particular, the most recent views about their empirical support [41, 43] provides the context within which this modelling work can be better appreciated.

## 7.    FINAL REMARKS

Process modelling is not only relevant in the context of the improvement of methods and tools to evolve software, that is in the realm of *how* to achieve software evolution, but also within the investigation of the *what* and *why* of the evolution process. In order to illustrate this, an after having provided a necessary background, the chapter described a systems dynamics simulation model that can serve as the core of a tool to support decisions regarding allocation of personnel to evolution activities over the application lifetime. More generally, formalisation of concepts and principles developed over the years [1, 8, 9, 10, 11, 12] has the potential to facilitate their further extension and unification, leading to a theory of software evolution and a long sought conceptual framework [13].

Simulation process modelling has been pursued in the software engineering community for many years [19]. The approach suggests that even when processes are executed and managed by people, process models are a source of insight, provide rational for decision making. The local process will, at each instant in time, be the result of and reflect *local* decisions in the context of locally perceived circumstances. Process modelling at an aggregated, high level of abstraction, can offer the basis for a tool to assist managers to recognise and control the various influences on long-term behaviour. By taking these into account, they may direct effort to activities that otherwise would have been neglected. As argued in this chapter, the achievement of a minimum level of complexity management and control activity is required to maintain the rate of system evolution at the desired or required level. Control and mastery of system evolution is vital in a society increasingly reliant on ageing software in which increased size, more *interdependent* functionality, larger numbers of integrated components, more control mechanisms, a higher level of organisational interdependency are likely to lead to decrease in evolvability. Process modelling in general may be able to control key evolutionary attributes, identify counterintuitive behaviour and take appropriate action. As society relies increasingly on software, planning and management of complex, dynamic and ever more widespread and integrated evolution processes is becoming increasingly critical.

## ACKNOWLEDGEMENTS

Thanks are due to Professors Dewayne Perry (U. of Texas) and Wlad Turski (U. of Warsaw), Dr. Paul D. Wernick (U. of Hertfordshire) and to the FEAST industrial collaborators for their valuable inputs to the research which this book chapter reports. The work reported was in part funded by UK EPSRC, grants GR/K86008 (FEAST/1, 1996-1998), GR/M44101 (FEAST/2, 1999-2001), GR/L07437 and GR/L96561 (Senior Visiting Fellowships).

**REFERENCES** - * indicates that the reference has been reprinted in [1]

[1]   Lehman MM, Belady LA (eds.). *Software Evolution - Processes of Software Change*, Academic Press: London, 1985

[2]   Kemerer C, Slaughter S. An Empirical Approach to Studying Software Evolution. *IEEE Transactions on Software Engineering 1999*; **25**(4): 493 – 509

[3]   Godfrey MW, Qiang T. Evolution in Open Source Software: A Case Study. *In Proceedings of the International Conference on Software Maintenance* – 2000: IEEE Computer Press; 131 – 142

[4]   Rajlich VT, Bennett KH. A Staged Model for the Software Life Cycle, *Computer* 2000; July: 66 - 71

[5]   *Feedback, Evolution and Software Technology*, http://www.doc.ic.ac.uk/~mml/feast [December 2001]

[6]   Koestler A. *The Act of Creation*, Pan Books Ltd: London, 1970; 176 - 177

[7]   Lehman MM. Process Modelling: Where Next?, Most Influential Paper of ICSE 9 Award, *Proceedings 19th International Conference on Software Engineering-1997*, Boston; 549 – 552. Also in Hunter RB, Thayer RH (eds.). *Software Process Improvement*. IEEE CS Press, 2001

[8]*  Lehman MM. *The Programming Process*. IBM Res. Rep. RC 2722. IBM Res. Centre: Yorktown Heights, NY 10594; Sept. 1969

[9]*  Lehman MM. Programs, Cities, Students, Limits to Growth?, Inaugural Lecture, Imperial College, London, 14 May 1974. In *Imperial College of Science and Technology Inaugural Lecture Series 1970 - 74*; **9**: 211 - 229. Also in Gries D (ed.), *Programming Methodology*, Springer, 1978: 42 – 62

[10]  Lehman MM, Ramil JF. Rules and Tools for Software Evolution Planning and Management. *Annals of Software Engineering 2001*, special issue on Software Management; **11**(1), 2001: 15 – 44

[11]  *id*. Software Uncertainty. In Bustard D, Liu W and Sterritt R (eds.), *Soft-Ware 2002*, LNCS 2311, Springer: Berlin, 2002; 174 - 190

[12]  Lehman MM. Feedback in the Software Process. *Information and Software Technology* 1996. Special issue on Software Maintenance; **38**(11): 681 – 686

[13]  Lehman MM, Ramil JF. Towards a Theory of Software Evolution - And its Practical Impact, invited lecture, *Proceedings of International Symposium on the Principles of Software Evolution ISPSE 2000*; Kanazawa, Japan, Nov. 1-2

[14]  Osterweil L. Software Processes are Software too. *Proceedings 9th International Conference on Software Engineering-1987*. Monterey, CA; 2 - 12

[15] Osterweil L. Software Processes are Software too, Revisited: An Invited Talk on the Most Influential Paper of ICSE 9. *Proceedings 19th International Conference on Software Engineering-1997*. Boston, MA: 540 – 548

[16] Podoroznhy RM, Osterweil LJ. The Criticality of Modeling Formalisms in Software Design Method Comparison. *Proceedings 19th International Conference on Software Engineering-1997*. Boston MA: 303 - 313

[17] Wirtz G. Using a Visual Software Engineering Language for Specifying and Analysing Workflows. *IEEE International Symposium on Visual Languages 2000*: 97 – 98

[18] Boehm BW, Sullivan KJ. Software Economics: A Roadmap. In Finkelstein A (ed.). *The Future of Software Engineering*. IEEE Computer Press, 2000: 321 – 343

[19] Kellner MI, Madachy RJ, Raffo DM. Software Process Simulation Modelling: Why? What? How?, *Journal of Systems and Software 1999*; **46**(2/3): 91 - 106

[20] Forrester JW. *Industrial Dynamics*, MIT Press: Cambridge, MA; 1961

[21] Forrester JW, Senge P. Tests for Building Confidence in System Dynamics Models, In Legasto AA Jr., Forrester JW, Lyneis JM (eds.). *System Dynamics*. TIMS Studies in the Management Sciences **14**. North Holland: New York; 1980, 209 – 228

[22] Coyle RG. *System Dynamics Modelling - A Practical Approach*. Chapman & Hall: London, 1996; 413 pp.

[23] Abdel-Hamid T, Madnick S. *Software Project Dynamics - An Integrated Approach*, Prentice-Hall: Englewood Cliffs, NJ, 1991

[24] *Vensim – The Ventana Simulation Environment*, Version PLE32 Version 5.0b, Harvard, MA, 2002, Personal Learning Edition (PLE) downloadable from http://www.vensim.com/ [July 2002]

[25] Zurcher FW, Randell B. Iterative Multi-Level Modeling - A Methodology for Computer System Design. *Proceedings IFIP Congress 1968*, Edinburgh, Aug 5 – 10: D-138 – 142

[26] Wirth N. Program Development by Stepwise Refinement, *Communications of the ACM 1971*; 14(4): 221-227

[27] Lehman MM and Ramil JF. Software Evolution and Software Evolution Processes, *Annals of Software Engineering 2002*. Special issue on Process-based Software Engineering, **14**. In press.

[28] Baumol WJ. Macro-Economics of Unbalanced Growth - The Anatomy of Urban Cities, *Am. Econ. Review* 1967; June: 415 - 426

[29]    Griswold WG. *Program Restructuring as an Aid to Software Maintenance*. Doctoral dissertation. Department of Computer Science and Engineering. University of Washington. 1991

[30]    Fowler M. *Refactoring: Improving the Design of Existing Code*. Addison-Wesley Longman: New York; 1999, 461 pp.

[31]    Zuse H. Software Complexity Measures and Models. De Gruyter: NY; 1990

[32]    Riordan JS. An Evolution Dynamics Model of Software Systems Development. In *Software Phenomenology - Working Papers of the (First) SLCM Workshop-Aug. 1977*, Airlie, Virginia. Pub ISRAD/AIRMICS, Comp. Sys. Comm. US Army, Fort Belvoir VI, Dec 1977; 339 - 360

[33]    Aoyama M. Metrics and Analysis of Software Architecture Evolution with Discontinuity. In Aoyama M *et al.* (eds.), *Proc. 5th Intl. Workshop on Principles of Software Evolution, IWPSE 2002*, in association with ICSE 02, May 19 – 20, Orlando, FL.: 103 - 107

[34]    Chapin N *et al.* Types of Software Evolution and Software Maintenance, *J. of Software Maintenance and Evolution: Res. and Practice* 2001, **13**(1); 1 - 30

[35]    Christie AM. Simulation in Support of CMM-based Process Improvement, *J. of Systems and Software* 1999, **46**(2/3): 107 – 112

[36]    Goldenson DR, El Eman K, Herbsleb J, Deephouse C. Empirical Studies of Software Process Assessment Methods, in El Eman K and Madhavji N H, *Elements of Software Process Assessment & Improvement*, IEEE Computer Society, Los Alamitos, California 1999: 177 – 218

[37]    Wernick P, Lehman MM. Software Process White Box Modelling for FEAST/1, *Journal of Systems and Software* 1999, **46**(2-3): 193 - 201

[38]    Chatters BW *et al.* Modelling A Software Evolution Process: A Long-term Case Study. *J. of Software Process: Improvement and Practice* 2000; **5**(2-3): 95 - 102

[39]    Kahen G, Lehman MM, Ramil JF, Wernick PD. System Dynamics Modelling of Software Evolution Processes for Policy Investigation: Approach and Example. *Journal of Systems and Software* 2001; **59**(3): 271-281

[40]    Aranda R *et al.* Quality Microworlds: Modeling the Impact of Quality Initiatives over the Software Product Life Cycle. *Am. Programmer* 1993; **6**(5): 52 – 61

[41]    Ramil JF, Smith N. Qualitative Simulation of Models of Software Evolution, *Journal of Software Process: Improvement and Practice* 2002; 7: 95 – 112

[42]    Ruiz M, Ramos I. A Dynamic Estimation Model for the Early Stages of a Software Project, *Proceedings of Workshop on Software Process Simulation and Modelling Prosim 2000*, Imperial College, London, 12-14 July

[43]     Ramil JF. Laws of Software Evolution and their Empirical Support, Invited Panel
         Statement, *Proc. ICSM 2002*, Montreal, Canada, 3 - 6 Oct 2002: 71

Chapter 5

# SOFTWARE PROCESS MODELLING:
*Socio-Technical Perspectives*

Patrick WATERSON, Stephan WEIBELZAHL and Dietmar PFAHL
*Fraunhofer Institute Experimental Software Engineering (IESE), Sauerwiesen 6, 67661*
*Kaiserslautern, Germany. E-mail: {waterson, weibel, pfahl}@iese.fhg.de*

**Abstract:**    In this chapter we describe how the socio-technical systems (STS) approach
has been applied to the software process, as well as attempts that have been
made to simulate and model the process as a whole. We also outline previous
attempts to use socio-technical criteria and guidelines in order to make
improvements to the process of constructing software. We first provide a
broad outline of the STS approach followed by a number of examples drawn
from the areas of COTS-based selection, the People Capability Maturity
Model (P-CMM), competency programmes and process simulation. We
conclude the chapter with a set of future research issues that are most likely to
occupy researchers in the coming years. These issues are drawn partly from
the theoretical literature within software engineering, as well as recent
developments within industrial practice.

**Key words:**    Process modelling; simulation; software engineering education; socio-
technical systems.

## 1. INTRODUCTION

The process of building software is by definition an activity that involves
people alongside more established technical considerations. Despite the
rather obvious nature of this statement it is still largely the case that human
aspects of the software process are mostly overlooked or in the most extreme
cases completely ignored. The lack of attention paid to human issues is
frequently cited as one of the main causes of large-scale software disasters
[see for example Gla97], as well as the fact that many software-based

systems are abandoned or fail to make a return on their initial investment [Lan95].

Aside from the failure of software systems many researchers and practitioners have also argued that there are many other grounds for readdressing the balance between the human and technical aspects of the software process. Within the area of requirements engineering for example, there has been a great deal of effort placed on involving end users and other associated experts and specialists as early on in the process of requirements capture. Similarly, much effort has gone into representing user requirements in terms of scenarios, and other types of formalism, such that they can be readily used and exploited by software developers [e.g., JiG94, HCI99]. In addition, many other roadmaps that have been developed in order to describe the future of software engineering highlight the need to develop competency development and educational programmes that extend beyond a traditional focus on technical aspects of educational curricula and cover in more detail human and social issues [e.g., FrK94].

At the heart of all of these considerations is the recognition that human issues play an overwhelming role in determining the success or failure of software systems. There is also widespread recognition that the productivity and efficiency of the software process is critical dependent upon human and social factors. Barry Boehm, one of the most well respected figures within software engineering for example, states in a recent text that:

> *"After product size, people factors have the strongest influence in determining the amount of effort required to develop a software product."* [BAB+00].

An outcome from these developments, whether it be in terms of requirements engineering or software engineering education, is that in the last decade a great deal of effort has been placed upon viewing software engineering and the software process from the point-of-view of a *socio-technical system (STS)* and applying the STS approach to the design of software systems [SoR97].

## 1.1   The socio-technical systems approach

In its simplest form the socio-technical systems (STS) approach stresses the importance of recognising a distinction between two sub-systems within the overall software process (the social and the technical) and the need to jointly optimise and design these in parallel. Figure 1 is a simple diagram showing the relationship between the social system (made up on people) and the technical system (made up of individual software systems). Proponents of the STS approach argue that improvements in the wider software process can only take place when the design of both social and technical sub-systems are considered to be complementary (for further details of the theoretical and historical background to the STS approach see [Wat04]). STS is itself based on a set of design principles that can be used to help design computer-based systems. Table 1 outlines a recent set of examples of such principles as they apply to system design [Cle00].

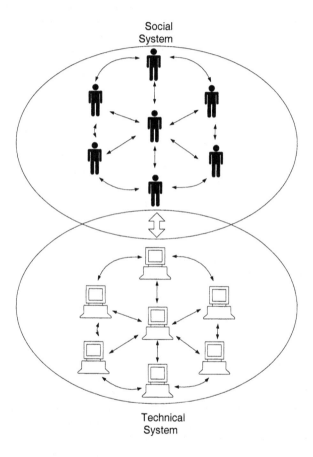

**Figure 1: Diagram of the software process as a socio-technical system**

Table 1: Example principles of socio-technical systems design [Cle00]

| Principle | Details |
|---|---|
| Design is systemic | All aspects of system design are inter-connected. Leaving out one part (e.g., human aspects) will inevitably lead to sub-optimal performance of the whole system. |
| Design is socially shaped | Design is subject to social movements and trends, these may sometimes manifest themselves as fads and fashions. |
| Evaluation is an essential part of design | Evaluation, although rarely undertaken, has several advantages, the chief one being that an organisation can learn from its mistakes and successes. |
| Design involves multidisciplinary education | There is a need for a diverse range of expertise and skills within design in order to bring about innovation, as well as viewing design from several perspectives. |

The aim of these principles is not to act as some kind of prescriptive guide as to how to design and balance the interface between social and technical aspects of system design. Instead, the principles are intended to act as guidelines and heuristics for software personnel, including managers, when implementing and evaluating changes to the software process. For example, the first principle (design is systemic) conveys the need to address all aspects of design in parallel, rather than leave some issues (e.g., social and organizational concerns) to a later stage where there is a danger that due to time pressure, budget restrictions etc., they may be put aside or overlooked. Similarly, the last principle in Table 1 highlights the need for educational programmes that span a number of disciplines and competencies (i.e., in addition to more specialised technically-oriented knowledge or skills).

Two other aspects of the STS approach should also be highlighted, particularly since they have been widely applied within attempts to improve the software process. Firstly, the STS approach stresses the need to evaluate the result of any changes that are made to the human/technical system, allow time to reflect upon these, as well as including improvement cycles to take place over time. Secondly, proponents of the STS approach stress the need to actively involve all of those involved in the change in the process of decision-making relating to improvements to the human/technical system. One consequence of involving all of the stakeholders in the change process as early on as possible is that levels of ownership be improved and "buy-in" to the changes likely to take place.

## 1.2 The software process as a socio-technical system

One of the most salient characteristics of the STS approach to the software process is that it attempts to help to assess, improve and provide feedback to those involved in process change. Figure 2 outlines a generic model of the process improvement process as it is depicted in a recent textbook on software engineering [Som00]. As can be seen from Figure 2 one of the main areas in which the STS approach may yield benefits is in terms of providing guidance in designing and developing training and education programmes. Similarly, the approach may help to bring about process change and aid modelling efforts. Both the educational and modelling aspects are described in more detail in section 3 of the chapter. The specific focus of the STS approach towards understanding and improving the software process is centred on a number of other additional themes and associated research questions. Table 2 summarises some examples of these themes alongside the types of research questions that have recently attracted the attention of researchers in the field of STS and the software process. Table 2 is not intended as a comprehensive summary of the field of STS and the software process, rather it is an attempt to summarise some broad trends, (some of which are admittedly closer to the research interests of the present authors than others).

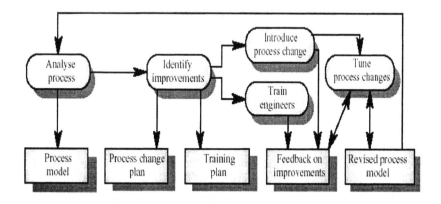

**Figure 2: The Process Improvement Process [adapted from Som00]**

Table 2: STS and the software process: Themes, example research questions and references

| Theme | Example Research Questions | Example References |
|---|---|---|
| Knowledge, skills and competencies | What types of knowledge and skills do software professionals need and how should these be taught? | [Sha00], [SWE01] |
| | What types of methods and techniques exist for the delivery of software education (e.g., in the work place)? | [DeH+03], [GWW04] |
| Human Resource Management (HRM) | How should people be allocated and given responsibility within software projects? | [SoB00], [AcJ03] |
| | How can the interrelation between human, technical and economic aspects of software projects be modelled or simulated? | [KMR99], [Mad04] |
| Participation and involvement in the software process | Who should be involved in the software process and when? | [PDC02], [Win+96] |
| | What is the most appropriate way in which to involve end users within the software process? | [HCI99], [O'NJJ99] |
| Evaluation/assessment | How can the effectiveness of the software process be measured and benchmarked over time? | [CHM02], [EDM+97] |
| | What strategies exist for changing and improving the process? | [CHM02], [Pau+93] |
| Communication and collaboration | How can effective collaboration between software personnel be achieved and integrated with the software process? | [KrS95], [Kyn91] |
| | What influence do individual, group and cultural factors have upon collaboration? | [Hof01], [Wal02] |
| Documenting the software process | What information needs to be documented during the process and how can this be made to be efficient and reliable? | [LSF03], [FoL02] |

Many of these themes have a long history within software engineering and other related disciplines such as human-computer interaction and the human factors of software development. Bill Curtis for example, in the work he and colleagues carried out in studying large-scale software projects, underlined the importance of specific types of knowledge (e.g., application domain knowledge) on the outcomes of software projects [CKI88]. Similarly, research aiming at increasing user participation and overall coordination between developers and other parties in the software process has a long history (e.g., [KrS95], [Kyn91]).

By contrast, other themes have achieved a more recent prominence. Documentation for example, whilst always proving to be a difficulty for most software engineers (e.g., in terms of maintaining documents relating to the software process), has been the subject of attention amongst followers of agile, or extreme programming where much effort has been given over to minimising the amount of paperwork and information stored during the software development process [Bec99].

We return to themes such as "Documenting the software process" and "Communication and collaboration" in section 4 of this chapter where we examine future research issues in more detail. In what follows we first review some STS aspects of the software process as they relate to "Participation and involvement" and "Evaluation/assessment" (section 2), these cover large-scale approaches (e.g., capability maturity models), as well as more specific research topics (commercial-off-the-shelf software selection). In section 3 we focus more specifically on two particular aspects of the research themes "Knowledge, skills and competencies" and "Human resource management", namely competency programmes and simulation of the software process.

## 2. STS AND THE SOFTWARE PROCESS: COTS SELECTION AND THE PEOPLE CAPABILITY MATURITY MODEL (P-CMM)

During the last two decades a good deal of effort within the software engineering community has been spent on increasing the productivity of software projects and the quality of the software they produce. In this section we review developments promoted by considerations of the human role in two software engineering domains. Both of the domains champion a participative approach to the software process, whilst at the same time providing comprehensive metrics and benchmarking tools for the evaluation of the process as a whole. The first (COTS-based selection) refers to socio-technical criteria that can be used to evaluate the various types of ready-made software that exist and can be integrated into larger systems. The second (The People Capability Maturity Model – P-CMM) is a much larger endeavour and involves guidelines, criteria and sets of organisational competencies that can be used the degree of process maturity of an organisation. P-CMM represents one of the most ambitious attempts to address socio-technical concerns in the course of bringing about changes to the software process as a whole.

## 2.1 Selection of Commercial Off-The-Shelf Systems (COTS)

COTS have been defined as "a software product developed by a third party for the purposes of integration into a larger system as an integral part (i.e., that will be delivered as part of the system to the customer of that system – i.e., not a tool)"[1]. COTS have proved to be popular amongst companies since they have been shown to reduce development cost and shorten time-to-market. However, the use of COTS also raises a number of risks such as using software that does not sufficiently satisfy the requirements [Och+00, MaN98]. There are a number of reasons why selecting COTS to fit the original requirements of the system proves to be problematic. Firstly, many organisations implement COTS into their software processes in an 'ad hoc' manner, this in turn makes planning difficult, lessons learnt from previous cases and systems are not learnt and appropriate evaluation tools and methods are not used [Kon96]. Secondly, the types of evaluation criteria used to assess COTS are often inadequate in that they tend to concentrate on technical capabilities in isolation and fail to include a consideration of human and business issues [Pow+97]. Despite the fact that many existing approaches fail to address so-called 'soft' aspects of COTS selection, there do exist a few exceptions. In particular the STACE (Socio-Technical Approach to COTS Evaluation) method [KuB99] explicitly attempts to address human and social issues.

### 2.1.1 The STACE method for COTS selection

The STACE method consists of four interrelated stages, these are: (1) requirements elicitation; (2) socio-technical criteria definition; (3) alternatives identification; and, (4) evaluation/assessment.

During the requirements elicitation high-level customer and system requirements are gathered through consultation with stakeholders. The process of consultation is designed to be as participative as possible and may involve activities such as consultation of documents (drawn from both the customer and the system), examination of domain knowledge, as well as

---

[1] www.cebase.org/www/researchActivities/COTS/definition.html

other activities such as analysis of the market to find out what other COTS alternatives exist.

During socio-technical criteria definition the high level requirements from the earlier phase are decomposed into a set of hierarchical criteria based partly upon customer needs and priorities. Part of the process involves consulting previous experience gained from past evaluation cases.

Alternative identification involves searching and screening for COTS products/technology that can later be evaluated in the evaluation stage of the method. Finally, in the evaluation stage the COTS alternatives are ranked according how well they match the socio-technical evaluation criteria. The evaluation stage itself may involve a number of data collection activities including analysis of documentation, interviews with users of the product and examination of sample outputs from projects that have used the products. A range of techniques such as card sorting and laddering [RuM95] may also be suitable for use during the evaluation stage.

One of the most interesting and important aspects of the STACE method are the socio-technical criteria since these involve explicit coverage of both human and technical issues, as well as involving stakeholders within the main stages of criteria selection and evaluation. The criterion-based and participative framework underpinning the method are, as we have seen in section 1 of the chapter, exemplary characteristics of the socio-technical approach and share much in common with other socio-technical methods and tools (e.g., see [WOC02] for an additional example).

### 2.1.2 The use of socio-technical criteria in the STACE method

Four types of STS criteria are involved in STACE, these cover: (1) technology factors; (2) functionality characteristics; (3) product quality characteristics; and (4) social-economic factors.

Technology factors include a number of considerations that may need to be taken into account, these include the intended functionality of the software (e.g., whether the technology should support distributed objects, real time processing etc.). In addition, other considerations such as performance (e.g., dependability, resource utilisation, usability), framework and architecture style, adherence to interface standards and security (e.g., the capability of the technology to provide a secure environment), may also be relevant.

Functionality characteristics and product quality characteristics cover a range of issues that include the type of environment that the COTS will be used in (e.g., in a banking or retail environment), as well as considerations focusing on quality (e.g., system dependability, maintainability).

The final set of criteria cover socio-economic factors and involve non-technical factors that should be considered during COTS selection. These non-technical factors range from operational criteria such as costs and overheads that come about as a result of implementing the COTS (e.g., training costs). In addition, there may well be a number of other non-technical considerations that need to be taken into account. Many of these may prove to be difficult to quantify, however, they may also prove to be a significant factor in determining the likely success/failure of the COTS. For example, management support and organisational politics may play a part in determining the extent to which user acceptance of the system is likely. In both cases, the result of considering these types of criteria may mean that more thought needs to go into managing the change from the old system to the new. Change management in itself is a difficult issue to resolve over a short time period and it may be that large-scale changes to the software process are necessary. In the next section we describe one of the most well known examples of a method that has been specifically designed in order to facilitate large-scale, longitudinal socio-technical process improvement.

## 2.2   The People Capability Maturity Model (P-CMM)

The People Capability Maturity Model (P-CMM)[2] came about in the mid-1990s as a result of work that had been carried out by the Software Engineering Institute at Carnegie Mellon University on process maturity frameworks for software organisations [Hum89, Pau+93]. Process maturity refers to "the extent to which an organisation's processes are defined, managed, measured, controlled and continually improved" [CHM02, pp. 515]. The range of organisational processes that the P-CMM addresses is extensive and covers areas of workforce management such as staffing (e.g., communication and coordination and workgroup development). These processes are themselves part of the main P-CMM maturity levels: Level 1 (initial); Level 2 (managed); Level 3 (defined); Level 4 (Predictable); and, Level 5 (Optimising). Within each of the various levels a set of goals associated with individual processes, as well as specific sub-components of the processes which are referred to as practices. Table 3 outlines some of the key process areas of the P-CMM.

---

[2] P-CMM and the IDEAL model are registered trademarks of Carnegie Mellon University.

Table 3: Process areas of the P-CMM

| P-CMM Maturity level | Focus | Process area |
|---|---|---|
| 5<br>Optimising | Continuously improve and align personal, workgroup and organisational capability | Continuous workforce innovation<br>Organisational performance alignment |
| 4<br>Predictable | Empower and integrate workforce competencies and manage performance quantitatively | Mentoring<br>Organisational capability management<br>Quantitative performance management<br>Competency-based assets<br>Empowered workgroups<br>Competency integration |
| 3<br>Defined | Develop workforce competencies and workgroups, and align with business strategy and objectives | Participatory culture<br>Workgroup development<br>Competency-based practices<br>Career development<br>Competency development<br>Workforce planning<br>Competency analysis |
| 2<br>Managed | Managers take responsibility for managing and developing their people | Compensation<br>Training and development<br>Performance management<br>Work environment<br>Communication and coordination<br>Staffing |
| 1<br>Initial | Workforce practices applied inconsistently | - |

The P-CMM primarily works by providing guidance on implementing the organisational processes listed in Table 3, it does not, however, specify the explicit workforce practices to be implemented. Rather, organisations are encouraged to align the practices to their own particular culture, history and environment. P-CMM makes use of the IDEAL model [GrM97][3], which in turn consists of five main components:

- Initiating – establish support and responsibilities for improvement.
- Diagnosing – identify the problems to be solved.
- Establishing – select and plan specific improvement activities.
- Acting – design, pilot, implement and institutionalise activities.
- Learning – identify improvements in IDEAL-based activities.

[3] www.sei.cmu.edu/ideal/ideal.bridge.html

The IDEAL model is applied within all of the maturity levels in Table 3, for each maturity level a specific process is examined using the five components of IDEAL: P-CMM also provides some guidance in terms of examples of how the sub-components of the processes (i.e., practices) can be implemented. Table 4 outlines some examples based the process of improving communication and coordination within Maturity Level 2 (Managed).

Table 4: Maturity level processes and associated practices

| Maturity level | Process | Example Practice |
|---|---|---|
| 2<br>Managed | Communication and Coordination | Interpersonal communication skills necessary to establish and maintain effective working relationships within and across workgroups are developed.<br>Examples of interpersonal skills that support working relationships include:<br>• Interpersonal communication and dynamics<br>• Active listening skills<br>• Group communication and dynamics<br>• Interaction protocols for specific situations. |

In order to illustrate the use of the P-CMM in more detail we briefly describe in the next section an example of its application in an industrial setting.

### 2.2.1 Using the P-CMM: An example

[CHM02, pp. 99-103] describes the use of the P-CMM at Lockheed Martin Missile Systems, a company that built command/control and logistics management systems. Lockheed Martin had been formed following the integration of a number of other companies (including IBM Federal Systems and divisions of Unisys) and was at the time of the P-CMM assessment just under five years old. The company decided to carry out a formal P-CMM assessment in order to establish a baseline of understanding regarding its current process-oriented practices, as well as gauging their strength and stability within the company. The longer-term goal of the assessment was to move the company toward attaining Level 3 maturity. One of the areas that Lockheed Martin chose to focus on as an area for improvement were communication channels within the company.

As a result of using the P-CMM the company decided to establish three types of communication channel in order to improve communication between employees and management:

- Open door – where employees could appeal to higher levels of management in the event that concerns were not resolved with their immediate manager;
- Speak up – where employees could anonymously engage in two-way communication with managers and seniors (e.g., raise questions, make comments or complaints);
- Skip level interviews – these provided an annual opportunity for employees to meet with managers in order to discuss for example, career interests or topics of concern within their work area.

Part of the reason these types of initiatives proved to be successful was that the improvements had been sponsored by senior managers as well as leaders within the human resources division of the company. Lockheed Martin also made a number of other changes to their training and development programmes, as well as their general Human Resource Management (HRM) strategy.

In the following section we examine these two areas in more detail and specifically describe two further areas that are important for STS work on the software process. One area concentrates specifically on competency development and the assessment of qualification needs, whilst the other addresses larger concerns, namely simulation of the software process as a whole.

## 3. STS AND THE SOFTWARE PROCESS: COMPETENCY PROGRAMMES AND PROCESS SIMULATION

### 3.1 Competency programmes

The qualifications, skills and competencies of the people involved in the software process are obviously an important determinant of the STS, since insufficient qualifications for a certain task might result in delays, increased costs, low software quality or even complete project failures. For instance, a lack of so called soft skills might be a source of communication problems, over-qualification might cause low motivation, and missing competencies might lead to inefficient or incomplete production of deliverables.

Compared to other scientific specialisms, the situation in software engineering is even more aggravated by the fact that the state-of-the-art changes frequently: new technologies, tools, standards and regulations are introduced every once in a while. Thus, the knowledge and skills of people gets outdated quickly, and continuous learning and training is required to keep up with technological development. Moreover, there has been, and still is, a shortage of computer-related professionals on the job market and thus companies need to find ways either to recruit suitable staff or to train the right competencies of the existing staff.

In summary, there is a need for systematic and precise analysis of both the skills and competencies that exist, that are required, and that will be required in the future. In this section, we describe an approach that represents steps towards such a skill gap analysis.

### 3.1.1  A framework for skill-gap analysis

Obviously, an important prerequisite for a skill-gap analysis is a specification of the skills and competencies that are required to fulfil a certain role in the software process. Various role-profile sets and skill portfolios have been proposed (see [NaS01] for a review of the literature and also [DiR01] for a case study). These skills can be analysed with different assessment methods, e.g., surveys, interviews, focus groups, Delphi-based/key-informant approaches, as well as the use of archival documents [Saw+98].

As an example of such an assessment approach we describe QUALISEM-People which is a set of methods, services, and tools to analyse the qualification needs of a software developing organization as well as overall educational and training needs [DeH+03]. QUALISEM-People systematically analyses and evaluates the qualification need by assessing the actual, target and preferred competence-based needs of employees. Such an analysis is intended to inform the management and human resource department about current, required and desired skills and competencies in order to plan qualification programs. The method is applied in six steps.

Firstly, skill profiles and questionnaires are selected from existing competence-based frameworks, depending on the current roles of the employees in the company. These include the so-called career-space framework[4] (a set of generic skill profiles in the Information and Communications Technology industry), work process oriented profiles of activities and competencies from the German APO initiative[5], as well as role

---

[4] www.career-space.com
[5] Arbeitsprozessorientiert Weiterbildung ("Work-oriented further education"), www.apo-it.de

oriented competencies in software engineering from the ESF-Baukasten[6]. Thus, QUALISEM-People covers not only subject matter knowledge, but also methods and tools skills, as well as intra and inter personal social skills.

Second, these standard profiles are tailored to the company's needs and preferences. In order to keep the questionnaire as short as possible skills and competencies that are not of interest, e.g., because they are probably not affected by the introduction of a new tool, might be removed. Additional aspects might be included because future projects or the company's strategy will require certain skills.

Third, the employees' skills and desires are assessed. In a self-assessment with a questionnaire the employees rate their actual skills and competencies individually and indicate their preference in acquiring these skills. In addition the manager might augment the results by providing the same data for each employee, too.

Fourth, the data is aggregated and analysed both on the individual level as well as on the group level by computing both the mean skill level and the difference between actual and target skill level based on the role profile. These results identify the qualification need and provide a prioritisation.

Fifth, the results are fed back to the employees and to the management in form of a summary report. Employees get their individual analysis, too.

Finally, the skill gap analysis can serve as basis for planning training and further education.

### 3.1.2 Experiences with skill-gap analysis

Applying QUALISEM-People in an industrial setting has yielded several interesting experiences and strengths, but also weaknesses of the approach. The method is very straightforward to apply and transparent to all participants. The fact that individual preferences are included in the analysis and that the assessment is anonymous and confidential, makes the employees feel very comfortable with the results and enhances the acceptance of the results.

However, there are limitations to the validity of the data, since QUALISEM-People considers answers to questionnaires only. Under certain circumstances (e.g., if there is an interest in presenting oneself in a better light) the picture would be more accurate if other data sources (e.g., observations, interviews, archival documents) are considered as well.

From a STS point of view, skill assessment should be seen as a continuous and iterative process rather than a single output: the skill gap analysis is part of the "analyse process" phase in the software improvement

---

[6] www.iese.fraunhofer.de/ESF-Baukasten/

process (Figure 2). It might either lead to a training of the engineers and/or to a process change. The results of the intervention are registered and fed back to another analysis cycle. Such a continuous improvement management enhances the precision and the interpretability of the analysis.

In the next section we examine in more detail approaches to the modelling of larger-scale competency programmes and their place within the wider software process.

## 3.2 Simulation of the software process: A tool for analysing and developing competencies in the software process

Personnel resources are an essential asset in developing a software product, as well as managing the associated software project and its processes. Figure 3 sketches the role of people in the context of the software process, reducing the complexity of actual projects and processes to its most fundamental entities: activities, artefacts, resources, and supporting materials [Lon93]. An activity can be characterized as follows: activities use the available resources and apply the supporting materials in order to transform input products (e.g., design documents) into output products (e.g., program code). Artefacts, resources, and materials can be further subdivided into sub-entities:

- Artefacts: engineering/development documents (e.g., requirements specification, design documents, program code, QA plans, test plans, test reports), service and user documents (e.g., service and user manuals, help texts), management documents (e.g., project plans, quality management plans, risk management plans).
- Materials: tools (incl. associated documentation), methods (incl. processes, policies, etc.), techniques (incl. guidelines, checklists, etc.).
- Resources: time budget, money budget, people (assuming certain engineering and management roles).

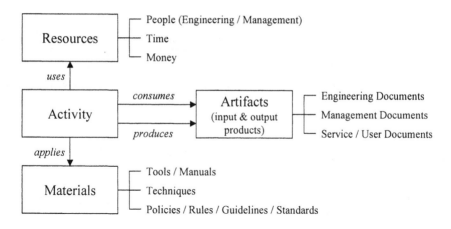

**Figure 3: Entities of software processes and their relationships**

Each of the entities is characterised by a set of attributes. The main objective of process engineering and project management is to set and control the attribute values in such a way that the business goals of the software organisation are achieved. Typical examples of attributes needed to capture project and process performance are the following:

- Attributes of artefacts: size, complexity, functionality, quality (incl. non-functional characteristics such as readability, maintainability, portability, testability, reliability, dependability, etc.), etc.
- Attributes of activities: duration, effort consumption, efficiency, etc.
- Attributes of materials: effectiveness, cost, comprehensibility, learnability, etc.
- Attributes of resources:
  - Time or money budget: size, allocation, availability, etc.
  - People: number, availability, cost/salary, motivation, exhaustion, exhaustion recoverage speed, productivity, ability to learn, experience, skills, competencies, etc.

Due to the complex interdependencies between all entities and their associated attributes, the design of development processes that are adequate for specific software development tasks in a specific software organisation is a rather complex task. As in other engineering disciplines, models are a powerful tool in supporting the process design task.

With the help of models, one can capture and describe the relations between subsets of attributes. Static models (either qualitative or quantitative) can help in two ways [BDR96]. Firstly, they can help in eliciting and describing relationships between attributes of process entities.

Secondly, they can help to establish quantitative cause-effect dependencies that may be used for evaluation and estimation purposes. In addition, dynamic models can be used to simulate the project and process behaviour, i.e. the interaction between attributes and entities at any given point in time. In many traditional engineering disciplines and management science, simulation is a well-established and commonly used tool, in software engineering it is currently becoming an accepted and more widely used tool to support process analysis and improvement, and project planning and control [Chr99][PfR01].

Particularly, process simulation can help to analyse and better understand the impact of people-related attributes on project performance (e.g., measured in terms of cost and duration) and product value (e.g., measured in terms of functionality and quality). Depending on the level of detail of the simulation model, the impact of role-specific or even individual skills/competencies [AcJ03] on certain activities and their associated outcomes, and the accumulation of these effects over the full duration of a project can be assessed. This type of analysis is useful in several ways, for example:

- To assess the impact of available engineering and management workforce on project performance.
- To compare alternative workforce allocations. Based on the comparison, the best allocation can be chosen.
- To assess the value of training, i.e., skill and competence development, by analysing how much an increase in skills/competencies (and the associated investment) would improve project performance. The advantage of simulation for this type of analysis is that in order to assess the effect of investments in training on global project performance parameters like product quality, project duration or effort consumption, only local effects need to be measured and further investigated, for example with the help of controlled experiments or qualitative research methods. An example of such a local effect would be the increase in design productivity and quality of software engineers in response to participating in training courses on a specific design method or tool.

Many process modelling and process simulation modelling approaches have been proposed in the literature [Acu+01][KMR99]. Since software development is a fundamentally human-based task, constituting a socio-technical system, the system dynamics approach is a particularly suited simulation approach to capture the people-related factors and their impact on software development performance.

The system dynamics analysis and simulation method was originally developed by Forrester in the late 1950s [For61]. In order to make the system dynamics approach more efficient in the domain of software development the method IMMoS (Integrated Measurement, Modelling and Simulation) has been developed [PfR02]. IMMoS provides comprehensive process guidance during model development, and describes how to re-use and integrate existing static models (e.g., process models and estimation models).

The philosophical position underlying the system dynamics method is what Senge and other researchers call system thinking [Sen90]. In system thinking, the behaviour of a system is considered as primarily being generated by the interaction of all the feedback loops over time. In order to analyse – and eventually change – the behaviour of observed objects in the real world, it is necessary to understand the important cause-effect relations of the factors that influence those variables that represent the observed behaviour. In system dynamics, these cause-effect relations are called base mechanisms. The union set of all base mechanisms is called a causal diagram. In order to be able to run system dynamics simulations the causal diagram has to be converted into a so-called flow graph. A flow graph is the pictorial representation of a set of mathematical equations. The application of system dynamics simulation has started with the work by Abdel-Hamid in the late 1980s [AbM91][ASR93]. In the meanwhile it has been applied with increasing frequency to many areas in the domain of software engineering since then [KMR99][Mad04].

Above, we pointed out that process simulation can be helpful in analysing the impact of human factors on project performance, and in assessing the value of training and skill/competence development within software organisations. In addition to that, process simulation and the development of process simulation models can become powerful in developing software management skills.

The following sub-sections describe three different approaches that can be useful in the scope of project management training.

### 3.2.1 Constructivist approach

With guidance from the trainer, trainees develop step-by-step their own process simulation model forcing them to make their own assumptions about cause-effect dependencies and the effectiveness of certain management policies explicit and, at the same time, providing them with a tool that helps them to validate these assumptions in a laboratory setting [Mor88][Ste94]. Moreover, this constructivist approach to management training can be performed in a team-work setting [Ven96], automatically triggering the exchange of opinions among trainees and thus implicitly developing social skills related to communication, negotiation, and group decision-making.

Even though the constructivist approach has proven to be very powerful with regards to learning effectiveness in other areas [Ven90], so far, not much experience with applying this approach to the field of software engineering has been reported in the literature. One reason for this might be the lack of knowledge about this approach in the context of software engineering training. Therefore, in the future, dissemination of experiences from other application domains has to be intensified and case studies proving the applicability of the approach in the field of software engineering need to be conducted.

### 3.2.2 Behaviourist approach - Individual setting

In a management game like setting, trainees are confronted with management-related tasks that they have to fulfil [Gra+92][Lane95]. Transferred to the software development domain, the simulation tool helps to generate realistic reactions to the decisions taken by the trainees and feeds them back to them [DrL99][PKR01].

This type of setting has been evaluated in very few studies [Pfa+03]. Initial findings indicate that the results of this approach are limited with regards to learning effectiveness if preparation before the start of the simulation game and thorough analysis of the trainees' decisions and the way how they impact simulated project behaviour are missing. Therefore, in future applications of this approach, more focus needs to be put on:

- An elaborate introduction of trainees into the problem scope that is covered (and reproduced) by the simulation model, and;
- Open and in-depth discussion on cause-effect relationships triggered by the policy decisions that were made by trainees.

### 3.2.3 Behaviourist approach - Group setting

In contrast to the individual setting described above, where group activities only apply during the preparation and post-hoc discussion phase, management games could involve several trainees playing at the same time, i.e. assuming several specific roles. In such a setting, each role's decisions might impact the performance of the activities under responsibility of other roles. In particular, the combination of local decisions, e.g. decisions independently made by sub-project managers (or other members of the management team) on the overall project performance can be analysed and demonstrated in the form of a collaborative management game. For example, the sub-project manager responsible for requirements elicitation and specification decides to not (completely) follow certain quality assurance procedures as described in the process handbook. Let's assume the prescribed type of inspection is not conducted to its full extent and not according to the defined method. With the help of the process simulation tool, the local impact of decreased quality of the requirements specification can be propagated into subsequent development activities (say, design, coding, testing) under responsibility of other sub-project managers. Now, these sub-project managers have to deal with a more difficult situation, which they most likely will not accept as soon as they realise that it is caused by decisions made in earlier development phases. The task of the overall project manager will be to moderate this situation, to make sure that the overall project performance is as good as possible, and that the project goals are achieved.

Similarly to the constructivist approach, not much experience is yet available on this type of behaviourist training in the domain of software engineering. Although much can be built upon available experience gained from individual learning settings (as described in the sub-section before), in order to assure the effectiveness of the collaborative group learning setting, again the training sessions have to be carefully designed and supervised.

## 4. STS AND THE SOFTWARE PROCESS: FUTURE ISSUES FOR RESEARCH AND PRACTICE

In this final section of the chapter we revisit some of themes outlined earlier in Table 2 and section 2 and 3 and consider these in terms of the developments that are already underway, or are likely to take place in the future.

### 4.1 COTS selection and maturity models

In terms of the work we have described on COTS selection criteria, techniques and methods in general, there is an outstanding need for more socio-technical work of the kind covered by the STACE method. Much of the COTS work focuses to this day on technical aspects of the software procurement process. Where selection criteria are applied they are most likely to address issues with regard to system compatibility and migration problems, as compared to a concern as to how the software will mesh, or conflict with the organisations culture and established mode of operation. Much more work needs to be carried out on the one hand developing STS inspired methods, but also addressing the well-known problems that exist in making such methods easy to use and cost-effective.

With regard to maturity models such as P-CMM, the outstanding need is not so much on the development side, since many types of models exist and their coverage of STS-related components is thorough, rather there is a need for careful evaluation and assessment of the introduction of interventions that are themselves based upon maturity levels. Whilst a number of case studies exist of the use of CMM, there are relatively few of the use of P-CMM so far. Without these types of evaluation studies it is difficult to assess the impact of large-scale process improvements, particularly as they take place over a period of several years. Likewise, there is a need to develop and evaluate the use of maturity models that are designed to be used in small to medium size companies. The available evidence suggests that models such as P-CMM are difficult to tailor to the particular requirements of small companies, and their effectiveness is more likely in larger enterprises.

## 4.2   Competency programmes

Skill gap analysis methods might be applied in at least three additional areas: first, such an analysis might be used not only to assess the skills and competencies of the current staff, but also to filter and select job applications automatically. The profiles of open positions would be compared to the profiles of the applicants. However, the applicants might obviously have a tendency to gloss over their skills. Thus, such a mechanism should be used for filtering or recommendation only. Nevertheless, this could support companies that have to evaluate thousands of applications.

A second application scenario is probably less biased: Skill gap analyses might also be used to filter offers in electronic job catalogues. Job-seekers could improve their search query by providing details about their skills and competencies.

Finally, a skill gap analysis might be the basis for automatically or semi-automatically provide training recommendations in an e-learning environment by checking for fulfilled prerequisites and required competencies.

All these applications already exist at least in simple variants. However, the validity of these analyses is still an open issue. Empirical studies are required to test the accuracy of predictions on skill gaps. This includes evaluation studies both on the granularity, coverage and completeness of the skill profiles as well as on the feasibility and accuracy of the assessment and analysis.

## 4.3 Process simulation

While the number of applications in software project and process management for planning, controlling, exploring and analysing improvement opportunities is increasing[7], process simulation still faces scepticism about whether it really can provide substantial contributions to solving the problems in software engineering. This scepticism is mainly due to the difficulties and often high costs associated with developing and maintaining valid simulation models. On the other hand, initial experiments have provided some evidence that process simulation can become a powerful tool in support of project management training.

In particular, the constructivist approach has yet proven its effectiveness in other areas than software development. What is needed in the future is the transfer of successful case examples from these areas into the field of software engineering education and training. Once case examples suited for software project management training have been developed, empirical studies need to be conducted in order to evaluate and improve. In order to keep effort for modelling before and during training sessions low, modularisation and tailoring concepts need to be developed and applied.

Regarding the usage of software process simulation in behaviourist approaches to project management education and training, more focus needs to be put on 1) introduction of trainees into the problem scope that is covered (and reproduced) by the simulation model, and 2) an open and in-depth discussion on cause-effect relationships triggered by the policy decisions that were made by trainees. For this purpose, guidance from learning theory and didactics needs to be exploited.

## 4.4 Other issues

Looking further into the future, aside from competency programmes or COTS selection for example, many other human-oriented aspects of the software process are worthy of more specific attention. In particular, we would point to two areas – software-based documentation and global software development.

One reason that the area of software-based documentation has recently come to prominence is due to the current vogue for agile, or extreme programming. This particular type of software development involves pairs, or small groups, of programmers developing systems over very short timescales and at the same time carrying out as little documentation of their activities as possible. Finding the right degree or extent of documentation

---

[7] See for example http://www.prosim.pdx.edu/prosim2004/

that should be carried out in agile environments presents one challenge for the future. Similarly, it has long been known that software documentation is hard to understand, and difficult to maintain. More recent studies have shown that documentation is especially important for learning about a system (e.g., [LSF03]) and how it can be used. Improving the usability of documentation, tailoring it to specific programming environments (e.g., extreme programming), and linking it to other activities important to software developers, are likely to be important research issues for the future and will no doubt have relevance for future perspectives on the software process.

One final area that deserves to be mentioned, partly because it is widely mentioned in software roadmaps aimed at predicting future developments, is the trend toward global software development. In terms of the software process more specifically, there are a whole host of factors that are likely to occupy research for the next few years. Not least amongst these factors will be the difficulties brought about to communication and collaboration patterns as a result of working across different national borders and cultures (e.g., East-West comparisons). Changes to collaboration patterns, the establishment of norms for collaboration and effective means of establishing working relationships across time zones are likely to be prominent topics for future research. These issues, together with the themes we have elaborated upon in the earlier parts of the chapter, are likely to make Boehm's comment (see earlier in the chapter – section 1) about the importance of people factors in the software process, even more relevant in the future as compared to the situation as it exists today.

## 5.    SUMMARY AND CONCLUSIONS

In this chapter we have only had space to focus upon a few of the possible aspects of the software process that are deserving of STS-based analysis. Many issues remain unresolved and at the present time difficulties exist in applying the STS perspective to the software process. Part of the problem relates to the fact that much work within software engineering as a whole has as yet, not adequately addressed the impact of social, organizational and behavioural factors upon the process of building and maintaining software. Whilst we have attempted to describe some valiant exceptions to this trend, it is still the case that psychological factors for example, whilst viewed as important if not crucial to the success of software, are not outlined in more detail or to a level of specificity where they can be operationalised, or easily understood, by those working in industry or academia. One reason for this is that definitions of what is meant by the "software process", for example, vary across different disciplines (e.g., software engineering, psychology, sociology). This naturally leads to confusion amongst researchers and frequent problems arising out of the lack of a common language with which to approach processes, the interfaces between processes, and software-based models as a whole. STS influenced approaches to the software process have come a long way in the last ten years (e.g., both the Capability Maturity Model and P-CMM initiatives have had a big impact upon research and practice), however, there remains a long way to go. Steps towards establishing a common inter-disciplinary language are perhaps one way forward, as are changes to software engineering education and training (i.e., more detailed coverage of human-centred and non-technical features of engineering software).

# REFERENCES

[AbM91] Abdel-Hamid TK, Madnick SE, *Software Projects Dynamics – an Integrated Approach*, Prentice-Hall, 1991.

[ASR93] Abdel-Hamid TK, Sengupta K, Ronan D, "Software Project Control: An Experimental Investigation of Judgement with Fallible Information", *IEEE Trans. on Software Engineering*, pp. 603-612, Vol. 19, No. 6, June 1993.

[Acu+01] Acuña ST, de Antonio A, Ferré X, López M, Maté L, "The Software Process: Modelling, Evaluation and Improvement". In: *Handbook of Software Engineering and Knowledge Engineering*, World Scientific Publishing, 2001.

[AcJ03] Acuña ST, Juristo N, "Modelling Human Competencies in the Software Process", *Proceedings of the International Workshop on Software Process Simulation Modelling* (ProSim), Portland, 2003.

[BAB+00] Boehm BW, Abts C, Brown WA, Chulani S, Clark BK, Horowitz E, Madachy R, Reifer DJ, Steece B, *Software Cost Estimation with COCOMO II*, Upper Saddle River: Prentice Hall PTR, 2000.

[BDR96] Briand LC, Differding CM, Rombach HD, "Practical Guidelines for Measurement-Based Process Improvement", *Software Process Improvement and Practice* 2 (4), pp. 253-280, 1996.

[Bec99] Beck K, *Extreme Programming Explained*, Addison-Wesley, 1999.

[Chr99] Christie AM, "Simulation: An Enabling Technology in Software Engineering", *CROSSTALK – The Journal of Defence Software Engineering*, pp. 2-7, April 1999.

[Cle00] Clegg CW, "Sociotechnical Principles for System Design", *Applied Ergonomics*, 31, pp. 463-477, 2000.

[CKI88] Curtis B, Krasner H, Iscoe I, "A Field Study of the Software Process for Large Systems", *Communications of the ACM*, 31 (11), pp. 1268-87, 1988.

[CHM02] Curtis B, Hefley WE, Miller, SA, *The People Capability Maturity Model: Guidelines for Improving the Workforce*, Boston: Addison-Wesley, 2002.

[DeH+03] de Haan D, Waterson PE, Trapp S, Pfahl D, "Integrating Needs Assessment within Next Generation E-Learning Systems: Lessons Learnt from a Case Study". In: M. Branda, H. Heiho & J. Multisilta (Hrsg.) *Abstract Book eTrain 2003. E-Training Practices for Professional Organisations*, IFIP Open Working Conference (S. 42). Tampere University of Technology, 2003.

[DiR01] Dingsøyr T, Røyrvik E, "Skills Management as Knowledge Technology in a Software Consulting Company". In: K-D. Althoff, RL. Feldmann & W. Müller (Eds.), *Advances in Learning Software Organisations (LSO 2001)*. Berlin: Springer-Verlag.

[DrL99] Drappa A, Ludewig J, "Quantitative Modelling for the Interactive Simulation of Software Projects", *Journal of Systems and Software* 46, pp. 113-122, 1999.

[EDM97] El Eman K, Drouin J, Melo W, *SPICE - The Theory and Practice of Software Process Improvement and Capability Determination*, IEEE Computer Society, 1997.

[For61] Forrester JW, *Industrial Dynamics*, Productivity Press, Cambridge, 1961.

[FoL02] Forward A, Lethbridge TC, "The Relevance of Software Documentation, Tools and Technologies: A Survey", *Proceedings of the ACM Symposium on Documentation Engineering (DocEng 2002)*, ACM Press, pp. 26-33, 2002.

[FrK94] Friedman B, Kahn PH "Educating Computer Scientists: Linking the Social and the Technical", *Communications of the ACM*, 37, 1, pp. 65-70. 1994.

[Gla97] Glass RL, *Software Runaways: Monumental Software Disasters*, New York: Pearson Education, 1997.

[Gra+92] Graham AK et al., "Model-supported Case Studies for Management Education", *European Journal of Operational Research* 59, pp. 151-166, 1992.

[GrM97] Gremba J, Myers C, "The IDEAL model: A Practical Guide for Improvement". *Bridge*, 3, 19-23, 1997.

[GWW04] Grützner I, Weibelzahl S, Waterson PE, "Improving Courseware Quality through Lifecycle Encompassing Quality Assurance", *Fraunhofer IESE Report*, Kaiserslautern, 2004.

[HCI99] Special Issue on Representations in Interactive Systems Development, Edited by P. Johnson, E. O'Neill, H. Johnson, *Human-Computer Interaction*, 14, 1/2.

[Hof01] Hofstede G, *Culture's Consequences: Comparing Values, Behaviours, Institutions and Organizations Across Nations*, 2nd Edition, Thousand Oaks CA: Sage Publications, 2001.

[Hum89] Humphrey WS, *Managing the Software Process*, Reading, MA: Addison-Wesley.

[JirG94] Jirotka M, Goguen J, *Requirements Engineering – Social and Technical Issues*, London: Academic Press, 1994.

[KMR99] Kellner MI, Madachy RJ, Raffo DM, "Software Process Simulation Modelling: Why? What? How?", *Journal of Systems and Software* 46, pp. 91-105, 1999.

[Kon96] Kontio J, "A Case Study in Applying a Systematic Method for COTS Selection", *Proceeding of the 18th International Conference on Software Engineering (ICSE '96)*, IEEE Computer Society, 1996.

[KrS95] Kraut RE, Streeter L, "Coordination in Software Development", *Communications of the ACM*, 38, 3, pp. 69-81, 1995.

[KuB99] Kunda D, Brooks L, "Applying the Socio-Technical Approach for COTS Selection", *Proceedings of the 4th UKAIS Conference*, University of York, McGraw Hill, 1999.

[Kyn91] Kyng M, "Designing for Cooperation: Cooperating in Design", *Communications of the ACM*, 34, 12, pp. 65-73, 1991.

[Lan95] Landauer TK, *The Trouble With Computers*, Cambridge, Mass.: MIT Press, 1995.

[Lane95] Lane DC, "On a Resurgence of Management Simulation Games", *Journal of the Operational Research Society* 46, pp. 604-625, 1995.

[LSF03] Lethbridge TC, Singer J, Forward A, "How Software Engineers User Documentation: The State of the Practice", *IEEE Software*, November/December, pp. 35-39, 2003.

[Lon93] Lonchamp J, "A Structured Conceptual and Terminological Framework for Software Process Engineering", *Proceedings of the Second International Conference on Software Process*, pp. 41-53, February 1993.

[MaN98] Maiden N, Ncube C, "Acquiring COTS Software Selection Requirements", *IEEE Software*, March/April, pp. 46-56, 1998.

[Mad04] Madachy RJ, *Software Process Dynamics*, to appear, 2004.

[Mor88] Morecroft JDW, "System Dynamics and Microworlds for Policymakers", *European Journal of Operational Research* 35, pp. 301-320, 1988.

[NaS01] Nakayama N, Sutcliffe NG, "IT Skills Portfolio Research in SIGCPR Proceedings: Analysis, Synthesis and Proposals", *Proceedings of the 2001 ACM SIGCPR*

*Conference on Computer Personnel Research*, San Diego, California, United States, pp. 100 – 113, 2001.

[Och+00]Ochs M, Pfahl D, Chrobok-Diening G, Nothelder-Kolb B, "CAP – Definition of a COTS Acquisition Process and Experience of its Application", Fraunhofer IESE Report, 2000.

[O'NJJ99] O' Neill E, Johnson P, Johnson H, "Representations and User-Developer Interaction in Cooperative Analysis and Design" *Human-Computer Interaction*, 14, 1/2 pp.43-91, 1999.

[Pau+93] Paulk MC, Curtis B, Chrissis MB, Weber CV, "The Capability Maturity Model for Software, Version 1.1", *IEEE Software*, 10, 4, pp. 18-27, 1993.

[PDC02] Biennial Participatory Design Conference (most recent – 2003 - Participation and design: Inquiring into the politics, contexts and practices of collaborative design work, PDC 2002 – the Participatory Design Conference, June 23-25, 2002, Malmö, Sweden, http://www.cpsr.org/publications/publications.html), 2003.

[PfR01] Pfahl D, Ruhe G, "System Dynamics as an Enabling Technology for Learning in Software Organizations", *Proceedings of 13th International Conference on Software Engineering and Knowledge Engineering* (SEKE), Skokie: Knowledge Systems Institute, pp. 355-362, 2001.

[PfR02] Pfahl D, Ruhe G, "IMMoS - A Methodology for Integrated Measurement, Modelling, and Simulation", *Software Process Improvement and Practice* 7, pp. 189-210, 2002.

[PKR01] Pfahl D, Klemm M, Ruhe G, "A CBT Module with Integrated Simulation Component for Software Project Management Education and Training", *Journal of Systems and Software* 59 (3), pp. 283-298, 2001.

[Pfa+03] Pfahl D, Laitenberger O, Dorsch J, Ruhe G, "An Externally Replicated Experiment for Evaluating the Learning Effectiveness of Using Simulations in Software Project Management Education", *Empirical Software Engineering* 8, 4, pp. 367-395, 2003.

[Pow+97] Powell A, Vickers A, Lam W, Edwards E. "Evaluating Tools to Support Component based Software Engineering", *Proceedings of the 5th International Symposium on Assessment of Software Tools*, IEEE Computer Society, Los Alamitos, 1997.

[RuM95] Rugg G, McGeorge P, "Laddering", *Expert Systems*, 12, 4, pp. 183-192, 1995.

[Saw+98] Sawyer S, Eschenfelder K, Diekema A, McClur C, "IT Skills in the Context of BigCo", *Proceedings of the 1998 ACM SIGCPR Conference on Computer Personnel Research*, Boston, Massachusetts, United States, pp. 9 – 18, 1998.

[Sen90] Senge PM, *The Fifth Discipline – the Art & Practice of the Learning Organization*, New York: Doubleday, 1990.

[Sha00] Shaw M, "Software Engineering Education: A Roadmap". In: *The Future of Software Engineering* (ed. A. Finkelstein), New York: ACM, pp. 371-380, 2000.

[SoB00] van Solingen R, Berghout E, "From Process Improvement to People Improvement – Enabling Learning in Software Development". In: *Project Control: The Software Factor* (eds. K. Maxwell, R. Kusters, E. Van Veenendaal and A. Cowderoy), Maastricht: Shaker Publications, 2000.

[Som00] Sommerville I, *Software Engineering (5^{th} Edition)*, London: Addison-Wesley, 2000.

[SoR97] Sommerville I, Rodden T, "Human, Social and Organisational Influences on the Software Process", Technical Report: CSEG/2/1995, University of Lancaster, Computing Department, 1995.

[SWE01] *Software Engineering Body of Knowledge* – (website: http://www.swebok.org/home.html), 2001.

[Ste94] Sterman JD, "Learning in and about Complex Systems", *System Dynamics Review*, 10 (2-3), pp. 291-330, 1994.

[Ven90] Vennix JAM, *Mental Models and Computer Models – design and evaluation of a computer-based learning environment for policy-making*, PhD Thesis, University of Nijmegen, 1990.

[Ven96] Vennix JAM, *Group Model Building*, John Wiley & Sons, 1996.

[Wal02] Walsham G, "Cross-Cultural Software Production and Use: A Structurational Analysis", *MIS Quarterly*, 26, 4, pp. 359-380, 2002.

[WOC02] Waterson PE, Older Gray MT, Clegg CW, "A Sociotechnical Method for Designing Work Systems", *Human Factors*, 44, 3, pp. 376-391, 2002.

[Wat04] Waterson PE, "Sociotechnical Design of Work Systems", To appear in: J. Wilson, E. Megaw (Eds.), *Evaluation of Human Work (3^{rd} Edition)*, London: Taylor and Francis, 2004.

[Win+96] Winograd T, Bennett J, De Young L, Hartfield B (Eds.), *Bringing Design to Software New York:* Addison Wesley, 1996.

# Chapter 6

# MOTIVATION AND PROCESS IMPROVEMENT

Watts S. HUMPHREY and Michael D. KONRAD
*Software Engineering Institute, Carnegie Mellon University.*
*E-mail: {watts, mdk}@sei.cmu.edu*

## 1. INTRODUCTION

Most discussions of people issues in software organizations concern the developers, their capabilities, and their motivations. However, lots of other people are involved in developing software and we must also consider their behavior. In this paper, we discuss people issues from a broad perspective. We address the principal issues concerning developers and their teams, and we also talk about the other people in the organization and how their behavior can affect the development work. Our objective is to show how the attitudes and concerns of the people in the entire integrated development community can help or hurt the work of developing, supporting, and enhancing software.

Since motivation and behavior are such enormous subjects, an in-depth discussion could easily fill several volumes. So, we characterize only the principal issues and discuss the key problems to be considered. Then we briefly characterize several improvement frameworks that help an organization address these people issues and key problems in a coherent and coordinated way. The Team Software Process (TSP$^{SM}$) and Personal Software Process (PSP$^{SM}$) address best practices for individuals and teams [Humphrey 1995, Humphrey 2002]. Capability Maturity Model® Integration (CMMI®) and the People CMM® address the broader organizational, management, and integration practices [Chrissis 2003, Curtis 2001].

---

® Capability Maturity Model, CMM, and CMMI are registered in the U.S. Patent and Trademark Office by Carnegie Mellon University.

## 2.  ORGANIZATIONAL OBJECTIVES

Before discussing motivation and behavior, it is important to discuss objectives. First, regarding motivation, what do we want the people, once motivated, to do and what people are we talking about? Second, what are the objectives we want their behavior to achieve? Typically, all development organizations strive to competitively and profitably meet their customers' needs and to do so according to the schedules and agreed costs. They must also maintain and build the organization's capability to continue to meet their customers' needs in the future.

This means that the entire organization must be focused on accomplishing one thing: motivating and supporting the developers and all related groups to perform, and continue to perform, the development job in a superior way. Therefore, as we discuss the typical problems in development organizations, we will define the steps required for all developers, teams, managers, and related groups to maximize development performance.

## 3.  HUMAN BEHAVIOR

One of the most useful and enduring frameworks for characterizing human behavior is Maslow's Hierarchy of Needs [Maslow 1954]. He ranked human needs in a five-level structure wherein each level provides the foundation for all of the higher levels. As shown in Figure 1, the bottom level is survival, or the need for food and shelter. Next comes health and safety. Third is membership in a group, and fourth is recognition and prestige. Maslow calls the highest level self-actualization. This level is where people are motivated by their own accomplishments, not merely by rewards and recognition.

The reason this hierarchy is important is that truly superior professional behavior is achieved by self-actualizing people. However, if these people are not adequately paid or otherwise rewarded, they will likely worry about recognition or continued membership in the group. In extreme cases, they could even worry about their health and safety. Under these conditions, they will have great difficulty performing at the self-actualizing level.

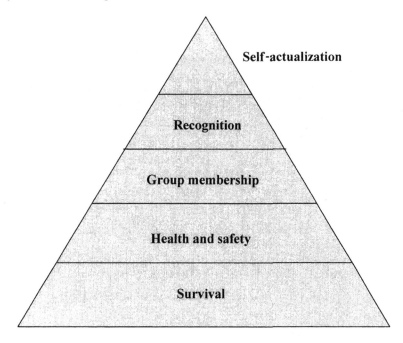

**Figure 1: The hierarchy of needs**

The needs hierarchy applies to all members in an organization—even its senior executives. When an organization's senior management is worried about the survival of the business, they are unlikely to devote much attention to industry leadership, corporate image, or superior product development. Furthermore, when senior management is not focused on superior performance, few if any people at lower organization levels will be either. Under these conditions, organizations cannot substantially improve their performance.

A second very useful framework for human behavior is called Situational Leadership [Hersey 1977]. This framework is particularly appropriate for software developers and other professionals. As shown in Figure 2, professional people's behavior can be characterized in a two-dimensional structure. The first, or task maturity dimension, concerns technical skills and abilities. Here, the task-mature developer says "Here is how I plan to do this job," while the immature one says "How do I do this job?" The second, or the relationship maturity dimension, deals with the professional's relationship with his or her peers and management. The relationship-mature developer says "How do you like my work?" while the immature one says, in effect, "How do you like me?"

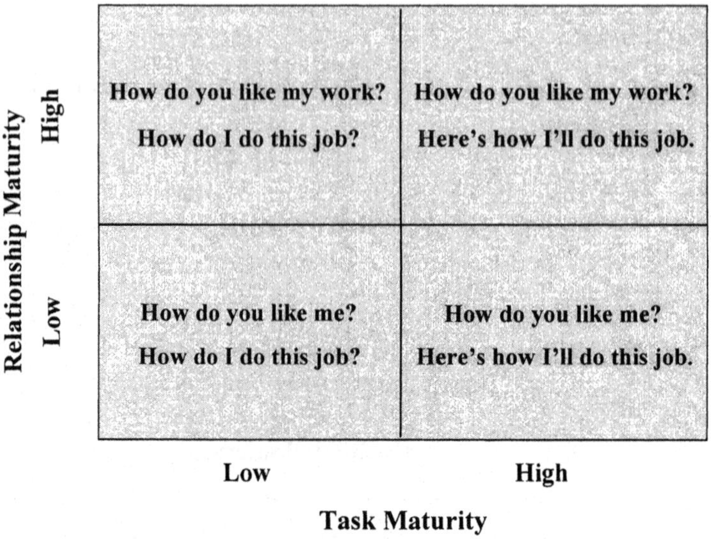

| | How do you like my work? | How do you like my work? |
|---|---|---|
| **High** | How do I do this job? | Here's how I'll do this job. |
| **Low** | How do you like me? | How do you like me? |
| | How do I do this job? | Here's how I'll do this job. |

**Relationship Maturity**

**Low**                              **High**

**Task Maturity**

**Figure 2: Task and relationship maturity**

## 3.1   The people involved

While many people are involved in or at least have an indirect relationship to the software and/or systems development process, we only address six people categories:

- developers
- the development teams
- related development and support people who interface with these developers (testing, configuration management, and quality assurance, for example)
- development team leaders and managers
- senior managers and executives
- customers or users of the products developed by the teams.

For each of these categories, we first discuss the motivational issues that govern behavior within each peer group; then, we address the interactions among these groups and some common relationship issues [Schein 1996]. Finally, we discuss how various process improvement initiatives impact these behaviors and relationships.

## 3.2   Developer and team behavior

While people's performance is influenced by many things, the Hierarchy of Needs and Situational Leadership models provide useful ways for identifying high performers and for helping managers more effectively guide and support their people. If the people are not properly trained for their jobs or they are not supported by appropriately skilled and able coaches and staffs, they will not likely be task mature. Similarly, if they are not properly compensated, appraised, and rewarded, they will not likely be relationship mature. In either case, their work will suffer. Also, if developers do not have reasonable control over their working environment and feel responsible for their own plans, processes, and methods, they will not likely behave as self-actualizing professionals.

While these conditions are simple to describe, they are difficult to achieve without preparation and guidance. However, when you know how, the conditions for high performance can be put into place rather quickly. And, once these conditions are actually in place and are supported and sustained, team performance is often exceptional.

In addition to the behavior patterns that are common to all developers, the members of development teams have another important trait: they view their team environment (i.e., the working environment, the technical challenges, and the rewards of building an important product) as the most important single aspect of their work. In fact, even developers who worked on projects that grossly overran their planned schedules and costs still viewed their projects as successful if their team environment was personally rewarding. This view of the team environment can give development teams a strong sense of membership and provide them with the reinforcement of peer recognition. This kind of supportive team environment is conducive to self-actualizing performance. We discuss the ways to achieve such performance a little later.

## 3.3   Related group behavior

The members of other related groups typically share the same general behavioral patterns as the developers, but they often do not work in the same cohesive and reinforcing team environment. In fact, these "other" professionals are often viewed by the developers as adversaries. For example, many development teams feel that the quality assurance (QA) group members are obstructionists and nit-pickers. They feel that these people are out to delay the job over unimportant details. Similarly, developers view the requirements and systems people as hard to please and possibly even a little arrogant. These people seem to developers to always change their minds while insisting that their current view is right and must be followed if the product is to have any chance of success.

The members of these other related groups, in turn, have problems with the developers. For example, they often feel that there is an invisible wall that separates them from development. Such separation can incite and exacerbate suspicion and distrust. This in-group/out-group situation can be destructive, not only for all of the individuals involved, but also for the project and its success.

A principal challenge in motivating and coaching other related groups is in devising ways to make them an integrated and coordinated part of the development effort so they can share in the motivational benefits of a cohesive team. We also discuss ways to do this in a later section.

## 3.4 Management behavior

Management behavior is much more complex, so we only touch on a few key points. First, managers behave according to the task and relationship maturity framework and have needs as characterized by the Maslow hierarchy. In general, when managers are relationship-insecure or have needs for recognition or membership, their behavior is likely to be destructive. One example is a very accomplished former developer named Tony. He reluctantly accepted the job of managing a small development group. Unfortunately, Tony believed that managers were infallible. Since he knew he wasn't infallible, he was unwilling to have his people see him make mistakes. He would work for hours in his closed office, figuring out what each of his people should do, and then call each of them in to issue orders. Even though he was highly insecure and was truly concerned about how well he was doing his job, his people viewed him as a tyrant. He was soon moved to a non-management position in another group and everyone was much happier.

When managers feel insecure or have needs for recognition or group membership, they may appear very accomplished to their superiors, but not to the developers who work for them. The developers will generally feel threatened in one way or another and be unable to operate at the self-actualizing level. The performance of development groups with relationship-immature managers will almost always suffer. Conversely, the relationship-mature manager will generally recognize the skills and talents of his or her developers, be willing to learn from them, and rely on them for information and technical guidance. The mutual trust that such a mature relationship brings allows open discussion of performance issues and risks, providing the manager with the insight and influence he or she needs to anticipate issues and resolve problems.

Managers, however, face a set of pressures that the developers do not. For example, if their department, division, or company is having financial problems, the managers may have goals that they are unable to (or at least unlikely to) meet. Often their jobs and those of their team will be threatened as well. Under these conditions, the relationship-mature manager will protect his or her people while attempting to maintain a productive working environment.

However, when managers are unsure of themselves, they are likely to be relationship-immature. They then react to business stresses in ways that increase their people's concerns. One of the most common reactions is to tell the developers, when they ask about the company's situation, that "Those dumb senior managers have screwed things up again" and that, as a consequence, the organization is in trouble. This, of course, causes the developers to worry even more about their jobs and makes it more difficult for them to continue to do superior work.

Even mature managers, when under severe business pressure, must often make quick decisions and can easily make mistakes, particularly when they have inaccurate or inconsistent information. We discuss ways to guard against these problems later.

## 3.5  Executive behavior

In many ways, executives can be viewed as just higher-level managers. They have the same maturity and needs problems as their subordinates and they also face the same pressures as the lower-level managers, only these pressures (e.g., the financial health of the corporation) are often much more threatening to them personally. The big difference between the executives and the managers that report to them is that the executives are typically out of touch with the working professionals. Therefore, they must count on these subordinate managers to keep them informed and to relay communication and direction. The consequence of being out of touch is that communications are often garbled and the executive's guidance is misunderstood. This can easily lead to confusion, and with confusion comes mistakes, mistrust, and inefficiency.

Executive problems are typically of two kinds. First, they often get late, incomplete, inaccurate, or even biased information. This inadequate information is often the cause of poor executive-level decisions.

Second, these executives must lead an organization that is managed by department heads who have overlapping and conflicting missions and objectives. Executives generally understand that every organization structure minimizes some conflicts and exacerbates others. These conflicts can often delay or distort the information that executives need to make timely decisions.

Even when the executive makes a sound decision, the conflicts among the subordinate managers can distort the communications needed to effectively implement it. In a sense, the executive problem concerns integration. By organizing their operations into separate departments, they disintegrate it. Their jobs as executives are to ensure that the work of these disparate functions is integrated into a coherent, competitive, and profitable business operation.

### 3.6   Customer behavior

While the customer and end user are not typically part of the development organization, their behavior can have a significant impact on the development groups. One quality maxim says that, "If the customer is willing to accept a poor-quality product, he will almost certainly get it." Where customers define challenging quality goals and establish measurement and tracking systems, supplier performance invariably improves, often by orders of magnitude. Such management and tracking can substantially increase the pressure on organizations to perform and it can be highly motivating to the professionals involved. Conversely, if the measurement and tracking systems are poorly managed or are not consistent with development practices, the customers' demands can waste a great deal of development time and damage the developer's motivation and performance.

The second way that customers can impact development work concerns the project's overall objectives. If the developers feel they are developing an important product and that it is for customers that they are truly anxious to satisfy, they will likely put their heart and soul into the work. On the other hand, if the customers are difficult to please and only seem to care about cost and schedule, the developers are not likely to exert maximum effort. The developers' perception of the customer can make a critical difference, since superior products are not produced by accident or by people who do not care.

### 4.   INTERACTIONS AMONG GROUPS

While highly-motivated and capable teams are those most likely to do superior work, few teams can be entirely independent of their surroundings. In sports, winning teams need an effective and capable support system. They need professional management and coaching, a trained and competent support staff, and the applause of a large and enthusiastic group of fans. The actions of all of these groups must be coherent and reinforce each other, both to help ensure a winning performance and to help the team recover quickly from temporary setbacks.

Development teams have similar needs. Management must not only demand superior performance, they also must recognize and demonstrate their appreciation for quality work and promptly address quality shortcomings. Just as in sports and the performing arts, superior development work requires informed and capable coaching. The coach's job is to recognize and applaud superior individual work, to diagnose performance shortcomings, and to know how to motivate individual team-member improvement. The coach also supports the entire team, sees where teamwork falls short, and knows how to motivate overall team improvement.

In development work, management's influence is critical to the team's success. Management's priorities define the team's priorities, and when management's words and actions are inconsistent or when different management levels provide conflicting guidance and direction, teams will be confused and their performance will suffer. The managers must not only be consistent, they must also know the performance they want, recognize it when they get it, and insist on corrective action when teams fall short. This must be true at every management level.

The team leader must motivate the performance of the team and all of its members. Similarly, higher-level managers must have consistent performance standards, require regular progress reporting, provide periodic feedback, and recognize both good and bad performance. At more senior management levels, reports will be less frequent and more concise, but these managers must still detect problems and obtain whatever detail is needed to ensure that corrective action is taken. However, managers at all levels must insist on superior work and applaud and reward such work when they get it.

The development team's interactions with related groups will also impact its performance. For example, requirements groups must define the product's characteristics. They must do this even when the users have only a vague idea of what they need. They must also communicate updates to the product's characteristics as the user needs become better understood. Conversely, the developers want complete information as soon as they can get it and requirements that are frozen for at least long enough to build the next product version. In fact, they will strenuously object whenever the requirements do change. Consequently, requirements groups tend to resist providing information to developers until they believe it represents what the users really need. These conflicting attitudes impede early agreement on the product's requirements and can substantially delay projects.

Systems design groups have similar relationship issues and must make trade-offs between conflicting needs and capabilities. They must often specify hardware capabilities to software groups and software performance to the hardware groups, sometimes before either group has started on the design work. The requirements and systems design groups are merely two examples of the many groups with which development teams must work. Other groups include testing, quality assurance, facilities, finance, configuration management, publications, and the release group. Each of these groups will have differing assumptions, goals, and motivations and these differing perspectives can easily cause confusion and discord. Unless properly managed and resolved, such problems often damage the quality and productivity of the team's development work.

The impact of customer relationships on team performance is much more difficult to characterize. In a sense, the customer can be viewed as the major source of pressure on the organization. The impact of this pressure is a function of the customer's power over the organization, the maturity of the management team, and the customer's attitude toward the development work and how it is done. Generally, the behavior of the team will depend on the way the team interacts with its management and the customer. The behavior of each of these groups can be characterized in terms of task and relationship maturity. The general nature of these behaviors is summarized in Tables 1 and 2.

As can be seen from Tables 1 and 2, the performance of development groups depends not only on the behavior of the team and all of its members, but also on the behavior of other related groups of people. In the following paragraphs we discuss the principal actions needed to build and maintain the team's relationship and task maturity, as well as the actions required to improve the maturity of the integrated environment in which the team operates.

## 5.    IMPROVING TEAM PERFORMANCE

Just as the performance of an organization depends on the performance and integration of its teams and related groups, so the performance of the teams and related groups depend on the performance and integration of their members. Therefore, to improve team performance, we must build both the task and relationship maturity of the members as well as the task and relationship maturity of the team as a unit.

Table 1: Task maturity characteristics

| Role | Mature | Immature |
|------|--------|----------|
| Individual Developer | • Uses defined methods<br>• Measures, plans, and tracks personal work<br>• Personally responsible for product quality | • Ineffective methods<br>• No plans and imprecise status measures<br>• Quality is a testing problem |
| Development Team | • Defined, effective, and consistent methods<br>• Detailed, measured, and tracked plans<br>• Measured, tracked, and managed quality goals | • Inadequate, inconsistent, or ineffective methods<br>• Poor plans or no plans and imprecise status measures<br>• No quality goals or measures |
| Related Groups | • Defined, effective, and consistent methods<br>• Detailed, measured, and tracked plans<br>• Measured, tracked, and managed quality goals | • Inadequate, inconsistent, or ineffective methods<br>• Poor plans or no plans and imprecise status measures<br>• No quality goals or measures |
| Management | • Plan-driven priorities<br>• Identified and managed risks<br>• Follow the process<br>• Negotiate commitments | • Crisis-driven priorities<br>• Deferred problems and issues<br>• Processes ignored<br>• Commitments missed |
| Executives | • Strategic focus<br>• The best way is always fastest and cheapest<br>• Reward quality work | • Tactical focus<br>• Problems fixed later<br>• Reward "fire-fighters" |
| Customer | • Clearly defined product objectives<br>• Measured and tracked project and process goals | • Vague or ill-defined objectives<br>• Undefined, unmeasured, and untracked project or process goals |

Table 2: Relationship maturity characteristics

| Role | Mature | Immature |
|------|--------|----------|
| Individual Developer | • Self-directed | • Management-directed |
| Development Team | • Self-directed | • Team-leader/management-directed |
| Related Groups | • Service-oriented | • Bureaucratic and rules-driven |
| Development Management Executive Management | • Rational management, fact-based decisions | • Directive management |
| Customer | • Trusting and fact-based relationship | • Contract-driven and rumor-based relationship |

The performance of individual development team members is determined by their personal practices. Similarly, the performance of the composite team is determined by the way the members perform individually and as a coherent group. For example, consider the conditions required to make a superior football team. First, all of the members must be superior individual performers, but they must also work together effectively. This effective teamwork requires that they have common goals and a mutually-understood and agreed-to set of rules and practices, as well as effective management and coaching support.

As shown in Figure 3, to improve development performance, we must similarly consider all of these elements. The Personal Software Process (PSP$^{SM}$) provides a framework for improving the task and relationship maturity of individual team members, while the Team Software Process (TSP$^{SM}$) provides a framework for improving the task and relationship maturity of the overall team [Humphrey 1995, Humphrey 2002].

## 5.1   Improving team member performance with the PSP

Each team member's task maturity can be considered as having three elements: technical skills, project skills, and quality management skills. While technical skills are critically important, they are generally addressed in the developer's education and training. Since personal skills in project and quality management have not typically been addressed in an orderly or consistent way by a traditional computer science education, the PSP was introduced by the Software Engineering Institute (SEI) to address this need.

---

[SM] Personal Software Process, PSP, Team Software Process, and TSP are service marks of Carnegie Mellon University.

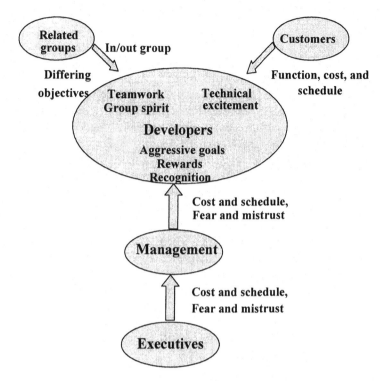

**Figure 3: Pressures on the developers**

The PSP shows developers how to follow a defined personal process, how to measure their work, and how to use these measures to make precise and accurate personal plans. The PSP also shows developers how to establish personal quality goals, how to measure their performance against these goals, and how to manage the quality of the products they produce. Once they have learned these skills and have the personal confidence that comes with such task maturity, developers can make accurate plans for their personal work and convincingly defend these plans with their team members, managers, and customers. This provides them with the foundation to operate in a relationship-mature way with their associates and to deal objectively with their customers and managers.

When developers have personal and team data and know how to use these data to make precise and accurate plans, they need not rely on emotion and intuition to manage their personal work. They can use historical data to support rational debates on the best courses of action. This approach provides them with the task and relationship maturity needed to participate effectively on a self-directed team.

## 5.2   Improving team performance with the TSP

Team task maturity consists of the same elements as individual task maturity: technical skills, project skills, and quality management skills. These team skills are built with the TSP when the team leader and all of the team members are coached and guided through a team planning and management process that builds and sustains self-directed teamwork.

In building self-directed teams, the TSP launch process starts by establishing team goals. After hearing their business goals from management, the team works under the guidance of a trained coach to select its team member roles, define the team's processes, and produce a complete team plan. The team, as a complete unit, then analyzes project risks and negotiates its plan with management.

The TSP has proven to be highly effective in building and guiding mature and capable development teams. These teams have consistently produced high-quality products, on schedule, and within budget. What is perhaps most important, the team members find that working on a self-directed TSP team is a truly enjoyable and rewarding personal experience [Davis 2003].

## 6.   IMPROVING ORGANIZATIONAL PERFORMANCE

As we have already observed, a development team's performance depends on the task and relationship maturity of other members and groups in the organization. To systematically improve the task and relationship maturity of all groups and individuals within the organization and to ensure that the work of each group integrates appropriately with that of other groups, the following actions must be taken.

- Instill good management practices in development teams and related groups and standardize the processes that these groups use.
- Establish and maintain a participatory culture where individuals and teams take responsibility for their own and their groups' performance.

## 6.1   Good management practices in development

If development teams and related groups do not plan and manage their work, they will not develop high task and relationship maturity or relate effectively with other development teams, related groups, customers, or suppliers. Unless development groups routinely plan their work and follow their plans, they will not consistently meet their commitments. Further, when development groups do not consistently meet their commitments, management, other related groups, and the customers, will not rely on or trust them. Finally, without trust, a cooperative and effective working relationship among groups is impossible. To build such a trusting relationship, the developers and their management must be trained, coached, and guided in performing effective personal and team management practices.

Effective personal and team management practices include estimating resources, developing plans, establishing commitments, monitoring projects, controlling quality, and managing risk. These practices also involve coordinating with other teams and groups. The critical human-resource management practices include performance management, rewards and recognition, and compensation. If organizations do not competently handle this key group of practices, their development staffs are unlikely to operate at the self-actualizing level.

The SEI has published a technical report that summarizes and analyzes the results from multiple case studies in which organizations have adopted TSP [Davis 2003]. Each of the individual case studies referenced in this report describe an organization's adoption of TSP as well as the benefits it has derived from its use. More case studies and impact studies are available on the SEI Web site (www.sei.cmu.edu/tsp/recommended-reading.html).

## 6.2   A family of improvement frameworks

To help organizations identify and apply sound management and development practices, the SEI has defined a family of complementary process frameworks. These processes include the full range of management, product development, people management, and support activities required to effectively operate a high-technology business.

By cooperatively defining, standardizing, and maintaining these processes, the various organizational units can establish shared expectations and identify interdependencies and relationships. This cooperation will further contribute to improving their task and relationship maturity.

The PSP and TSP cover the practices for individuals and teams, while Capability Maturity Model® Integration (CMMI®) and the People CMM® address the broader organizational, management, and integration practices [Chrissis 2003, Curtis 2001].

---

®   Capability Maturity Model, CMM, and CMMI are registered in the U.S. Patent and Trademark Office by Carnegie Mellon University.

In defining their processes, organizations should ensure that their standard processes support the formation, operation, and utilization of development teams. This requires a careful balance between little or no process guidance and overly-prescriptive standard practices. Each group should understand its role, have the flexibility to be creative, and feel responsible for defining and managing its own personal and team activities. To do this, organizations must understand precisely how the work is currently performed and decide on the most desirable team practices and integration structures. What decisions can be delegated? How will conflicts be resolved? Who will specify, define, and plan the work? By answering these questions, organizations can better manage their operations and more effectively utilize their people.

To enable the effective performance of defined processes, organizational management must identify, obtain, and develop critical development, management, and support skills. This requires an inventory of current competencies, future needs, and recruitment and development capabilities. By establishing administrative systems for routinely obtaining and maintaining critical skills, organizations can be assured that they will meet their evolving development needs.

For professionals and their management to operate at the self-actualizing level, they must achieve and maintain both task and relationship maturity. This, in turn, requires that the organization establish a culture in which individuals and teams participate in the decision making and share in the responsibility for personal, team, and organizational performance.

In general, people and groups perform consistently with their individual or group self interest. That is, they determine the actions that are most advantageous to them personally and then they act accordingly. This means that no organizational improvement initiative can be effective unless the rewards for the individuals and their teams reinforce and motivate the desired behavior. The organization must "fine tune" its performance management, rewards, recognition, compensation, competency development, and career policies and practices to align individuals' and teams' interests with those of the organization.

## 6.3  Improving organizational performance with the CMMI and the People CMM

CMMI and the People CMM provide a set of industry-proven practices for the management and engineering processes organizations need to improve their performance. These practices provide guidance to organizations that help them to create an environment and organizational infrastructure that enables teams and related groups to work together effectively. Such teamwork is a critical factor in achieving the organization's business objectives. The environment and infrastructure that enables teamwork also enables the work of TSP- and PSP-trained teams and individuals to be successful.

CMMI is a process improvement and best practices framework from which multiple capability maturity models can be derived. The People CMM is a single capability maturity model. Both CMMI models and the People CMM contain hundreds of practices. These practices are briefly described in each model, and interpretation and implementation suggestions are provided.

The practices of CMMI models are organized into the following 25 process areas. While CMMI comprises multiple models, each model addresses at least 22 of the following 25 process areas. This list is organized by maturity level:

### The Managed Level (Maturity Level 2)
- Requirements Management
- Project Planning
- Project Monitoring and Control
- Supplier Agreement Management
- Measurement and Analysis
- Process and Product Quality Assurance
- Configuration Management

### The Defined Level (Maturity Level 3)
- Requirements Development
- Technical Solution
- Product Integration
- Verification
- Validation
- Organizational Process Focus
- Organizational Process Definition
- Organizational Training
- Integrated Project Management
- Risk Management
- Integrated Teaming
- Integrated Supplier Management
- Decision Analysis and Resolution
- Organizational Environment for Integration

### The Quantitatively Managed Level (Maturity Level 4)
- Organizational Process Performance
- Quantitative Project Management

### The Optimizing Level (Maturity Level 5)
- Organizational Innovation and Deployment
- Causal Analysis and Resolution

The People CMM key process areas are:

**The Managed Level (Maturity Level 2)**
- Staffing
- Communication and Coordination
- Work Environment
- Performance Management
- Training and Development
- Compensation

**The Defined Level (Maturity Level 3)**
- Competency Analysis
- Workforce Planning
- Competency Development
- Career Development
- Competency-Based Practices
- Workgroup Development
- Participatory Culture

**The Predictable Level (Maturity Level 4)**
- Competency Integration
- Empowered Workgroups
- Competency-Based Assets
- Quantitative Performance Management
- Organizational Capability Management
- Mentoring

**The Optimizing Level (Maturity Level 5)**
- Continuous Capability Improvement
- Organizational Performance Alignment
- Continuous Workforce Innovation

Many organizations are implementing CMMI- and/or People CMM-based process improvement programs, and the benefits these organizations have obtained include better cost and schedule control, improved product quality, increased customer satisfaction, improved employee morale, and better integration with suppliers. In other words, these frameworks are helping organizations address many of the motivational and behavior issues described earlier.

There are several publications that summarize multiple case studies in which organizations have adopted CMMI or the People CMM [Goldenson 2003, Curtis 2001]. Each of the individual case studies referenced in these publications describe an organization's adoption of CMMI or the People CMM as well as the benefits derived from its use. More case studies and impact studies are available on the SEI Web site (www.sei.cmu.edu/cmmi/adoption).

## 7.   CONCLUSIONS

While CMMI and the People CMM help improve the task and relationship maturity of groups both inside and outside development organizations, they are not entirely sufficient for three reasons. First, developing and introducing defined and standard processes is a difficult task, and organizations often don't know where to start or how to accomplish the job in a reasonably short period of time. Second, these models provide high-level management and engineering guidance, not specific operational processes used by developers and their teams. Third, while high-maturity organizations have benefited from CMMI- and People CMM-based process achievements, they have not made all of the behavioral changes required to achieve the highest-maturity operation possible, particularly at the individual and team level.

The PSP and TSP frameworks were designed to address these shortcomings. To address the first problem, the PSP and TSP provide developers and their teams with explicit guidance on where to start and how to quickly implement many of the CMMI and People CMM practices at the individual and team level. Second, the PSP and TSP provide operational-level processes for individuals and teams that show them what to do and how to do it. Finally, the PSP and TSP practices were explicitly designed to guide the behavior needed to achieve a high-level of personal and team maturity for all aspects of the development work.

Conversely, the TSP and PSP are not entirely sufficient. They do not, for example, address the processes used by such related groups as systems design, configuration management, quality assurance, and the process improvement and support groups. The CMMI framework addresses these areas and identifies the overall process management practices required for a high-maturity integrated product development process. The People CMM addresses the people management practices needed to motivate and align team behavior with the organization's overall interests. Together, they provide the supportive environment required to most effectively use the TSP and PSP.

Thus, the good practices instilled by both CMMI and the People CMM are enhanced by the TSP and PSP, while the PSP and TSP benefit from the integrated technical and people-management environment provided by implementing CMMI and the People CMM.

The total set of high-maturity process management needs can be satisfied by introducing the PSP at the personal level, using the TSP to guide and manage teams, and using CMMI and the People CMM to institutionalize mature management practices, build effective relationships with customers and key suppliers, and establish standard processes for the development teams and their related groups. When organizations are driven to achieve real improvement and are not just obtaining a maturity level rating or an ISO certificate, they should implement CMMI, the People CMM, the PSP, and the TSP.

## ACKNOWLEDGEMENTS

This paper is based on the work of many people and we much appreciate all the work they have done to develop, refine, and transition these methods into general practice. While we cannot possibly mention all of these people, we particularly want to thank Bill Curtis, Jim Over, and Bill Peterson for their leadership in key aspects of this work. In addition, we have been fortunate to have a large group of expert reviewers who made many useful suggestions on this document. These people are Mary Beth Chrissis, Noopur Davis, Suzie Garcia, Caroline Graettinger, Jim McHale, Dave Kitson, Sally Miller, Julia Mullaney, Jim Over, Bill Peterson, Mike Phillips, and Marsha Pomeroy-Huff.

## REFERENCES

Chrissis, Mary Beth, Konrad, Mike, and Shrum, Sandy. *CMMI Guidelines for Process Integration and Product Improvement.* Reading, MA: Addison Wesley, 2003.

Curtis, Bill, Hefley, William E., and Miller, Sally. *The People Capability Maturity Model.* Reading, MA: Addison-Wesley, 2001.

Davis, Noopur, and Mullaney, Julia. The Team Software Process (TSP) in Practice: A Summary of Recent Results, Technical Report CMU/SEI-2003-TR-014, September 2003.

Goldenson, Dennis R., and Gibson, Diane L. Demonstrating the Impact and Benefits of CMMI: An Update and Preliminary Results, Special Report CMU/SEI-2003-SR-009, October 2003.

Hersey, Paul, and Blanchard, Kenneth H. *Management of Organizational Behavior.* Englewood Cliffs, NJ: Prentice Hall, 1977.

Humphrey, Watts S. *A Discipline for Software Engineering.* Reading, MA: Addison-Wesley, 1995.

Humphrey, Watts S. *Winning with Software: An Executive Strategy.* Reading, MA: Addison-Wesley, 2002.

Maslow, Abraham. *Motivation and Personality*. New York: Harper & Row, 1954.

Schein, Edgar H. Three Cultures of Management: The Key to Organizational Learning, *Sloan Management Review*, Fall 1996.

# Chapter 7

# MANAGING ORGANIZATIONAL CHANGE FOR SOFTWARE PROCESS IMPROVEMENT

Deependra MOITRA
*Infosys Technologies Limited, Bangalore, India. E-mail: deependra@moitra.com*

**Abstract:** Software process improvement has become a necessity for software intensive businesses for their competitive performance. However, managing change and revitalizing the organization for software process improvement is a considerable challenge. This chapter presents an analysis of the factors that enable and inhibit software process improvement, and presents a model and recommendations for successfully bringing about organizational change for software process improvement.

**Key words:** Software process improvement; change management; managing organizational change; change agent.

## 1. INTRODUCTION

These days, software and information technology are an integral part of almost every business. Increasingly, we are living in a world that is software enabled. Proliferation of software in all walks of life has heightened the demand on the profession and discipline of software engineering in terms of cost, quality, security, reliability, and timeliness. This, in turn, points to the need for addressing software and organizational processes – the underlying infrastructure and environment for carrying out the development, delivery and maintenance of software. Over the last decade, there has been a phenomenal growth and maturity in the discipline of software engineering. It is now established that provided a strong and optimal software development process, many measurable benefits will result (Herbsleb et al. 1994, Paulish and Carleton 1994, Pitterman 2000). This belief has gained strength as software process improvement success stories from around the globe with evidence of improved cost, quality and delivery performance have been reported.

While the rationale for software process improvement (SPI) is quite straight forward, success is often difficult to come by owing to a lack of shared context, clear objectives and ineffective approaches to managing organizational change (Moitra 1998).

## 2.    SOFTWARE PROCESS IMPROVEMENT (SPI)

Increasing competition and the resulting quest for software excellence has brought about a dramatic focus on SPI. With a view to derive business benefits such as improved quality, lower cost, compressed development cycle time, and increased customer satisfaction, many software organizations have installed an SPI initiative. A plethora of SPI models such as SW-CMM, ISO 9000, Trillium, SPICE, Bootstrap, etc. emerged on the scene and have been adopted by organizations (Zahran 1998). However, the instances of software organizations truly achieving success in their SPI efforts are still small in number. It may be noted that most organizations who fail with SPI don't publish their experiences. Often, failure to align the SPI initiatives with the business objectives and ineffective organizational change management are the reasons for the paucity of success.

Software processes – broadly defined as a set of steps, methods, procedures, techniques, and tools employed to develop, deliver and maintain software – have a direct impact on the quality of the software and business performance. It is therefore only natural to focus on improving and optimizing software processes. However, unlike hardware processes, which when fine-tuned and automated yield consistent output quality, software processes have a strong dependency on human factors, especially knowledge, competency, and attitude of people (Humphrey 1989). Unfortunately, this distinction is often ignored when designing and deploying software processes and while considering software process improvements. Consequently, even though the human and organizational dimensions and the associated "soft" aspects have a vital influence on SPI (Stelzer and Mellis 1999, Moitra 1998), SPI initiatives often turn out to be very mechanical in nature.

Software process improvement is about migration from the current state of process maturity and capability to a desired state, entailing refinements in the procedures, methods and tools (Humphrey 1989). It is also about transition of individual and team behaviors and attitudes into more supportive forms – fact often ignored while planning SPI. The transition in behaviors and attitudes into a more supportive state characterized by enthusiasm, commitment and involvement is actually a very crucial element for the success of an SPI program, and this requires a careful crafting and managing of the underlying organizational change. Organizational change for SPI is really challenging because it involves dealing with people with different socio-cultural orientations and their myriad motivations, backgrounds, preferences, and expectations. In section 4, I discuss the problems, challenges and influencing factors for managing organizational change for SPI.

## 3.   BRIEF OVERVIEW OF THE LITERATURE

Although the software engineering literature contained treatments on software process and its importance, I believe it was only with the publication of Watts Humphrey's landmark book (1989) that software process improvement attained a distinct identity and importance within the discipline of software engineering. Humphrey's work received tremendous reception across the globe, resulting in many companies adopting his recommendations and achieving success (Humphrey et al. 1991, Brodman and Johnson 1996, Diaz and Sligo 1997, Wohlwend and Rosenbaum 1994, Pitterman 2000). As the success stories spread and software process improvement gained momentum, several scholars and professionals reported structured end-to-end approaches for planning and implementing SPI. Two pieces of work that dealt with a systematic approach to SPI that I found particularly helpful are books by Grady (1997) and Zahran (1998). Notably, Zahran (1998) provides a useful classification of strategies for implementing organizational changes for SPI, in addition to five different kinds of change associated with SPI (p. 206).

However, in as much as SPI became a business necessity, successfully managing an SPI program emerged as a significant business challenge. Successfully managing organizational change became an important consideration for success of SPI programs much like any other major organizational change initiatives. While many excellent sources exist in the literature on SPI, the literature associated with managing organizational change for SPI appears scarce. There are very few publications exclusively dealing with managing change for SPI. Wiegers (1996) discusses some pragmatic perspectives on ten issues related to SPI and offers solutions to address them. Stelzer and Mellis (1999) discuss success factors related to organizational change in SPI based on their study of several ISO 9000 and CMM-based software process improvement programs, whereas Moitra (1998) provides an experiential account of the problems and challenges in SPI and suggests a recommended approach. In his narrative and insightful article, Allen (1995) shares his successful efforts in change management for SPI and distills many important lessons. Others (Humphrey 1989, Humphrey 1997, Grady 1997, Zahran 1998, Juran 1995) touch upon various aspects of change management. Two insightful executive perspectives on the structure, dynamics and success factors of SPI and change management are contained in interviews with Norm Kerth (1996) and Sanjiv Ahuja (1999). Finally, in his book, *Anticipating Change*, Weinberg (1997) presents the systems thinking approach to dealing with change in organizations.

Outside the realm of software engineering and management literature, however, there has been much work on managing organizational change that I have found very useful. Many of these are directly relevant for managing organizational change for SPI, although when applied with some background in software engineering the overall approach becomes stronger. Hutton (1995) is an excellent resource for anyone wanting to assume the challenging role of a change agent and deals with the subject with a quality management perspective. Kanter and Stein (1992), Katzenbach et al. (1996), and Kotter (1996) offer end-to-end perspectives on managing organizational change, whereas Duck (2001) discusses how human and emotional forces can be leveraged to fuel organizational transformations. Robbins and Finley (1997) provide a detailed, analytical account of why change does not work and offer ways to successfully deal with change management. Building further on their learning organization theory, Senge et al. (1999) present a comprehensive systems thinking-based approach to effecting and sustaining change in organizations.

In their influential publication, Beer et al. (1990) explains the fallacy of commonly adopted programmatic change approaches and offers six steps to effective change. In another insightful article, Schaffer and Thomson (1992) discuss the importance of results-driven change programs and emphasize the need for employees to experience continual success in improvement programs. A comprehensive framework and approaches to organizational change along with models for implementing change were presented by Mintzberg and Westley (1992). Chatman and Cha (2003) show how organizational culture can be effective leveraged, whereas Repenning and Sterman (2001) offers some insightful perspectives and lessons drawn from their research on process improvement in manufacturing. Other useful works in the context of change management include (Branstad and Lucier 2001, Prastacos et al. 2002, Ascari et al. 1995, Thomson 1998).

Managing change for SPI is not really different from managing other kinds of organizational change, although familiarity with the nuances of software business and development processes do help a great deal. As I mentioned above, there are many excellent resources on SPI in general but specific literature on managing organizational change for SPI is rather scarce. In this chapter, I synthesize my research findings and experiences gained in managing SPI initiatives to provide an integrated approach to managing organizational change for successful SPI. Specifically, I discuss what is involved in SPI, describe the sources of resistance and inhibitors for SPI, and present a pragmatic approach to managing organizational change for SPI. In addition, I describe the characteristics of a successful *change agent* – the person who leads the change initiative, and discuss the associated skills and behaviors. Emphasis is placed both on the hard and soft aspects of organizational change for SPI, including the human dimension.

## 4. PROBLEMS AND CHALLENGES IN ORGANIZATIONAL CHANGE FOR SPI

Change in the organizational context refers to transition to a desired state within a defined timeframe, and requires a managed process to bring about the desired change (Hutton 1995, Kotter 1996). Several factors come into play regarding the dynamics of organizational change for SPI. Resistance to SPI stems from various sources and the problems of different nature impede the organizational change. In what follows, I discuss the problems and the sources of resistance to SPI efforts in organizations. It may be noted that my primary focus is on the human side of the organizational change, a.k.a. the "soft" factors that impact the change process. A deeper understanding of these factors will help understand why some of the organizational change drives for SPI don't succeed and how these factors influence the change process.

*Lack of Context and Vision.* Human being relate to information and action well when there is a clarity of context and purpose. A majority of the SPI programs don't succeed because the context for change and the objectives of the SPI program are not clear and shared among the stakeholders (Beer et al. 1990). Context provides the background and reasons for SPI, whereas the objectives define what needs to be improved, how much and when. I have observed that a majority of the SPI initiatives are often driven from a technical perspective without a clear vision for SPI and well-established business case. This creates a lack of commitment and sense of urgency at the executive level (Kotter 1996). Benefits are frequently described in terms of cost reduction instead of showing the impact on the business as a whole.

A clear context provides a sense of purpose and direction, and brings about the necessary alignment among the stakeholders. For example, when the business need is to reduce cycle time, then this objective must be clearly established in the light of the context, stating why cycle time reduction is essential for the competitiveness of the organization. Oftentimes, the context is either very generic or nonexistent, leading the stakeholders to believe that SPI would be a nice thing to do. However, establishing a shared context alone is not sufficient. Having established the context, it is necessary to architect a vision for SPI – defining the desired improvement (the "to-be" state) with the expected benefits and a timeline in which the specific process improvements should be accomplished.

*Focus on Compliance.* In most organizations SPI is merely about compliance to a process improvement model or system such as CMM or ISO 9000 with "certification" being the eventual goal (Wiegers 1996, Moitra 1998). In my interactions with many companies, I have observed that focus on effectiveness and "improvement" measured by business results is often missing. Most organizations embrace process improvement models because it is fashionable to do so or because their competition is doing so. Frequently, organizations do not understand how a specific process improvement model fits into their business environment and whether embracing it will yield the desired benefits. Typically, in such cases, most organizations tend to emphasize conformance than building commitment for continuous improvement. As a result, when people are asked to support an SPI initiative without a shared context and well-defined objectives, their participation becomes "mechanical" – they are not committed to the cause and hence don't get involved in the SPI journey. Also, more often the commitment fades over time if early results are not communicated. Once an SPI initiative has stalled it is very difficult to restart.

*Short-Term Focus.* This is another cause of failure in SPI. It is first important to understood that change is a time consuming process, and hence is best brought about gradually and systematically. However, when organizations take a tactical approach to SPI for quick gains, their focus shifts to compliance with a model or a system, with the SPI initiative becoming a marketing instrument (Moitra 1998, Wiegers 1996). In such cases, SPI is not integrated with the business strategy of the organization and seldom yields any real improvement in business performance.

*Lack of Sense of Urgency.* When SPI vision and objectives are formulated, a sense of urgency in execution to realize the intended objectives is very vital for success of the SPI effort. A quick succession of incremental results reinforces belief in SPI in the minds of the people, generates a sense of accomplishment, and catalyses involvement. However, I have found that most SPI initiatives start with much fanfare but eventually die out without achieving results, and often the lack of sense of urgency is the cause for failure. I have noticed that many organizations consider SPI as a nice thing to do as opposed to treating it as a business priority. Unless SPI is a business priority, it will not result in management involvement and attract a sense of urgency. Moreover, only with a continued sense of urgency, the change and the momentum can be sustained and the improved processes institutionalized.

*Political Dimension.* SPI requires change in the organizational culture, people's mindset and work practices, and while it is known that change is necessary for progress, people resist change. Change requires people to transition through a phase of discomfort or unfamiliarity, and individuals do not want to move out of their comfort zones. In essence, change causes an upheaval in the organization and demands adapting to new structures and new order of things. In order to resist change, people play "games" and resort to numerous political tactics. Moreover, the political dimension also comes into force because of power struggle amongst some key people within the organization, and due to ego and turf issues (Moitra 1998). After all, processes demand certain way of working, acquisition of new competencies, usage of new technology and tools and also embracing new behaviors.

*Resistance to Change.* "No body likes change except a baby with wet pants," so goes a popular saying. Even though progress can happen only through change, most people resist change, either actively or passively. Change implies that people are forced out of their comfort zones. New approaches threaten their familiarity with the "old ways" of doing things. They also feel threatened in their established positions of expertise in the old process and resist change to maintain their power base.

In the context of management of organizational change for SPI, usually resistance comes from the line staff and middle managers but often these people are not involved in envisioning and implementing the change. As a result, the necessary buy-in from people from the trenches does not exist. Unfortunately, most change agents fail to understand the anatomy of resistance. Resistance to change stems from one or a combination of the following: uncertainty and skepticism about the effectiveness of the new processes; loss of control or prominence within the organization; and a perception about increased overhead and demand on their time. Many times the change agents are unable to establish the meaningfulness of the planned change for the practitioners – What's in it for them? How does it help them heighten their performance and deliver better software? (Zahran 1998, Hutton 1995, Humphrey 1997). If an SPI program is perceived as a dictate and desire from the management without its relevance and implications established for the people in the front line, resistance to change is inevitable – either directly or passively.

*Lack of Change Agent Buy-in.* Interestingly, I have observed that there are situations where the change agent himself (or herself) does not buy into the SPI objectives and the associated organizational change agenda. Quite often such situations arise because management entrusts the organizational change responsibility to someone who himself does not subscribe to the change vision but gets on to the job because of the organizational mandate. In such cases, the change agent's heart and mind are not aligned with the SPI and organizational change agenda, and often he does not know what he is trying to accomplish and why (Moitra 1998). In other words, the selection of the change agent is an important success factor many organizations tend to overlook.

*Ineffective Communication.* Most SPI initiatives do not gain momentum and eventually do not succeed because of the lack of effective communication. Clear communication of the context and objectives of SPI, regular communication to motivate and engage the employees, and also periodic highlighting of success stories is vital for success of the program. Regular communication keeps the stakeholders aligned to the agenda and objectives of the SPI program. More importantly, structured communication on what roles individuals can play and how they can help in the SPI journey is a very effective way of ensuring across-the-board engagement (Beer et al. 1990). Under-communication prevents momentum building and dilution of SPI intent.

Individuals need to get a clear articulation of why the envisioned change is needed and what's in it for them. People identify best with their individual needs and interests, and communication is crucial to making sure that people align themselves with the organizational needs and interests as well. My experience in observing and advising several software companies suggests that communication, which is the most vital link in the entire SPI journey, is often inadequate and neglected, affecting involvement and engagement of the people, without which the real change cannot happen.

*Lack of Project Management Approach.* The very objective of managing organizational change for SPI is to realize certain improvements and benefits for business within a specific timeframe. Because of the complexities and challenges involved in managing change and to deliver a sense of progress and achievement, it is necessary to *projectize* a change management program for SPI (Grady 1997). In many organizations, such a project management approach does not exist and in those where it does, often the spirit of project management is not seen in the organizational culture, especially when it comes to SPI, even though formal process improvement plans might exist.

*Quality of the People.* The people dealing with quality assurance and process improvement are often seen as a hindrance than help. The main reason for such a perception, I find, is that the quality and process professionals often fail to relate to the realities and needs of software development. Their positioning, therefore, tends to be viewed as theoretical – away from the realities of the business (Moitra 1998). On the other hand, since software development has strong dependency on human factors and individual knowledge and competencies, the quality of the development staff and managerial behavior also has bearing on the outcome of an SPI effort. The quality of the change agent is also a critical success factors. He or she must have recognition and esteem within the organization. Often the position of change agent is seen as an *overhead* role and assigned to people who have spare time and typically are not the opinion leaders of the organization.

*Lack of an Integrated Approach.* SPI is about achieving software excellence, but SPI alone won't help achieve higher business performance. For true software excellence, overall organizational maturity is essential. Organizational maturity requires focus on three fundamental dimensions of an organization: process, people and technology. Growth in the process dimension requires simultaneous growth in the people and technology dimension as each one of these have an impact on the growth of the other. But most organizations tend to treat the process dimension in isolation, thus receiving only sub-optimal benefits at best.

In addition, I have found that the belief based on the acquired experiences from the past organizational change initiatives could also adversely influence the SPI efforts, especially if the past initiatives did not succeed.

## 5. MODEL FOR MANAGING ORGANIZATIONAL CHANGE FOR SPI

Now that I have identified the factors that affect or influence organizational change management for SPI, I offer a pragmatic approach to guide the change initiative. Figure 1 presents the model for organizational change, which involves four stages:

- Preparation/Readiness

- Planning
- Implementing
- Institutionalizing.

It also emphasizes the role of communication as well as management involvement throughout the change process in the SPI journey.

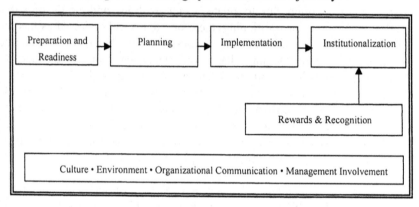

**Figure 1: Model for managing organizational change for SPI**

Preparation. This phase is about preparing for change for SPI. First, a vision for the desired change should be developed, which should be based on what processes need improvement, why and in what order of priority. Typically, a formal assessment of the "as-is" state is done to determine the areas that need improvement. It is very critical that the envisioned change is strongly aligned to the company's business goals. It is also essential to establish clarity on what implications would the envisioned change have on the company's business performance when realized (Reifer 2002). The vision for change for SPI can come from senior management, middle management, and quality managers or even from the development staff. Irrespective of where it comes from, it is absolutely vital that the senior management understands the need and implications of the envisioned change and buys into it. In addition, in this stage sufficient due diligence is required to figure out what will be the cost of the desired change. Also, all the key people within the organization should be involved right from this stage and for firming up the change vision, because the task of mobilizing commitment and involvement should begin from the *Preparation* stage itself. It is also the time when the organization-wide communication about the envisioned change and its compelling need for the business should begin and must be done by the senior management.

At this stage, the organization needs to assess as to whether it is ready for embarking on the change initiative for SPI. The key thing is to determine if the organizational environment is conducive for change. The senior management of the organization needs to ensure that they will remain committed to the change program and that SPI will remain a priority for them for as long as it takes to achieve the results.

In addition, at this stage it is highly recommended that a senior management member be identified as the sponsor for the SPI initiative with accountability for the success of the program. The next step is to identify a *change agent*, who will have the responsibility to plan out and implement the change. It is very critical that the identified change agent has a good understanding of the business and software engineering, and has a good credibility within the organization. Change agent's credibility and relationships with people across the organization have a strong influence on the success of the SPI program. Elsewhere, in this chapter we discuss the specific skills and competencies for a successful change agent.

Planning. In the *Planning* stage, the key activities include formulating measurable objectives for SPI aligned with the change vision, and *projectizing* the SPI effort. This involves breaking down the SPI effort into manageable and logical milestones with timelines, and roles and responsibilities for executing the change agenda. Besides planning for SPI, the project plan should also cover in depth as to how the new or improved processes will be deployed and what deployment mechanisms will be employed. A very important step in this phase is validating the *implementability* of the plan – Is it feasible? Is it possible to accomplish the SPI goals in the timeline planned? Would the necessary resources and attention be available throughout? Also, the project plan should account for the organization wide training needs for SPI and correspondingly have a training plan.

When the plan has specific actions formulated and outcome of each action defined, the SPI Project Plan should be made visible to all in the organization, so that people not only know how the change vision is going to be realized but also can volunteer to help make the change happen. Socialization of the plan and buy-in from all concerned in the organization is absolutely crucial for success of SPI efforts. SPI communication strategies for the senior management should be designed to show them the business benefits of the SPI program, whereas for the development community the communication strategy should additionally focus on what SPI means to them. If the management buy-in of the SPI plan is strong, then they will help create a 'market' for the plan and this will, in turn, ensure the necessary top-down cascading of SPI vision and goals.

Usually, most change programs fail because of lack of middle management support and involvement in SPI, so it is a prerequisite for the success of the program that middle level managers are engaged in the planning process and completely buy into the SPI objectives. Middle management involvement and contributions throughout the SPI journey should be designed into the plan.

The SPI project plan should also answer the following: How the progress of the SPI initiative will be reviewed, and how improvement will be assessed? For this, at this stage it is necessary to define metrics for reviewing the progress of the SPI program and to measure the success of the overall SPI efforts. It must be kept in mind that data on progress and improvement will go a long way in strengthening people's belief and involvement in the SPI program. The SPI project plan should also have a communication plan, including frequency and mode for the organization-wide communications. Communication is not about top-down communication or information dissemination; it is about two-way communication aimed at seeking across-the-board employee involvement, collaboration and building commitment for SPI.

The implementation approach in the plan should emphasize and ensure line staff involvement, particularly the middle management. For working on each major action for SPI, a cross-functional team involving the line staff should be established. In addition, I have found it helpful if SPI actions are included in the performance objectives of the line staff and the middle managers.

An effective communication to all employees about the SPI objectives and the need for change is immensely helpful. Communicate what precisely is the need for change, why, share the SPI strategy and plan with them, and articulate how SPI will help them in terms of efficiency, productivity and performance. I have found a focus on individuals and those in the frontline of development very useful, because when collectively the individual performance improves through SPI the organizational performance improves. Pay attention to the suggestions and concerns raised as you communicate about SPI, and factor them appropriately as you refine and baseline the SPI plan. It pays to work towards involving those sounding negative, pessimistic and opposing – focus on how their negativity and skepticism can be turned around by making them part of the solution and challenging them to deliver on the improvement agenda. Bottoms-up involvement and initiatives are tremendously effective in SPI, and that's the focus and purpose of communication.

Implementation. In this stage, the focus is on operationalizing the plan and realizing the SPI objectives. As prioritized in the SPI project plan, the objective in this phase is to accomplish each SPI milestone on time, quantifying and communicating the benefits of improved processes, and continuing to gain and sustain momentum.

It is usually recommended that the new or improved processes be tried in a pilot setting before their wide scale deployment. However, my experience suggests that whether to pilot a process or not should be carefully evaluated based on several factors. Piloting helps in several ways: it provides an indication of the level of support and enthusiasm for the change, allows insights into the magnitude and complexity of change, allows to experience early wins, helps in gaining experience in managing change, and above all, gives an indication of the performance of the new process. Based on experiences and learning acquired during a pilot, alternate or improved strategies for organization-wide deployment can be crafted. On the other hand, the pilot experience and its performance can affect the employee motivation and the momentum of the change program, especially if the pilot is not successful, leading to resistance and skepticism for SPI. It must be noted that the failure of the pilot may not always be due to lacunas or deficiencies in the new process; the failure could be due to lack of support and cooperation as a result of ego and turf issues.

Many SPI experts assert that organizational-wide roll out of the new processes must be preceded by a well-planned pilot. However, I have not found this to be necessary. Whether to adopt a piloting approach to implementation or not should be viewed in the light of the following considerations (Kanter and Stein 1992):

- Extent to which change (SPI) and its implications are clearly understood. If the intended process change is vital for the organization and its implications are well understood across the board, then it might be okay to directly go in for an organization-wide deployment. However, before deployment, the process(es) must be critically reviewed by all the stakeholders who will be affected by it to rule out any adverse impact. To ensure this, many companies I have interacted with involve a cross-section of the various stakeholders in reviewing the process before baselining and releasing it.
- Level of support and enthusiasm for SPI and change. This is a function of conviction and shared belief in the organization that improvement in processes is necessary. When process improvement is carried out with the involvement of the line staff, who provide inputs, expectations and directions for improvement, conviction and belief in the new process will be naturally high. As a result, there will be support and enthusiasm for adopting the new processes. When

such conducive environment exists, and when the new process is believed to be critical for the business (e.g. risk management process), a pilot may not be always necessary.

- Magnitude and complexity of change for SPI. If the magnitude and complexity of the changes for SPI are significant, particularly in case of highly business critical processes (e.g. defect and change management), or when it is not clear how the new process will interact with the environment, or when there is a potential of productivity dip attributable to new process introduction, a pilot is recommended.

- Prior experience in managing SPI within the organization. If the prior experiences with SPI suggests that a restricted roll out of the new process to assess its impact will be necessary, or if an alternate deployment approach would potentially maximize the chances of adoption and success, then a piloting approach should be considered.

- Urgency for SPI as it relates to company's business. Specific business conditions may warrant an across-the-board deployment of some key processes (e.g. project management), not allowing the time for a pilot, or when it is strongly felt that the new process will invariably positively contribute to the business, planning for a pilot will only delay the benefit from the new process to the larger organization.

During implementation phase, management support and involvement is very important because implementation requires transition from one practice or process to another, introduction of new processes, etc., and this may lead to several problems like dip in the productivity, increased resistance, frustration, and political maneuvering. Such transitions could be very demanding and stressful, and by being involved and supportive, management ensures that there are no morale and motivation issues. This is also a good way of demonstrating management commitment and interest in SPI.

It also pays to be flexible in the approach to implementing the process changes, particularly flexibility to incorporate changes in the SPI plan based on line staff inputs. However, it is important to make sure that the focus is on results defined in the plan. A good approach is one that focuses on ownership building and creates short-term wins. This increases the confidence level of the project team members in the effectiveness of the new processes and further secures their commitment towards the need for process improvement (Schaffer and Thomson 1992). This, in turn, creates a multiplier effect and gives birth to process improvement ambassadors in the organization. Also, it is always good to have alternative approaches – they come in handy during moments of crisis. One must simultaneously strive to develop infrastructure – both 'soft' (environment, culture, attitude, etc.) and 'hard' (tools, workflows, etc.) – in the organization that will enable people to perform and implement the new process without 'pain.'

Establishing a reward and recognition system to recognize the individual and team contributions is an essential ingredient of a SPI program. When people are appreciated and recognized for their contributions, it not only heightens their enthusiasm and commitment but also encourages others to get involved. Rewards can be both monetary and non-monetary, and a well thought out combination of both can be installed. To unleash creativity and innovation, such awards as "the best process improvement suggestion" are very effective.

Institutionalizing. In this phase, the focus is on making sure that the change (improvement) is permanent and pervasive within the organization. This stage, therefore, is about making sure that the improved processes go beyond the pilot stage (if there is one) and are deployed across the organization to derive the intended business benefits. Success of this stage requires entire organization's involvement at a grass roots level in adopting the new processes. Formation of focus groups to work on and propagate the improved processes is a very helpful strategy to adopt. Essentially, the idea is to clone the change agent and create many of them, focusing on various aspects of SPI to institutionalize the change. Again, measurements should be performed to establish effectiveness of the new processes and constantly communicated to the people, which aid in conviction about the change and invites involvement of the people. The change agent's job in this phase becomes more demanding and involves ensuring the new processes are used across the organization and the quest for continuous improvement is intensified (Moitra 1998).

## 6.    ROLE OF CULTURE IN SPI

Depending on the dominant organizational culture, a specific SPI strategy should be chosen. Zahran (1998) provides some helpful perspectives on the kind of SPI strategies that would be appropriate for different kinds of organizational culture. However, whatever be the organizational culture, it has a significant influence on change initiatives. Leaders and their behaviors shape the organizational culture, and I have found that a participatory culture has the most positive influence on SPI. Especially with regard to SPI, first and foremost, leaders need to demonstrate genuine interest in SPI and establish its criticality and relevance for business success. Second, leaders need to understand SPI and its implications, and need to involve themselves in the SPI journey. Mere commitment for resources and budgets does not establish leaders' interest and seriousness about SPI. So, the culture building (for SPI) has to happen from the top, and without the engagement of senior leaders SPI can never truly succeed.

As I mentioned above, a participatory culture is vital for SPI. When people are involved in conceiving and guiding the change and in making decisions, they get emotionally involved and assume ownership for success (Chatman and Cha 2003). Unfortunately, most SPI programs tend to emphasize conformance, and this is never effective. People do not like to follow instructions and complying to things without knowing why should they do something and what is in it for them. Focus on commitment building, on the other hand, is very effective. To mobilize people's commitment, establishing and communicating a context for change and SPI is necessary. When the context is established and shared, it is equally important to highlight that the success won't materialize without each individual's commitment, involvement, and contributions. When people understand why they are doing what they are doing and how does it help them improve and perform better, they align their energies to the SPI cause. They become emotionally involved in the process of change. Therefore, strategically it is very important to capitalize on the emotional reservoir existing within the organization, because an emotional engagement can truly fuel the change program (Thomson 1998).

Another determinant of organizational culture for SPI is reaction to failure. An organizational environment where involvement and initiatives are rewarded and risk-taking is encouraged is an ideal environment for SPI. The culture of the organization, which tolerates failures to a reasonable extent, allows individuals to take initiatives and contribute without fear of failure. Also, the ability to constructively confront and openly communicate constitutes a positive SPI culture.

Yet another culture influencer is how the company does recruitment. Building a culture is one thing, and sustaining it is another. The process of sustaining company's culture is very challenging, because it requires the leaders to make continuous investment in it. As the company grows and acquires talent, it is essential that the new recruits be hired with value systems and orientations that will align with company's value system and culture. And, once onboard, it must be ensured that the new employees are completely immersed into company's value system, culture and SPI philosophy through a structured assimilation program. A technically well-qualified person with no process orientation or regard for processes can have very negative and destabilizing influence on the SPI program, and hence company's recruitment philosophy and processes must ensure that any candidate under consideration will culturally fit in the company. In the companies I have worked for and in my own hiring efforts, I have always particularly assessed candidates for their "process centricity" and attitude towards process improvement.

A simple way to assess whether your organizational culture is conducive for change and SPI is to take an inventory of the various attributes of the organizational environment as shown in Table 1, and see whether the overall valuation is positive (Thomson 1998).

Table 1: Inventory of the attributes of organizational culture

| Positive Attribute | Negative Attribute |
| --- | --- |
| Enthusiasm | Selfishness |
| Passion | Hatred |
| Commitment | Politics |
| Collaboration | Leaders not practicing what they |
| Trust | preach |
| Mutual respect | Jealousy |
| Pride | Internal competition |
| Joy | Apathy |
| Motivation | Command and control |
| Focus on excellence | Focus on compliance |

## 7.    THE CHANGE AGENT

Change agent is a management representative responsible for driving the SPI program and ensuring that the defined organizational and process changes fall in place to realize the intended benefits (Allen 1995). A successful change agent is someone who has a solid understanding of the business, reasonably good understanding of software engineering, is passionate about excellence, and possess a commitment for process improvement. It is very important that the change agent has good credibility and relationships across the organization (Hutton 1995). I believe that a leader's credibility is a function of his technical and business competence and his attitude and behavior, which means that an effective change agent has to demonstrate leadership traits in both these dimensions.

Change agent's role is very critical in any change program, as his/her abilities and attitudes have significant influence on the people's attitude towards the change. Therefore, the selection of the change agent merits a careful consideration. My research suggests that a successful change agent ought to demonstrate the skills, attitudes and characteristics as shown in Table 2 to be effective (Moitra 1998).

Table 2: Competence profile of effective change agent

| | |
|---|---|
| **Skills and Competence** | • Deep cross functional understanding of the business<br>• Knowledge of software development processes<br>• Knowledge of software process improvement and total quality management principles<br>• Strong ability to sell and influence<br>• Strong negotiation skills<br>• Strong conflict management skills<br>• Ability to manage emotions<br>• Ability to establish credibility and gain respect<br>• Good listening skills<br>• Ability to deliver on objectives (project management)<br>• Value-based leadership<br>• Good trouble shooter<br>• Ability to inspire, energize and motivate<br>• Good coaching abilities<br>• Ability to work across organizational layers<br>• Manages diversity well |
| **Attitudes** | • Optimistic<br>• Proactive<br>• Strong belief in the SPI goals and their importance<br>• Respect for others |
| **Characteristics** | • Persistence<br>• High confidence<br>• Perseverance<br>• Flexibility<br>• No fear of failure<br>• Good relationship management<br>• Enthusiastic, passionate, and driven<br>• Practices what he/she preaches and walks the talk<br>• Not driven by credit taking for success/results<br>• High emotional quotient<br>• Trustworthy |

## 8.  SUCCESS FACTORS FOR ORGANIZATIONAL CHANGE FOR SPI

Managing organizational change for SPI is quite a challenge because it requires aligning people from across the organization towards a common cause. There are several success factors for SPI (Wiegers 1996), but the most fundamental is senior management's passionate belief in SPI and their behavior and attitude towards it. Of course, a good change management strategy crafted around a strong vision is necessary to align people to SPI objectives and channel their energies. Before embarking on the change program for SPI, company's management must ensure that SPI will remain their priority irrespective of how the other business priorities evolve, and this happens only when SPI is tightly linked to business benefits and competitiveness. Therefore, establishing compelling reasons for SPI and ensuring that the reality does not contradict the planned changes is very crucial. This also gives the much-needed authenticity to the SPI program.

Bringing about the necessary change is a gigantic and daunting task, which cannot be accomplished without involvement of all the people in the organization. A thorough assessment of organization's capacity and capability for change, and the urgency associated with the need for change, is an essential ingredient for the success of the change program. The selection of the change agent is equally important, because this individual becomes the voice and face of the change. SPI requires a supportive and participatory culture, which promotes collaboration and excellence. A conducive organizational climate, therefore, is a necessary condition for launching an SPI program. A culture founded on strong value system and supported by leadership behavior should also be augmented with other organizational aspects such as employee motivation and morale, job design and compensation, etc. An unhappy and de-motivated employee will have no energy and inclination to contribute to SPI.

Organizational structure also has an influence on SPI success. When organizational structures give empowerment but do not emphasize accountability and organization building, they tend to have a negative impact as far as SPI is concerned. This is because such organizational structures encourage people to pursue their own agendas, building resistance, affecting teamwork, and lack of support for SPI. Hence, organizational structures that establish clarity of roles and responsibilities and promote mutual accountability are effective.

As I have emphasized throughout the chapter, constant, focused and effective communication throughout the duration of the SPI program is absolutely vital for its success. Establishing effective measures and metrics for gauging and communicating the progress of SPI is thus very important.

Since successful change programs can be launched and sustained only with an organization-wide involvement of people, it is essential that individual needs and motivations are understood and then aligned to the SPI objectives. My research suggests that one of the following four provides the fundamental motivation for people to progress and succeed: knowledge, power/prominence, money, and fear. I certainly do not recommended using fear in any form to drive people involvement in SPI programs. Also, except seeking involvement and giving a sense of ownership perhaps not much can be done to give 'power' or prominence to all individuals. However, acquisition of new knowledge and its relevance for the individual career and performance can surely be a motivation for people in SPI. Similarly, appropriate rewards and recognitions definitely help in motivating people to participate and contribute to SPI, and encourage them to take initiatives and go the extra mile. Finally, I consider emotion as the fuel that can really fire true performance and believe that change programs targeted at SPI should focus on capitalizing on the emotional reservoir existing within the organization (Duck 2001).

---

### CHECKLIST FOR SUCCESSFULLY MANAGING ORGANIZATIONAL CHANGE FOR SPI

1. Is SPI one of the top 3 priorities for the management for at least next 3 years?
2. Is there a well-understood business case with anticipated corporate benefits?
3. Is the context for change and SPI established?
4. Is a vision for change formulated?
5. Has the "as-is" state of the process effectiveness been assessed? Have the gaps and desired improvements been identified in order of priorities?
6. Are clear and specific goals and priorities for SPI established?
7. Does a communication plan exist? Do people know why the change has been envisioned, and what's their role in the entire SPI journey?
8. Have the people from the development community been involved in creating the change vision and SPI plans?
9. Is there a management sponsor who has the bottom line accountability for the success of the SPI program?
10. Is a change agent with organization-wide visibility and credibility across the organizational layers identified?
11. Are mechanisms defined to ensure management involvement on an on-going basis?
12. Are measures to gauge progress of the SPI defined and made known to all the stakeholders?
13. Is a training plan defined for the people to acquire the new skills?
14. Are development staff and line managers involved in improving the identified processes and executing the change?
15. Are rewards and recognition planned for those contributing to the SPI journey?
16. Are individual objectives formally linked to the SPI objectives?
17. Is there a forum for exchange of ideas and suggestions for SPI?
18. Have workshops aiming at providing guidance for SPI been planned for all levels for organizations, including the senior management?
19. Does a formal project plan exist for SPI with milestones, timelines, and review mechanisms?
20. Are review mechanisms defined to assess the progress and impact of change?
21. Have all the key risk factors been identified and addressed through mitigation and contingency plans?

## ACKNOWLEDGEMENTS

In addition to the two anonymous reviewers, I thank my professional colleagues, Karl Wiegers and Wolfgang Strigel for their critical comments and helpful suggestions on this chapter.

# REFERENCES

Allen, C.D. 1995. Succeeding as a Clandestine Change Agent. *Communications of the ACM*, Vol. 38, No. 5, pp. 81-86.

Ascari, A., Rock, M. and Dutta, S. 1995. Reengineering and Organizational Change: Lessons from a Comparative Analysis of Company Experiences. *European Management Journal*, Vol. 13, No. 1, pp. 1-30.

Beer, M., Eisenstat, R. and Spector, B. 1990. Why Change Does Not Work. *Harvard Business Review*, November-December, pp. 158-166.

Branstad, P. and Lucier, C. 2001. Zealots Rising: The Case for Practical Visionaries. *strategy+business*, Issue 22, 1st Quarter, pp. 1-12.

Brodman, J.G. and Johnson, D. 1996. Return on Investment from Software Process Improvement as Measured by US Industry. *Crosstalk*, Vol. 9, No. 4, pp. 23-29.

Chatman, J.A. and Cha, S.E. 2003. Leading by Leveraging Culture. *California Management Review*, Vol. 45, No. 5, pp. 22-33.

Diaz, M. and Sligo, J. 1997. How Software Process Improvement Helped Motorola. *IEEE Software,* Vol. 14, No. 5, pp. 75-81.

Duck, J.D. 2001. *The Change Monsters: The Human Forces That Fuel or Foil Corporate Transformation and Change*. Crown Business, New York.

Grady, R.B. 1997. *Successful Software Process Improvement*. Hewlett-Packard Professional Books, Prentice Hall, New Jersey.

Herbsleb, J., Zubrow, D., Siegel, J., Rozum, J. and Carleton, A. 1994. Software Process Improvement State of the Payoff. *American Programmer*, Vol. 7, No. 9, pp. 2-12.

Humphrey, W. S. 1989. *Managing the Software Process*. Addison-Wesley, New York.

Humphrey, W., Snyder, T. and Willis, R. 1991. Software Process Improvement at Hughes Aircraft. *IEEE Software*, Vol. 8, No. 4, pp. 11-23.

Humphrey, W.S. 1997. *Managing Technical People: Innovation, Teamwork and Software Process*. Addison-Wesley Longman, Reading, Massachusetts.

Hutton, D.W. 1995. *The Change Agent's Handbook: A Survival Guide for Quality Improvement Champions*. Tata McGraw-Hill, New Delhi.

Interview with Norm Kerth. 1996. Leading from a Powerless Position. *IEEE Software*, September, pp. 106-108.

Interview with Sanjiv Ahuja. 1999. Laying the Groundwork for Success. *IEEE Software*, November-December, pp. 72-75.

Kanter, R.M. and Stein, B.A. 1992. *The Challenge of Organizational Change: How Companies Experience It and Leaders Guide It*. Free Press, New York.

Katzenbach, J., et al. 1996. *Real Change Leaders: How You Can Create Growth and High Performance at Your Company*. Nicholas Brealey, London.

Kotter, J.P. 1996. *Leading Change*. Harvard Business School Press, Boston, MA.

Mintzberg, H. and Westley, F. 1992. Cycles of Organizational Change. *Strategic Management Journal*, Vol. 13, pp. 39-59.

Moitra, D. 1998. Managing Change for Software Process Improvement Initiatives: A Practical Experience Based Approach. *Software Process – Improvement and Practice*, Vol. 4, No. 4, pp. 199-207.

Paulish, D.J. and Carleton, A.D. 1994. Case Studies of Software Process-Improvement Measurement. *IEEE Computer*, Vol. 27, No. 9, pp. 50-57.

Pitterman, B. 2000. Telcordia Technologies: The Journey to High Maturity. *IEEE Software*, July-August, pp. 89-96.

Prastacos, G., Söderquist, K., Spanes, Y. and Wasswenhove, L.V. 2002. An Integrated Framework for Managing Change in the New Competitive Landscape. *European Management Journal*, Vol. 20, No. 1, pp. 55-71.

Reifer, D.J. 2002. *Making the Software Business Case: Improvement by Numbers*. Addison-Wesley, New Jersey.

Repenning, N.P. and Sterman, J.D. 2001. Nobody Ever Gets Credit for Fixing Problems that Never Happened: Creating and Sustaining Process Improvement. *California Management Review*, Vol. 43, No. 4, pp. 64-88.

Robbins, H. and Finley, M. 1997. *Why Change Does Not Work*. Orion Business Books, London.

Schaffer, R. and Thomson, H. 1992. Successful Change Programs Begin with Results. *Harvard Business Review*, January-February, pp. 80-89.

Senge, P., et. al. 1999. *The Dance of Change: The Challenges to Sustaining Momentum in Learning Organizations*. Currency Doubleday, New York.

Stelzer, D. and Mellis, W. 1999. Success Factors of Organizational Change in Software Process Improvement. *Software Process – Improvement and Practice*, Vol. 4, No. 4, pp. 227-250.

Thomson, K. 1998. *Emotional Capital*. Capstone, Oxford.

Weinberg, G.M. 1997. *Quality Software Management: Anticipating Change*. Dorset House Publishing, New York

Wiegers, K.E. 1996. Software Process Improvement: Ten Traps to Avoid. *Software Development*, Vol. 4, No. 5.

Wohlwend, H. and Rosenbaum, S. 1994. Schlumberger's Software Improvement Program. *IEEE Transactions on Software Engineering*, Vol. 20, No. 11, pp. 833-839.

Zahran, S. 1998. *Software Process Improvement: Practical Guidelines for Business Success*. Addison-Wesley Longman, Sussex.

# Chapter 8

# A WORKSHOP-ORIENTED APPROACH FOR DEFINING ELECTRONIC PROCESS GUIDES
*A Case Study*

Torgeir DINGSØYR[1], Nils B. MOE[1], Tore DYBÅ[1] and Reidar CONRADI[2]

[1]*SINTEF Information and Communication Technology, [2]Norwegian University of Science and Technology. E-mail: {Torgeir.Dingsoyr, Nils.B.Moe, Tore.Dyba}@sintef.no ; Reidar.Conradi@idi.ntnu.no*

**Abstract:** We introduce electronic process guides, and discuss their role in software engineering projects. We then present existing methods for constructing electronic process guides by defining a set of common processes for a company. Different approaches from the software engineering and management science are presented. We then go on to propose a new way of dealing with process description in software engineering: using process workshops as a tool to reach consensus on work practice. The main reason for this is to get realistic descriptions with accurate detail as well as company commitment in an efficient manner. We describe our workshop-oriented method to define processes, which we have used in small software companies, and show examples of results.

**Key words:** Electronic process guide; process workshop; process model; software process improvement.

## 1. INTRODUCTION

The way we develop and maintain software, or the software process, has long been regarded as crucial for software quality and productivity (Lehman & Belady, 1985). Most quality systems and software process improvement initiatives prescribe recommended processes for the developers and organization to follow. We therefore need to describe the relevant processes.

In the 1990s there was a lot of work on defining formal and rather sophisticated process modeling languages, and associated tools for process execution and evolution. However, in spite of substantial efforts by academia and partly industry (Derniame et al., 1999) and creation of several conference series (Oquendo, 2003), the attitude was too formal to have a practical impact. In fact, most companies prefer rather simple process models - such as IDEF0 (National Institute of Standards and Technology, 1993), proprietary ad-hoc formalisms (e.g. the one used for Rational Unified Process), or even quasi-formal diagrams using a document-producing tool like Word (Becker-Kornstaedt et al., 2001).

We can draw two lessons from this: formal modeling of processes may easily be overdone and is anyhow not enough to ensure developer motivation and hence process conformance. Second, automated enactment should be used with great care. To our knowledge, there are no success stories of enactment in an industrial context, apart from stable and mature domains like configuration management and testing. Knowledge-work, like software development seems to be extremely difficult to support with enactment.

A more practical approach to process work for companies, is to make such process descriptions available as electronic process guides (EPGs) on the company Intranet. Our recommendation is that the developers should be involved in such processes, both to work as recommended and to contribute to the process models. Otherwise, there will easily be a too large gap between the official process model and the actual process, leading to poor process conformance. This has happened in many organizations with elaborate quality systems, that are hardly respected by (or applicable for) the rank and file (Conradi & Dybå, 2001). A balance must therefore be found between discipline (obeying formal routines) and creativity (Glass, 1995) (actual development with much improvisation (Dybå, 2000)).

This chapter reports on the experience with developing of an electronic process guide in a Norwegian medium-size company with rather strict requirements on their software processes. To increase process awareness by the developers, process workshops were run to collect experience that could lead to better process descriptions. This kind of participatory design has a strong Scandinavian work and research tradition.

The issue we would like to discuss in this chapter is our suggested method for organizing process workshops. Interesting questions are which organizing elements make a well-working process, and how the process can be designed to increase process guide usage in the future. We will describe how this was done in an example company, and discuss experiences from using this method, compare it to other possible approaches, and conclude with advice for organizing similar workshops.

Now, we present electronic process guides in further detail and then describe important issues in employee participation which we build on in designing process workshops. The rest of the chapter is organized as follows: section 2 introduces the research method. Section 3 describes our workshop-oriented method to define software processes, which we have used in several small and medium-sized software companies. We present a case study of results from conducting process workshops in a satellite software company. Section 4 discusses findings from the case study in relation to existing theory, and section 7 concludes the chapter.

## 1.1 Electronic process guides

Effectively disseminating process knowledge to process participants is crucial in any software process improvement effort. Process participants need effective guidance when process conformance is important, when a process changes frequently, and when new personnel join a project.

Traditionally, this has been the realm of large organizations, and the way of describing and communicating processes has focused on printed standards and handbooks. However, such handbooks are more often seen as dust collectors than software process improvement facilitators, and especially so in small and medium-sized companies.

For process guides to be useful, increasingly more software companies not only tailor their process guides to the specific needs of the company, but also make them available on the company's intranet. This way the traditional process handbook shifts from a bulky pile of paper to a flexible on-line structure allowing easy access to all relevant information by means of an electronic process guide (Scott et al., 2002).

A process guide can be seen as a structured, workflow-oriented, reference document for a particular process, and exists to support participants in carrying out the intended process (Kellner et al., 1998). Whether in the form of a printed handbook or an electronic version, a process guide should include the following basic elements:

- Activities: descriptions of "how things are done", including an overview of the activities and details regarding each individual activity.
- Artifacts: details regarding the products created or modified by an activity, either as a final or intermediate result of the activity or as a temporary result created by one of the steps.
- Roles: details regarding the roles and agents involved in performing the activities.

- Tools and Techniques: details regarding the tools and techniques used to support or automate the performance of an activity.

A common way to describe processes is to describe process *entry*, *tasks*, *verification* and *exit*, where *entry* and *exit* are criteria needed to be fulfilled and the *tasks* describe activities, roles, artifacts, tools and techniques. This is commonly referred to as the ETVX model.

Based on these elements, Kellner et al. (1998) have proposed a set of basic requirements and design principles for EPGs. Most importantly, an EPG should provide all the information elements and relationships contained in a good paper-based process guide. In addition, it should capitalize on diagrams, tables, and narrative to provide an effective user interface. Also, it should make extensive use of hyper-links to support flexible navigation and direct access to supporting information such as examples and templates.

However, the potential of EPG's can only be realized when key capabilities are not only adopted, but also infused across the organization. This is complicated by the fact that there is considerable scepticism among software developers to learn from and adhere to prescribed process models, which are often perceived as overly "structured" or implying too much "control" (Conradi & Dybå, 2001). Therefore, we cannot expect such infusion of EPGs unless they are perceived as useful and easy to use in daily practice and consistent with the existing values, past experience, and needs of the software developers (Davis, 1989; Venkatesh & Davis, 2000).

## 1.2   Employee participation

Conradi and Dybå (2001) showed the importance of employee participation during the development and introduction of formal software routines and that such routines must be supplemented by collaborative, social processes to promote effective infusion and organizational learning.

This insight is not new. Employee participation and the way people are treated, has been noted to be a crucial factor in organizational management and development ever since the famous productivity studies at Western Electric's Hawthorne plant in the 1920s (Mayo, 1933; Mayo, 1945). The results of these studies started a revolution in management thinking, showing that even routine jobs can be improved if the workers are treated with respect.

Since then, participation and involvement has been one of the most important foundations of organization development and change (Cummings & Worley, 2001; French & Bell, 1999). Participation is also one of the fundamental ideas of Total Quality Management (Crosby, 1979; Deming, 2000; Juran, 1992). Similarly, participation has always been a central goal and one of the pillars of organizational learning. For example, autonomous work groups (Trist, 1981), quality circles (Ishikawa, 1990), survey feedback (Baumgartel, 1959; Neff, 1966), quality of work life programs (Davis, 1977), search conferences (Emery & Purser, 1996), and cultural analysis (Denison & Spreitzer, 1991; Schein, 1992) are all predicated on the belief that increased participation will lead to better solutions and enhanced organizational problem-solving capability.

What can be learned from these prior studies is that people tend to support what they have participated in creating, or to use Berger and Luckmann's (Berger & Luckmann, 1966) words: "it is more likely that one will deviate from programmes set up for one by others than from programmes that one has helped establish oneself."

An important aspect of participation is "co-determination", i.e. the direct participation of workers in decisions about what should best be done at their own level. Within the context of software development, no one is more expert in the realities of a software company's business with respect to the day-to-day details of particular technologies, products, and markets than the software developers and their first-line managers are. Hence, it is important to involve all those who are part of the software process, and have decisions made regarding the development of EPGs by those who are closest to the problem.

Consequently, and in order to get realistic descriptions with accurate detail as well as company commitment in an efficient manner, we involve all relevant employee groups in defining processes by using process workshops as a tool to reach consensus on work practice.

## 2. METHOD

The research reported in this chapter is from a large industrial research project, Software Process Improvement through Knowledge and Experience (SPIKE), where many companies cooperate with research institutions and universities in improvement activities. The collaboration is based on finding common improvement and learning goals, and working together to obtain the goals. The communication between contact persons in the companies and researchers (and data collection) is through meetings (minutes, observation, and pictures), telephone calls, and e-mail communication. The researchers usually stay two-day visits in the participating companies in order to also get into the informal arena in the company, and not just collaborate in official meetings.

This research method is a form of action research (Greenwood & Levin, 1998), where the researchers and participants from the companies had common goals: to improve software development, and learn from that experience. Together with the company, we discuss how improvement activities can be organized, and try it out in a cogenerative learning process. That the process is cogenerative means that both company "insiders" and researcher "outsiders" are able to reflect on actions performed. A communication arena is established with regular meetings between researchers and the quality responsible in the company. In this case, the process workshops were a solution suggested by researchers for a problem the quality department had: to improve documentation of the core processes of the company. We organized feedback-sessions after performing the process workshops for cogenerative learning.

Potential problems with this type of research are that it can easily be biased, in that everyone is interested in reaching the goals that are set up. Thus, we do not know if the same results would be achieved with another set of researchers, with other people from the company, or with another company in the same situation. But action research is a way to get interaction with companies in a way that would not be possible if it was not so much in the company's interest.

The case company was selected because they were putting much effort in software process improvement, and was thus a candidate for participation in the SPIKE project.

## 3.    DEFINING PROCESSES IN A MEDIUM-SIZE COMPANY

We first describe the company where we carried out research, and then present our work with process workshops in this company.

### 3.1  A satellite software company

Since the company was founded in 1984, they have delivered turnkey ground station systems, consultancy, feasibility studies, system engineering, training, and support. The company has been working with large development projects, both as a prime contractor and as a subcontractor.

Customers range from universities to companies like Lockheed Martin and Alcatel to governmental institutions like the European Space Agency and the Norwegian Meteorological Institute.

Most of the software systems that are developed are running on Unix, many on the Linux operating system.

The company possesses a stable and highly skilled staff, many with master's degrees in computer science, mathematics or physics, and have what we can describe as an "engineering culture". Approximately 60 people are working in the company, and the majority is working with software development. Projects are managed in accordance with quality routines fulfilling the European Space Agency PSS-05 standards and ISO 9001-2000.

The company had an extensive quality system, but the system was cumbersome to use because of the size – and because it existed partly on file and partly on paper. As a part of being certified according to ISO 9001-2000, the company decided to document all main processes in the company. We worked with the company in defining the processes for software development.

## 3.2 Defining requirements for an EPG

We started out with an initial workshop. The goal of this workshop was to define the different existing project types in the company, and to decide the format and most important requirements for the process guide. The company defined four main project types, and they chose the most common one as a starting point for the following workshops. Product development was the most common project type, and the size of this project type was typically 1000-4000 work hours. Other project types was customer controlled development projects, delivery projects (integration of existing components, and configuration), maintenance projects, and studies. Typical activities for product development projects were either customizing an existing product for a customer, developing a new system for a customer, or an internal project with a mixture of new development and integration of existing products. After the project types were defined and product development was chosen as a starting point, the most important requirements were defined. The process guide should provide:

- Description of tasks for the most important roles in a project
- Checklists for each main process
- Templates for all documents produced
- Descriptions of best practice
- Access to all tools needed in the project (e.g. a requirement and a bug track system).

In addition to these "functional" requirements a few non-functional requirements were defined during the first workshop. The most important such requirements were that it should be: easy accessible, as simple as possible, and up to date.

### 3.3   Discussing processes: The process workshop

We ran a total of six process workshops focusing on different parts of the development process. The workshops involved people from the market and quality department as well as the development unit.

In the first process workshop for product development, "initiation" was the one the company wanted to start with. The initiation process was defined to include "offer", "follow-up" and "blast off".

We followed the same pattern for each workshop, which we describe below with examples of output from the first workshop. See (Ahonen et al., 2002), for a discussion of a similar group process technique.

The workshops differed in length, but would usually last half a day. The researchers acted as moderators and secretaries. In addition to a meeting room, the workshop required a collection of yellow stickers in different colors, and walls that were covered with paper, where we could attach stickers and draw figures. A digital camera was useful to document the results of the workshop. We also found it useful to bring large process worksheets, based on the ETVX model: a sheet with boxes for input, activities, output, roles and related documents involved in the process (see Figure 2).

We defined process(es) in six steps and five sub-steps as shown in Figure 1.

As the initiation of projects is an interface between different parts of the organization, it was important to bring together people from marketing, quality assurance and the development department. We started the workshop by giving a 15-minute presentation of what we were going to do, and put a large sheet with a figure of the process worksheet (as in Figure 2) on the wall – one for each process that would be discussed in the meeting.

For each sub-process we wanted to define, "offer", "follow-up" and "blast-off", we went through the sub steps:

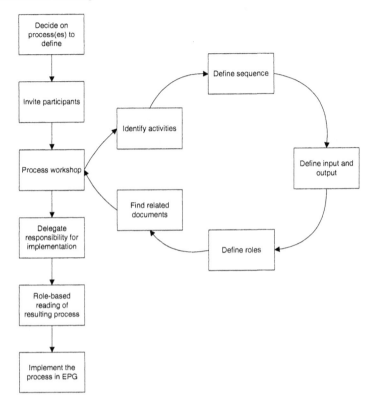

**Figure 1: Steps to define a process in a workshop**

*Identified activities.* We brainstormed on the main activities of the process by using the KJ process (Scupin, 1997) (after Japanese ethnologist Jiro Kawakita) and documented the result. The KJ is a creative group technique to organize and find relations between seemingly unrelated ideas. We did this as follows:

- We gave each participant a set of yellow stickers and a thick pen. We asked them to write suggestions for activities on each yellow sticker in large letters. People got time to document 5-10 ideas.
- We asked each participant to present her suggestions: attach each sticker on a wall, and describe the activity. No-one was allowed to criticize or discuss the ideas at this point.
- Grouped the suggestions: the participants came forward to the wall and organized the yellow stickers into groups. We asked them to state why they chose to move the stickers.

- Formulated headings: we found new suitable headers that described the stickers in each group. The headings were formulated to make sense to people who have not participated in the workshop.
- We documented the diagram on the wall with groups and supporting activities on stickers.

During this work, several interesting discussions came up, and several important problems and misunderstandings were solved. Especially marketing and project managers had different views on initiation, but were able to agree on a common process during the workshop.

Because we wanted to get through three sub-processes in half a day, we used time boxing which limited discussion. However, we were able to produce an extensive material in the time slot for each sub-process.

The main activities identified in this step for the "blast-off" sub-process were:

- Appoint project manager
- Organize "Handover meeting"
- First project analysis
- Allocate resources
- Prepare for kick-off meeting
- Internal kick-off.

*Defined the sequence of the activities.* We took the activities from the previous phase, made a sticker for each. Then, we placed them on the activities-field of the process worksheet, where time goes from left to the right. We found a suitable workflow between the activities.

*Defined input and output.* We found documents or artifacts that must be available to start the sub-process, and which documents that mark the end of the sub-process. We used stickers with other colors than for the activities to mark input and output, and attached them on the process worksheet on the wall together with the activities. Conditions that must be satisfied to begin or exit the sub-process can be described in checklists.

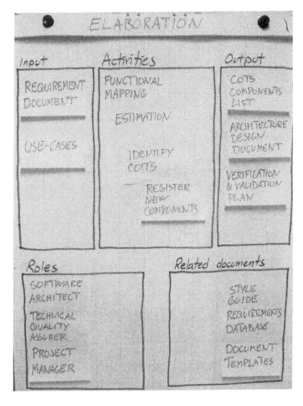

**Figure 2: A process worksheet with input, activities, output, roles and related documents defined**

*Defined roles.* We brainstormed on which roles should contribute in each activity and found the following roles for the "blast off" phase: project manager, quality assurance, development responsible, technical responsible, product committee, bid manager, purchasing manager, logistics expert.

*Related documents.* We identified documents that either already existed in the company, or new documents that would be helpful in carrying out the activities. Such documents were templates, checklists and good examples of input or output documents.

The researchers documented the process workshop by taking notes of stickers in different categories, and by the use of pictures (as in Figure 3).

**Figure 3: A workshop participant adds an activity to a process worksheet**

We found it helpful to ask the people who participated in the process workshop to read the result and comment on it (see (Shull et al., 2000) for an example of such a technique in requirements inspection). We assigned the most typical roles that were involved in the processes to people – and asked them to find if there was information that was lacking or irrelevant for this role in the description. This reading resulted in a number of modifications and clarifications on the process description.

Finally, two people in the company were responsible for making a draft process guide, based on the overall description of the processes which are developed in the workshop. Each activity was then described in much more detail than what appeared in the workshop minutes – the participants gave feedback on these before the processes were implemented in the process guide, as shown in Figure 4.

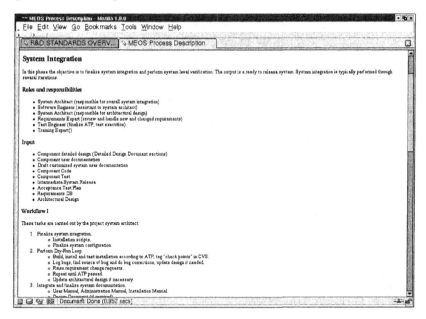

**Figure 4: A screenshot of a part of the resulting electronic process guide on the company Intranet**

## 3.4    Following work

After the first version of "initiation" was accepted and implemented in the process guide, the company was ready for the next workshop. After initiation it was natural to focus on product development. This process was defined to include the sub-processes: "specification", "elaboration", "component construction", and "system integration". Also for these processes, input, activities, output, roles, and related documents involved in the process were defined.

After the two main processes, product development and initiation were defined, the company was ready to release the first version of the process guide. The enthusiasm was high after the workshops. It was therefore important to give the workshop participants feedback through a running system even if it was not complete. Waiting for the perfect and complete process guide would take too long and could kill the enthusiasm. While implementing and releasing the process guide, the company conducted process workshops on project closure, product release, delivery and competence registration.

These seven first workshops had from 4-6 participants (researchers not included), and 20 persons (1/3 of the employees) from the company participated in one or more workshops. The workshops lasted from 2 hours (workshop on format and requirements of the process guide) to 6.5 hours. The participants did not need to prepare themselves before the workshops. The company used:

- 168 work hours for seven workshops
- 40 work hours on supplementary work after workshops
- 208 work hours for implementing the process guide
- 223 work hours for implementing project tracking tools in addition to the guide
- 38 work hours on documentation.

The total cost of developing the first version of the process guide was 1049 work hours.

The two researchers used 10 work hours each including preparation and supplementary work for each workshop.

## 4.    DISCUSSION

In this section, we would like to discuss our experience with conducting process workshops, and elaborate on strengths and weaknesses of applying such an approach.

We believe that participation and involvement is critical to achieve improvement in any organization, and see the process workshop as an arena which is open for many of the employees to take part in. Further, we see the process workshops as an arena where representatives from various departments can meet and discuss which will give participants a broader view of how work is conducted in the organization. Finally, we see the process workshop as an arena for collective reflection and learning, where employees can share experience on how they usually solve tasks, and discuss efforts to help them solve the tasks more efficiently.

It is not the intention in this paper to "prove" that process workshops are more suitable than other techniques in eliciting process descriptions. We do not yet have sufficient experience with the resulting process descriptions to investigate that issue. We will rather point out some elements that we noted when conducting the workshops which can be useful for other approaches in the future. However, we note the findings of Ahonen et al. (2002), who report that a similar workshop-technique for modeling software processes both increased the knowledge of the real process and identified points of improvement.

First, we noted that the people who participated in the workshops were contributing with many new perspectives on the processes. For example, one of the people in the quality department in the company had already made a draft version of a process description before organizing a workshop. He found that the workshop produced a number of activities, roles, and also input and output-documents that he did not think of himself.

The brainstorming sessions with yellow stickers worked well to get all participants involved in the process. We have experienced that software developers often can be quite introvert people; and the workshops gave them the opportunity to participate more actively in discussions. Using the stickers gives each participant approximately the same time to present experience.

The workshop provided an arena for cross-functional discussion in the company, and there were several discussions between for example the market and software development departments on how issues were to be handled. We think many clarifications were made that would not have appeared if it had not been for these workshops.

We were satisfied with using the simplified version of the ETVX "process worksheets" in the brainstorming sessions. Using the worksheet gave an easily understandable visual presentation of the results and the connection between different elements of the result. None of the participants in the workshops we organized said they found the ETVX sheets inappropriate.

During the sessions we used time boxing in order to generate ideas for all sub-processes and sub-process elements. Because of limited time, we had to stop some discussions to move to the next process element. In an organizational learning sense, one could argue that we should have had more space for free "dialogue", which would elicit more of the tacit knowledge from the people involved. However, using time boxing generated a "flow" in the workshop. We had the impression that none of the participants got bored or stopped engaging in discussions because the topic was irrelevant, which might have happened if we had allowed for more time.

Another aspect that gave a lot of feedback on the results was the role-based reading of the results of the workshop. Assigning roles to people was a good tool in discovering inconsistencies, for example that a role was missing in one sub-process description or that a document relevant to a role appeared in one sub-process as output and not as input in another sub-process later. It also gave us general feedback of the wording of the names of roles, documents and activities.

We claim that the workshops provided an arena for participation which was consistent with existing values, past experience and also with the needs of the company employees.

Further, the process workshops were fairly efficient in terms of resources spent to design the process guide. We do not think using other approaches such as process experts conducting interviews or purchasing existing "canned" processes would have come out cheaper for the company. Other approaches would also probably require more tailoring, and would not involve the employees to such a large degree. It would also put less focus on the learning aspects through reflection on own practice, which are evident in group-work.

On the basis of the workshops conducted, we can recommend other companies wanting to develop electronic process guides to organize a set of workshops using the brainstorming techniques, the ETVX sheets and the role-based review.

## 5.    CONCLUSION AND FURTHER WORK

From the previous discussion of how process workshops worked in the case study of the satellite software company we can conclude:

- Process workshops conducted in the way described provides an open forum for reflection and learning about own work methods.
- Process workshops are an efficient method for discussing and agreeing on a set of work processes.

Further work in this area will be to follow the acceptance, usage and impact of this process guide in the satellite company. We would also like to further develop the process workshop by introducing other group-based techniques and methods. One possible future activity would be to focus more on the "verification" part of ETVX, which we think would be useful when processes are more established.

## ACKNOWLEDGEMENTS

This work was conducted as a part of the SPIKE research project, supported by the Research Council of Norway. We are very grateful to our contact persons in the satellite company for providing a stimulating environment in the project and to the participants in the process workshops for a positive attitude towards new work methods.

# REFERENCES

Ahonen, J. J., Forsell, M., & Taskinen, S.-K. (2002). A Modest but Practical Software Process Modeling Technique for Software Process Improvement. *Software Process Improvement and Practice*, 7(1), 33-44.

Baumgartel, H. (1959). Using Employee Questionnaire Results for Improving Organizations: The Survey 'Feedback' Experiment. *Kansas Business Review*, 12, 2-6.

Becker-Kornstaedt, U., Neu, H., & Hirche, G. (2001). Software Process Technology Transfer: Using a Formal Process Notation to Capture a Software Process in Industry. In V. Ambriola (Ed.), *Proceedings from the Eight European Workshop on Software Process Technology (EWSPT'2001)* (pp. 63-76): Springer LNCS 2077.

Berger, P. L., & Luckmann, T. (1966). *The Social Construction of Reality: A Treatise in the Sociology of Knowledge*. Harmondsworth: Penguin Books.

Conradi, R., & Dybå, T. (2001). An Empirical Study on the Utility of Formal Routines to Transfer Knowledge and Experience. In V. Gruhn (Ed.), *Proceedings of the European Software Engineering Conference 2001 (ESEC'2001)* (pp. 268-276): ACM/IEEE CS Press.

Crosby, P. B. (1979). *Quality is Free: The Art of Making Quality Certain*. New York: McGraw-Hill.

Cummings, T. G., & Worley, C. G. (2001). *Organization Development and Change*. Cincinnati, Ohio: South-Western College Publishing.

Davis, F. (1989). Perceived Usefulness, Perceived Ease of Use, and User Acceptance of Information Technology. *MIS Quarterly*, 13(3), 318-339.

Davis, L. (1977). Enhancing the Quality of Work Life: Developments in the United States. *International Labour Review*, 116 (July-August), 53-65.

Deming, E. W. (2000). *Out of the Crisis*. Cambridge, Massachusetts: The MIT Press (first published in 1982 by MIT Center for Advanced Educational Services).

Denison, D., & Spreitzer, G. (1991). Organizational Culture and Organizational Development: A Competing Values Approach. In R. Woodman & W. Posmore (Eds.), *Research in Organizational Change and Development* (Vol. 5, pp. 1-22.). Greenwich, Connecticut: JAI Press.

Derniame, J.-C., Kaba, B. A., & Wastell, D. (1999). *Software Process: Principles, Methodology, and Technology*. Springer Verlag LNCS 1500.

Dybå, T. (2000). Improvisation in Small Software Organizations. *IEEE Software*, 17 (September/October), 82-87.

Emery, M., & Purser, R. E. (1996). *The Search Conference*. San Francisco: Jossey-Bass.

French, W. L., & Bell, C. H. J. (1999). *Organization Development: Behavioral Science Interventions for Organization Improvement.* Upper Saddle River, New Jersey: Prentice-Hall.

Glass, R. L. (1995). *Software Creativity.* Prentice Hall.

Greenwood, D. J., & Levin, M. (1998). *Introduction to Action Research.* Sage Publications.

Ishikawa, K. (1990). *Introduction to Quality Control.* London: Chapman & Hall.

Juran, J. M. (1992). *Juran on Quality by Design: The New Steps for Planning Quality into Goods and Services.* New York: Free Press.

Kellner, M. I., Becker-Kornstaedt, U., Riddle, W. E., Tomal, J., & Verlag, M. (1998). Process Guides: Effective Guidance for Process Participants. *Proceedings of the 5th International Conference on the Software Process*: Computer Supported Organizational Work, Lisle, Illinois, USA.

Lehman, M. M., & Belady, L. A. (1985). *Program Evolution - Processes of Software Change.* Academic Press.

Mayo, E. (1933). *The Human Problems of an Industrial Civilization.* Boston: Harvard University Press.

Mayo, E. (1945). *The Social Problems of an Industrial Civilization.* Boston: Harvard University Press.

National Institute of Standards and Technology. (1993). *The Standard for Integration Definition for Function Modelling (IDEF0).*

Neff, F. W. (1966). Survey Research: A Tool for Problem Diagnosis and Improvement in Organizations. In A. W. Gouldner & S. M. Miller (Eds.), *Applied Sociology* (pp. 23-38). New York: Free Press.

Oquendo, F. (2003). Software Process Technology. *Proceedings of the Ninth International Workshop, EWSPT'2003*, Helsinki, Finland.

Schein, E. H. (1992). *Organizational Culture and Leadership.* San Francisco: Jossey-Bass.

Scott, L., Carvalho, L., Jeffery, R., D'Ambra, J., & Becker-Koernstaedt, U. (2002). Understanding the Use of an Electronic Process Guide. *Information and Software Technology*, 44, 601-616.

Scupin, R. (1997). The KJ Method: A Technique for Analyzing Data Derived from Japanese Ethnology. *Human Organization*, 56(2), 233-237.

Shull, F., Rus, I., & Basili, V. R. (2000). How Perspective-Based Reading Can Improve Requirements Inspections. *IEEE Computer*, 33(7), 73-79.

Trist, E. (1981). *The Evolution of Socio-Technical Systems: A Conceptual Framework and an Action Research Program*. Toronto, Ontario: Ontario Quality of Working Life Center.

Venkatesh, V., & Davis, F. (2000). A Theoretical Extension of the Technology Acceptance Model: Four Longitudinal Field Studies. *Management Science*, 46(2), 186-204.

# Index